MW01493795

If you're ready to shake off the shackles of imitation worship this book is for you! *The Book of Mormon for the Least of These, Vol. II* disrupts spiritually damaging institutionalized patriarchal interpretations by creating a space that helps those who have desired more from the gospel to question, examine, and reconnect spiritually. This book is a valuable resource for those who desire discipleship with Jesus in the margins.

—Tamu Smith
coauthor of *Can I Get an Amen?*
Celebrating the Lord in Everyday Life

As the authors note of King Benjamin's famous sermon, the Book of Mormon "addresses the rich, the poor, the people burning themselves out in justice work, and those who create narratives to further marginalize people." Salleh and Olsen Hemming's kind and determined voices amplify the Book of Mormon's clarion call to repentance and justice. The perceptive readings in this volume help us find ourselves in the text, invite us to a more expansive understanding of God's love, and challenge us to share that love with all of God's children.

—Kristine Haglund
author of *Eugene England: A Mormon Liberal*

Get out of the way and into the Word! This book is a captivating resource that allows us to experience the Book of Mormon through a social justice lens. Passages we have heard dozens of times become a fresh read as Salleh and Olsen Hemming's commentary breathes life, liberation, and the pursuit of consciousness onto each page. *The Book of Mormon for the Least of These* unapologetically moves us beyond the altar call to lay down our burdens and pushes us to lay down our biases. More than a source to examine the Word, this book is a tool to engage in the work.

—Zandra Vranes, coauthor of
Can I Get an Amen?
Celebrating the Lord in Everyday Life

If you think the Book of Mormon has nothing left to teach you about Christian discipleship, think again. Fatimah Salleh and Margaret Olsen Hemming have produced another superb volume of mind-expanding, soul-stretching, love-enhancing, and action-inspiring readings of Restoration scripture. *For the Least of These* has become one of my go-to Book of Mormon commentaries.

—Patrick Mason
author of *Restoration: God's Call
to the 21st-Century World*

The Book of Mormon

of Mormon

For the Least of These

VOLUME 2
MOSIAH – ALMA

BY COMMON CONSENT PRESS is a non-profit publisher dedicated to producing affordable, high-quality books that help define and shape the Latter-day Saint experience. BCC Press publishes books that address all aspects of Mormon life. Our mission includes finding manuscripts that will contribute to the lives of thoughtful Latter-day Saints, mentoring authors and nurturing projects to completion, and distributing important books to the Mormon audience at the lowest possible cost.

The Book of Mormon

For the Least of These

VOLUME 2
MOSIAH – ALMA

By Fatimah Salleh
and Margaret Olsen Hemming

The Book of Mormon For the Least of These, volume 2: Mosiah–Alma
Copyright © 2022 by Fatimah Salleh and Margaret Olsen Hemming

For information contact
By Common Consent Press
4900 Penrose Dr.
Newburgh, IN 47630

Cover art: "Line Faces" by Mikenzi Jones (@kenzistudioco on Instagram)
Cover design: D Christian Harrison
Book design: Andrew Heiss

www.bccpress.org
ISBN-13: 978-1-948218-58-0

10 9 8 7 6 5 4 3 2 1

For those who seek for God and work for justice

CONTENTS

PREFACE

I think it is important to know that Margaret and I wrote most of this volume during the COVID-19 pandemic. We wrote during the deaths of George Floyd, Ahmaud Arbery, Breonna Taylor, and so many others. We wrote during a tumultuous political season that hurt family ties. We wrote with our children's virtual learning classrooms right next to us.

And then there were times when we did not write.

We stopped writing to grieve when loved ones went on to their heavenly homes and we could not attend their funerals and mourn with our community. When the heaviness of this life got too weighty, we allowed ourselves to just not write. Then we would check back in with each other and see if either of us felt ready to step back into it. We told each other that we would not apologize for life's happenings. We would not apologize for our children interrupting us as we worked. We would not apologize if we just could not muster the energy and needed to reschedule.

At one point, I asked Margaret if it was worth even writing this volume. I remember feeling done with so much of the work I was doing around racism and social justice. I felt deeply exhausted and considered retreating, or completely leaving this project. I have to be honest, this book seemed like something I did not need to do anymore. As a black brown mother living during these last turbulent years, I felt tender with grief, frustration, anger—and just plain fed up. In a hard conversation with Margaret, she reassured me that this book was still needed and that, at our pace, we could get it done. I believed her. And, in return, she shielded me. She took on most, if not all, of the outside communication related to this book. She consulted and spoke with scholars, our publisher, editors, and fielded anyone wanting to speak with me in regards to the book. Margaret's friendship, not to mention her brilliance, is the main reason this book is done. Plain and simple.

To know the backdrop of this volume is important because in this commentary, we tried to not look away. If we did not understand how God was at work in the text, we conveyed that mystery. We may have been hard on religious and political leaders in the Book of Mormon because we sat in a time, much like the peoples of the Book of Mormon, where both political and religious leadership needed to be brave, just, and visionary. So please, as always, consider what we offer as something dynamic and evolving.

—Rev. Dr. Fatimah Salleh
March 2022

As Fatimah noted, this volume emerged during the COVID-19 pandemic, meaning that our children were home with us for much of the time. Their presence and the childcare that came with it was so constant that I am unable to separate it from the work of the book. My kids and foster kids were on my mind, in my heart, and in my lap for every moment of writing.

Learning from and working with Fatimah is one of the great joys and honors of my life. The crises and pressures of the past several years have forced me to repeatedly reassess what is most important. I chose to continue this project not only because I believe in the work, but because my time with Fatimah is invaluable to me. While steadfastly calling for greater justice, she offers abundant grace and love to those around her. She is wise, generous, and kinder to me than I deserve. So while this book is a reflection of the period of instability, injustice, and conflict in which we live, it is also a tribute to a meaningful and important friendship. I have only gratitude.

—Margaret Olsen Hemming

March 2022

INTRODUCTION

In the introduction to Volume One of this series, we expressed the importance of reading the Book of Mormon through the lens of social justice and liberation theology and described the necessity and value of this type of interpretation. While the Book of Mormon has been analyzed in many different ways—including symbolically, historically, and as a work of literature—never before has it been the subject of a verse-by-verse reading focused on issues of the oppressed. Given that holy text has so frequently been used throughout history to further oppress people who already stand at the margins, the absence of an alternative reading seems striking. Reading scripture with the intent of finding and amplifying messages of liberation and justice offers hope and relief to the least of these.

The response to our first volume using this interpretation of the Book of Mormon was extraordinary. We received messages from readers around the world, particularly from women, BIPOC, and queer folk. Many told us that for the first time in their adult lives, they felt excited by and drawn to the Book of Mormon. In personal conversations, people tearfully told us they had prayed for a book like ours for many years. While we had hoped the book would resonate, we were overwhelmed and humbled by the impact readers described. We struck a chord and identified an urgent gap in the discussion.

At the same time, we felt disappointed, though not surprised, to also hear from those who felt we had no right to publish a study of the Book of Mormon. Those respondents questioned our authority to interpret scripture. These comments strengthened our conviction that not enough commentaries about the Book of Mormon have been written by women and people of color. Our faith community needs to see these populations speaking about scripture. Every person engages with holy text through the filter of their own personal experiences, culture, and family background, whether or not they are conscious of it. Women have distinctive questions and insights to raise about the Book of Mormon. People of color have particular issues that may resonate with their experiences in the world. Knowledge is, in part, a matter of perspective. We hope this book encourages all readers, whatever their background and experiences, to ask and wrestle with questions different from the ones they have previously considered.

●

What does it mean to read the Book of Mormon for the least of these? Liberation theologian Miguel A. De La Torre wrote that, "Reading the Bible from the margins of society is not an exercise that reveals interesting perspectives on how other cultures read and interpret biblical texts. To read the Bible from the margins is to grasp God in the midst of struggle and oppression."[1] Similarly, the work of reading the Book of Mormon through the lens of social justice can feel heart-rending and disturbing. The Book of Mormon is, fundamentally, a tragedy and a book about loss. It poses big questions about where and how God shows up in periods of terrible violence and heartbreak, particularly in the books of Mosiah and Alma. This text demands that readers not look away from the existence of war, rape, torture, and oppression in our world. The term "bondage" appears 66 times in the Book of Mormon, almost entirely in the books of Mosiah and Alma. This speaks to the horrifying reality of slavery and the damage

1. Miguel de La Torre. *Reading the Bible From the Margins*. Maryknoll, NY: Orbis Books, 2002.

it inflicts on people's bodies and souls. The Book of Mormon does not tolerate the excuse of ignorance, asking us to examine the worst parts of human behavior and wrestle with the question, "How does an omniscient and all-loving God allow these things to happen?"

Our approach evaluates status-quo readings of well-trodden stories and interrogates less-typically discussed stories for important truths. We examine leadership models and the idea of prosperity gospel, extrapolating the spiritual definition of what it means to "prosper in the land." In addition, we show further evidence for the ways Nephites and Lamanites are constructed identities meant to stoke racism and animosity, and not ethnic differences. The books of Mosiah and Alma return again and again to the concept of community: how to build it, how it fractures, and what happens when people choose themselves over others. The people of Zeniff leave and Mosiah welcomes Limhi and Alma's people to the land of Zarahemla. The sons of Mosiah form loving friendships with people they previously considered enemies. The Zoramites evict a portion of their own people, then declare war on those who offer them sanctuary. The Anti-Nephi-Lehies establish the land of Jershon, which becomes a beautiful place of safety for anyone who needs it, regardless of nationality or background. The Nephites struggle again and again with dissenters who chose their own interests over their people. In these discussions, we often refer to "beloved community," which references the Rev. Dr. Martin Luther King's phrase for an ideal where everyone strives to benefit the common good, seeks justice for all people, and helps build an integrated society. We could, and sometimes do, also call this Zion. The books of Mosiah and Alma offer beautiful and sometimes tragic collisions of people and how their complicated interactions sometimes come close to, and often fail, to meet this ideal. The tragedy of the Book of Mormon is that ultimately, the people choose their own interests over beloved community. This may also be the tragedy of our modern time.

Story-telling and letters also feature prominently in the books of Mosiah and Alma. Characters frequently separate in these books—

Alma the Elder is in Lehi-Nephi while Mosiah is in Zarahemla; Ammon is with the Lamanites while Alma the Younger is in Ammonihah; Moroni and Helaman face different fronts of the war—and story-telling and letters serve to share their experiences with each other (and the reader). Thus, while the record in the first third of the Book of Mormon seems directed toward an unspecified future reader, the text of Mosiah and Alma frequently shows the characters communicating to one another. These sections emphasize the spiritual power of narrative and memory work. The stories preserved in this holy text have equal value to the sermons and doctrinal explanations. When Ammon finds Limhi and when Limhi's people and Alma's people return to Zarahemla, one of the first things they do is sit down together and read one another's records and tell their histories. The preservation of these stories on brass plates—the very existence of the Book of Mormon—speaks to the sacredness of story-telling, particularly as a part of community.

This volume analyzes what gets often referred to as "the war chapters" of the Book of Mormon, which some skip over. As we show, passing over these chapters is a lost opportunity. The frequently violent events of these books and the principal characters often struggle with what role God plays in that violence. When things go well for the Nephites in battle, they see God directing their military strategy. When they fall under siege and slowly starving to death, they wonder if God has abandoned them. When they suffer under the burdens of enslavement, they see God's punishment. When they walk free into the wilderness, they speak of God's miracles. In this volume, we have carefully tried to not strip God from other people's narratives. Particularly in dark times, people must be allowed to interpret divine intervention in their lives in their own way. At the same time, we can recognize it as their truth without accepting their interpretation as universal truth. This is how they experienced God, not necessarily the totality of truth about God. Whether or not we accept how they interpret the events of their lives, the narrators of the Book of

Mormon ask us to sit with them in difficult questions about how the divine interacts with a world that includes so much suffering.

As you read Volume Two in this series, we hope you will consider which voices in our society speak with spiritual power but get widely ignored. Frequently, the most important and powerful perspectives come from the margins of society—from brave Lamanite queens to an unnamed maid acting as a spy to the Anti-Nephi-Lehi community modeling how to welcome refugees. We also hope you will see how God shows up in the unlikeliest of places and in the most harrowing times. Finally, we hope the world will see the Book of Mormon as a tragic warning of the perils of choosing power and self-interest over humility, compassion, and justice. As Alma discusses, joy and sorrow often coexist. The clarion call of this volume is of the urgent need to dedicate ourselves to building beloved community. We pray that it may offer a word of healing and liberation for a wounded world.

MOSIAH

Mosiah 1:2–4

Lehi seems to have taught all of his children, including his daughters, how to read and understand their scriptures and history. Since in surrounding verses Mormon and Benjamin repeatedly use the more exclusive word "sons," it would be reasonable to expect that if Lehi had taught only his boys, they would have used that instead of the word "children" in verse 4. We know almost nothing about Nephi's sisters, but this verse gives us a tiny insight into their lives. Interestingly, while many of the authors of the Book of Mormon introduce themselves by referencing their fathers, Nephi is the only one who invokes his mother as well. With only small amounts of information about the women in these families and societies, readers have to piece together what these women's lives were like during these times and places. In Nephi's family, at least, there is some evidence that mothers and sisters were treated with some degree of respect.

Mosiah 1:5

When Benjamin tells the origin story of the Nephites and describes the importance of the plates, he passes down the idea of separation between the Nephites and Lamanites. The value that he gives the plates is based on a comparison to the Lamanites: we need the plates so that we are not like them. This is a less effective way of teaching the worth of knowledge. His language sets up the Nephites as superior to the Lamanites, mostly based on the decisions of their ancestors. It's worth noting that Benjamin's language possibly comes from his own social location as a reaction to his personal experiences in war with the Lamanites.[1] Lingering anger from the violence he witnessed in that war could fuel the disconnection he feels toward them, affecting the way he is interpreting scripture.

Benjamin's history also ignores the active role that his ancestors played in the Lamanites not having the plates. Nephi took the plates with him when he departed into the wilderness. That was a justifiable action given his situation. But to criticize the Lamanites for not having the plates when your own folk have some responsibility for the current status ignores the historical account.

Mosiah 1:10–12

This is clearly a highly ritualistic theocracy. Although Mosiah is inheriting the throne simply through birth, Benjamin invokes God's approval of this highly conventional system at the end of verse 10. While royalty throughout time has claimed divine rights, it's worth questioning whether this was true or whether this structure simply smoothed the transition of power. The Book of Mormon itself suggests an argument against a divine sanction of birthright to political office by Mosiah's later decision to replace the monarchy with a system of judges[2] and the violent conflict the Nephites wage to avoid the installment of a king a few years later.[3]

Benjamin also uses religiously-tinged ritual here to create a unified identity for the different groups of people now living in Zarahemla. In verse 10, he refers to them as separate groups, not using the umbrella term of Nephites. And in verse 12, he writes that he will give them a new name. Most commentators connect these verses to Mosiah 5:7–11

---

1. Omni 1:24
2. Alma 29
3. Alma 51

and agree that this new name is "Christ."[4] This is a powerful idea of the people choosing to be Christians rather than Nephites, Mulekites, or other nationalities. Their unified identity would be lives centered on the divine. There appears to be some ceremonial work here as the people gather together, receive a common name, and recognize their new king.

Mosiah 1:16

Here, again, the sword of Laban and the plates are named together— this time also with the Liahona. The Liahona has not been named in text since the time of Lehi, although the sword of Laban has been mentioned repeatedly as being an important part of Nephite society. A sword is certainly much easier to use than the Liahona, which requires obedience, faith, and asking questions. We might imagine that it was used to lead Mosiah to Zarahemla, but we cannot know for sure.

Nephite identity stems from a relationship to their holy text, according to Benjamin in verse 5. He also says they used the sword to acquire that text, and now those two objects are held closely together. By linking these objects, the unsubtle message is clear: violence is an inherent part of the nation's origin story. They believe they have survived through the sword since the beginning. It is hard to imagine that this would not affect the way the Nephites engage with the Lamanites.

Mosiah 2:4

Modern women readers of scripture must do additional work to decipher where they belong and where they are left out, a labor encapsulated in verses like this one. "Men" is sometimes used as a gender-neutral reference to everyone, as it is used at the end of this verse. However, in the middle it reads that men were appointed to be

---

4. Joseph F. McConkie and Robert L. Millet. *Doctrinal Commentary on The Book of Mormon, Vol. II*. Salt Lake City, UT: Bookcraft, 1988, 132–33.

teachers of the people. Are women included in that statement? Given that this is an ancient, patriarchal civilization, probably not. But it is a possibility. Women have to delineate when they are being included and excluded in a way that men do not when studying scripture. Men have the privilege of being the norm. This gendered language appears heavily throughout this chapter, with Benjamin repeatedly referring to "my brethren," when he almost certainly means everyone in attendance, and "the man" or "that man" to refer to any individual.

Mosiah 2:5–6

Mormon gives a surprisingly detailed account of the physicality of this gathering: how the people gathered, where they slept, and how their tents were situated. The information gives us an interesting insight into Nephite society. While the scriptures describe buildings and cities made of stone and metal, the fact that every family owns a tent large enough for their extended family points to a more nomadic existence than we might imagine. Tents belong to people who move and travel often. Nephi's statement that his "father dwelt in a tent"[5] is a pithy way of describing the conditions of living in wilderness spaces. People still gathering in large tents signals a society that is transient on occasion. While at times the writers of the Book of Mormon will criticize the Lamanites for being nomadic,[6] here we learn that, at least to a certain extent, the Nephites were also a people who sometimes lived itinerant lives.

Mosiah 2:8

Towers represent literal and symbolic tools of power. They can harm or help folk, and therefore need to be treated carefully. The Rameump-

---

5. 1 Nephi 2:15
6. Alma 22:28

4

tom,[7] king Noah's tower,[8] and the Tower of Babel[9] were used out of pride and sowed division among the population. But towers can also aid people in hearing the words of the prophets. When towers appear in the scriptures, consider why they are being built, what messages are being shared from them, and who they serve. How is the person speaking from the tower wielding the additional power that the tower lends them? Who is allowed access to that power?

Mosiah 2:9

Benjamin immediately starts out with a call for faithfulness, telling the people that he did not gather everyone together so that they could ignore him or find fault in what he has to say. He asks the people to open their ears, hearts, and minds all at once because he will speak about the mysteries of God. While Nephi called the gospel "plain" and "easy to the understanding of all men,"[10] Benjamin references the unfolding of the mysteries of God, describing a process that sounds much more difficult. For Nephi, the gospel may have been easy to understand, but for Benjamin, things appear more complicated. Neither perspective is necessarily superior, and both may be experienced in this life.

Benjamin's use of the heart and mind working together sounds like the exhortation to "seek learning, even by study and also by faith."[11] The mental wrestling that we do should go hand in hand with emotional engagement with holy texts. Also, the scriptures often use physical descriptions to refer to spiritual experiences. To walk with God, we need to understand that the physical and the spiritual are connected. This metaphorical language helps us understand that this journey will be a whole body experience.

---

7. Alma 31:21
8. Mosiah 11:12–13
9. Genesis 11:1–9
10. 1 Nephi 14:23
11. Doctrine and Covenants 109:7

Mosiah 2:10-11

Just as other Book of Mormon prophets have done, Benjamin addresses his own fallibility. Near the beginning of his speech, he reminds his listeners that he is merely human. He starts by naming his social location and stating, "I am nothing more than a mortal man" (v. 10). The prophets of the Book of Mormon do not try to censor their own mortality. This is radical in its own way. It is hard to imagine any leader today beginning a speech with an acknowledgement that they struggle with "infirmities in body and mind" (v. 11). This beautiful testament shows that Benjamin, like everyone else, struggles. He ties himself to the people, reminding them that the only thing separating him is being born into royalty and holding a leadership position.

Notice that Benjamin acknowledges that his status as king came from being the son of his father and from the will of the people, not from divine appointment. He says that this power came to him through his family inheritance. Simultaneously, he describes how God has sustained him through the responsibilities that came with that power. Finally, Benjamin tells the people exactly what he has been able to do with that political power through God's support: serve the people. This is an extraordinary statement and an excellent example for anyone with privilege. Benjamin sees that his initial status and power was an inheritance, something he received because of the circumstances of his birth. He did not use his power to hoard more power. He knew that having privilege meant being called by God to serve with all the resources that he had been given. By exercising his privilege correctly, he was able to better fulfill his call.

Mosiah 2:12-17

Notice that in the list of egregious sins, slavery is listed at the top. Was slavery something that Benjamin's people struggled with? We know that the Nephites came into the land of Zarahemla and instituted their own government, language, and culture.[12] It would follow the patterns of history for them to have also considered enslaving the people of Zarahemla. Instead, Benjamin is gathering them together, uniting them under one name,[13] and reminding them of the responsibilities that each person bears toward God and their fellow humans. He has given them his example of laboring with his own hands so that he never puts anything on them that is "grievous to be borne" (v. 14). That is a beautiful way of using power to build community.

Benjamin also makes clear that he is not giving this speech for the purpose of boasting or shaming. He is trying to teach them how to construct beloved community. He explains that the way to stand before God with a clear conscience means using every part of our gifts and resources to serve. His life experience referenced in verse 17 and subsequent wisdom imparts that any privilege comes with the responsibility of serving others.

Mosiah 2:18–19

The charismatic voice here is reminiscent of Black churches in the United States. The use of rhetorical questions, the injunction to give praise, and the reminder that our lives and breath exist on borrowed time, sound like rhetoric used by traditional Black pastors. By opening our ears to the varied voices of Book of Mormon prophets, readers can understand how God moves with different people, speaking in a still, small voice at some times and shouting alleluias at another. Being willing to hear those different voices allows the spirit to speak to us in a greater variety of ways.

Mosiah 2:22–24

Because Benjamin never clearly defines his understanding of the words "bless" and "prosper," readers might misinterpret these words

---

12. Omni 1:17–19
13. Mosiah 1:12

in a way that sanctions prosperity gospel and a transactional God. A deeper, more beautiful understanding of his intent is that he wishes to remind listeners not to boast of their blessings because everything good that they have ultimately comes from God.

Prosperity gospel certainly does not fit with the experiences of the Nephite people, nor with the rest of Benjamin's sermon, which makes this interpretation a poor understanding of this scripture. Traditionally, we tell the story of the Nephites as an example of the "pride cycle": keep the commandments, amass wealth, become prideful and stop keeping the commandments, suffer bad consequences. But, crucially, it does not always happen that way. The origin story of this people is one in which a family kept God's commandments and, as a direct result, lost all of their land and possessions and had to flee into the wilderness. Benjamin's own father, Mosiah, had to flee out of the promised land. He ventured into the wilderness and, finally, to Zarahemla, apparently because the Lamanites took over the land. These people kept the commandments and still lost everything. The idea that God immediately blesses those who are obedient simply does not fit with the lived history of this people. Believing that following the commandments entitles us to blessings will inevitably lead to disappointment. That does not appear to be how God works. We are not "paid" by a vending machine God who dispenses prosperity as a reward for obedience. To be blessed by God does not always, to our mortal eyes, look like a blessing. Sometimes keeping the commandments will move us into greater risk or worse situations.

Mosiah 2:25–26

There is a noted teaching tactic that tells people of their worthlessness so that they can see themselves in light of the greatness of God. It needs to be used carefully. Some folk—those who regularly receive praise, honor, and reward from society—may need to be humbled to recognize how dependent they are on God. Other folk—oppressed populations, people who are already told by society that they are worth nothing—need to be reminded of how God sees them and values them. Any spiritual leader needs to be in tune with their audience to know what will best serve the community. For someone like Benjamin, who was born into power and prominence, this kind of theology is great for molding him into a person who gives his life to service. Yet, this posture that has kept him close to God may not work for someone who has been deeply disenfranchised. That person may be brought to God through seeing how good and powerful they are and knowing that God is ever mindful of them.

Mosiah 2:27–28

These evocative verses come from someone in a powerful position of leadership publicly examining his own judgment with God. Benjamin says that he will have blood on his hands if he has not used his privilege and political power in the ways that God has commanded him. He would have blood on his hands without having directly and intentionally harmed anyone—having committed a sin of omission.

We have seen this sentiment before. Jacob wrote multiple times about feeling an almost oppressive sense of responsibility for his people.[14] This pattern indicates that if we do not fulfill the service that God has called us to, we are held accountable in some way for others' suffering. Some people's call will include a divine accountability for how they are using the resources they have to help people. Where they have any kind of power, they are also responsible for how they used that power. God gave king Benjamin a personal commandment, not a suggestion, that they are liable in this way. Once we grasp the seriousness of this, we can understand why Benjamin goes to such effort to communicate with his people one more time before his death. He needs to make sure that he has done everything in his power to fulfill the responsibilities that came with his privilege. Benjamin hopes he will find peace with a "just God" through

---

14. 2 Nephi 9:44; Jacob 1:19

consecrating a life of service. Note that Benjamin emphasizes the justice, not the mercy, of God in this moment. A just God holds people accountable. For Benjamin—a man who was born into and lived a life of privilege—the ability to worship a just God in the eternities is closely linked to what he has done with his power.

Mosiah 2:31

The way Benjamin mixes ideas of his own laws and God's commandments is problematic. Humans can establish laws. Prophets can reveal commandments. But all commandments are of God and the prophets reveal them. Benjamin seems to acknowledge this in some way, as he says, "ye shall keep the commandments of my son, or the commandments of God which shall be delivered unto you by him." He seems to be clarifying that the commandments of his son are actually the commandments of God, spoken by the son. But that clarification is not enough, given that he has now referenced his own commandments and his father's commandments. He has gotten too close to blurring the line between the dictates of humans and God. The tendency for humans to conflate kings and/or prophets with God ought to make him additionally careful of that line. Sometimes leaders make policies or laws that are not of God but insist that they are commandments, often with tragic results. We need to take care to distinguish between God and any human. Given that Benjamin introduced his speech with the reminder that he is fallible and not "more than a mortal man,"[15] he might agree with this criticism.

Mosiah 2:32–36

Obedience, like any other quality, is not inherently virtuous. Obedience can be misguided. It can be given to an "evil spirit" (v. 32). The goodness of obedience lies in how we wield it.

---

15. Mosiah 2:10

Blessed, *prospered*, and *preserved* are three different things and wisdom's path does not always lead to all of them. You may be blessed. You may prosper. You may be preserved. Benjamin is right in saying that we "may" have these things because none of them are certain. Insisting that wisdom's path will always lead to good fortune necessarily excludes God from the lives of those who suffer. As we examine world history, or even the text of the Book of Mormon, we see righteous people who have to wander in the wilderness, endure prison, feel terrible pain, struggle with grief, and face death. Wisdom's path will not always look like blessings, prospering, and preservation.

Mosiah 2:37–38

In Hebrew and in Greek, *righteousness* can be translated as *justice*. Substituting these words can give a slightly different meaning to these verses: those who go contrary to God's laws become an enemy to justice. Verse 38 gives further clarification: divine justice is a person waking up to what they have done wrong. When a person obeys evil and lives an unjust life, that person is acutely aware of the harm they have caused in the presence of God. That in itself is anguish. Benjamin's description sounds like Hell. Here, Hell is basically being aware of the injustice that you have caused, being sensitive to ways in which you have not lived your life for the good of others or answered your call. Divine justice is knowing how we have hurt people or failed to use what we had to help them.

Mosiah 2:40

It seems as if Benjamin goes out of his way to avoid including women in this list of listeners while trying to be inclusive with his language here as he speaks of "ye old men, and also ye young men, and you little children who can understand my words." This is an excellent example of why women sometimes feel that the Book of Mormon does not speak to them.

Mosiah 2:41

Again, Benjamin conflates righteousness and temporal prosperity. We can hope he intends an eternal view, one in which people are blessed and happy in the afterlife. But that is not really what it sounds like when he explicitly states that "they are blessed in all things, *both temporal and spiritual*" (emphasis added). Of course, sometimes obedience leads to wonderful blessings. But sometimes it does not appear or feel as if our obedience is moving in blessing or happiness. Sometimes we may pay tithing and still come up short in our bills. Sometimes good mothers have postpartum depression. Sometimes faithful people have debilitating medical conditions. So while we consider the blessed and happy state of some, we can also hold that this is not always the case for everyone. A prophet's singular voice may sometimes be too limiting for a God bigger than we understand. But we need to be careful about prophets using language or making promises that guide people toward not seeing God in all the avenues of our lives or toward attempting to hold God to one kind of mortal experience. The lives of the righteous may not look blessed and happy.

Mosiah 3:4–5

The angel tells Benjamin to feel joy because Christ is coming soon . . . in 124 years. God's time is not our time. None of the people who hear Benjamin's speech will be alive for Christ's birth, let alone for when Christ comes to the Nephites and Lamanites. And yet, they should be happy. This is reminiscent of Enos writing that his soul could rest because the Nephite records would eventually reach the Lamanites, even though the Nephites would still die out.[16] As the psalmist wrote, "joy cometh in the morning,"[17] whether or not we see the morning. So much of social justice work is building toward a distant joy. We

---

16. Enos 1:16–17
17. Psalms 30:5

have to trust that long perspective, believing that God will come, that there will be relief in the end, even if we do not witness it. In the darkest of times, we can know who God is and what God has promised, and we can take joy in that.

Mosiah 3:8

Benjamin describes the miracles and extraordinary life and lineage of Jesus, shown to him by an angel. And then the angel names Mary. Jesus was as much Mary's son as he was God's.

Mosiah 3:9

Cross-reference this verse with the end of Mosiah 2, where Benjamin writes about "the blessed and happy state of those that keep the commandments of God."[18] Here, we have the angel correcting Benjamin's earlier statement: Christ will offer salvation through a sinless life and a consecrated death, and yet the people around him will "say that he hath a devil, and shall scourge him, and shall crucify him." That does not seem like being blessed "in all things, both temporal and spiritual." It does not sound like prospering or being preserved. The Savior of the earth shows us the juxtaposition of living righteously and still living through pain and grief. We can do everything right and still have horrible things happen. Another mention of this is an additional sign of how imperative this message is.

Mosiah 3:11

Benjamin has already made it clear that the current generation of Lamanites are uneducated about the faith of their ancestors and do not have holy texts to teach them.[19] So when the angel teaches that those "who have died not knowing the will of God concerning them," the angel seems to be deliberately referencing the Lamanites. The

18. Mosiah 2:41
19. Mosiah 1:5

great majority, if not all, of the Lamanites alive in this era do not know the gospel. The Nephites do not seem to apply this teaching to the Lamanites, but it is an important element in understanding the relationship between the two peoples. This appears to nudge Benjamin and his people to see the Lamanites the way God sees them—as beloved children covered by Christ's Atonement.

Mosiah 3:17

Writing that there is only one name through which salvation comes is like saying that a person can only leave the city through the gate, but there are 500 gates. Christ has over 100 names in the Book of Mormon alone.[20] Ironically, king Benjamin gives Christ a new name in this very verse: "Lord Omnipotent," a name which emphasizes Christ's unrestricted power and understanding. While Benjamin has admitted to his own fallibility, God sees all.

Mosiah 3:19–21

Benjamin preaches very intentionally to children through his talk, and particularly in these verses. He establishes that they cannot sin and that they are covered by the Atonement. He also encourages the people to be like children, which echoes Christ's teachings about the innocence and obedience of children.[21] Benjamin's connection with children seems interwoven with his theology. Maybe it comes from personal experience and the likelihood that he is a grandfather. Possibly there have been questions among the people about original sin and whether children are held culpable. There's also the possibility of some grief or struggle behind this connection: maybe Benjamin has had a young child die in his life or maybe there has been disease

---

20. Susan Ward Easton. "Names of Christ in the Book of Mormon." *The Ensign*, July 1978.
21. Matthew 18:24

among the people. We do not know the social and personal context of these words, but they seem deeply embedded in Benjamin's heart.

Mosiah 3:26–27

Benjamin closes his talk with a warning about the eternities—that post-judgment, those who are separated from God will be beyond the reach of mercy forever. For a Christian, any claim about a complete ending or a point of no return should be viewed with some suspicion.[22] Christians believe in a divinity who shattered the false notion of an irreversible end (death). They believe in a God who enacted an Act II when everyone thought the play was over. We should not impose timelines on God's power and mercy.

The text itself offers an interesting pushback to Benjamin's claim of a final end. Notice that Chapter 3 ends with an "Amen," intended to close his sermon. But in the first verses of chapter 4, Benjamin gazes at the crowd and sees that the people need him to speak a little longer and give more guidance. The remainder of Benjamin's speech—all of chapters 4 and 5—was unplanned and well beyond "the end" of what he initially believed he needed to say. And yet those additional chapters, the Act II, arguably contain some of the most beautiful and important words of the entire Book of Mormon. Jesus will do the same thing in 3 Nephi: he concludes his words, then looks around at people and their needs, then continues on. With God, there is always more to be had. We believe in a God of surprises and the endings that turn into new beginnings. Some of the most stunning things happen after the amen has been said.

Mosiah 4:3

The Book of Mormon contains several examples of a kind of collective repentance, where everyone present experiences an almost simultane-

---

22. Doctrine and Covenants 19 offers additional Restoration text about God's eternal nature.

ous change of heart. We typically think of repentance as an individual experience, yet this text gives us multiple stories of an entire society repenting together. In this case, the people rely on an atonement that has not yet occurred—their trust is in the prophetic promise.

Mosiah 4:4

Jacob repeatedly referred to his people as "beloved brethren."[23] Here, Benjamin uses an even more beautiful address: "My friends and my brethren, my kindred and my people." This language is more inclusive, more welcoming of every person present in the crowd.

Mosiah 4:8–9

Benjamin begins with a more absolutist theology, proclaiming a singular model for all people to reach God. Yet he almost immediately contradicts himself, following his more narrow teachings about how God operates in the world with the admission that God is far too powerful and wise for humans to fully understand. He writes, "believe that man doth not comprehend all the things which the Lord can comprehend" (v. 9). So even though he is drawing this line around God, he simultaneously acknowledges that he cannot draw that line because his understanding is limited by his own mortality.

Mosiah 4:11–16

Again and again, Benjamin returns to the language of the weakness of humans. He comes up with almost as many ways to describe the worthiness of the people as other prophets come up with ways of naming and describing God. But in these verses, we begin to understand the purpose of this theme.

Verse 11 reminds the people of their unworthiness. But after seeing his people lying on the ground in fear and grief, Benjamin knows

---

23. A few of many examples include 2 Nephi 9:1, 3, 39; Jacob 4:2–3, 18

that simply knowing their own frailty is not transformative. Verses 12 and 13 are an ending point, the place where all this language about humility leads. First, Benjamin makes the connection between God's glory and truth and justice: "ye shall grow in the knowledge of the glory of him that created you, *or* in the knowledge of that which is just and true" (v. 12, emphasis added). That "or" indicates that the two things are synonymous. And then, when we know the glory of God—also defined as understanding truth and justice—"ye will not have a mind to injure one another, but to live peaceably, and to render to every man according to that which is his due" (v. 13). We build peace and give all people what is right by knowing justice and truth.

This is a moving crescendo for Benjamin. Knowing our own nothingness compared to God is not an end in itself. This step leads us to love God and then to use that love to build beloved community. Letting go of pride allows us to accept a world frame of justice because we no longer believe that we are entitled to what we have. Justice and truth walk together because we work for justice when we understand the truth that all we have comes from God, not because we earn or deserve it. Accepting that truth allows us to let go of our own privileges and embrace community. All of Benjamin's statements about unworthiness and nothingness work toward this crucial idea: that we have to be so deeply invested in humility that we are able to witness God's love in our lives, which then translates to love and sacrifice for one another.

And then finally, Benjamin very specifically tells us what we will do if we have faced the truth of our own unworthiness and translated that into a love for others. The first category is about children: we will not let them go hungry or naked. We will teach children about the healing, transformational power of God and to love and serve one another. Secondly, we will never let others stand in need if there is any possible way we can help them. We will not turn people away who ask for assistance. Notice that all of this is said as "ye will"—as in, it will happen, not that it might. It is a natural consequence of undergoing the process Benjamin has already described. If we understand our reliance on God, we *will* do these things.

Mosiah 4:17-19

Despite our Christian responsibilities, we sometimes denigrate the needy. This powerful section describes the narratives we use to exonerate ourselves. Rather than facing our own selfishness and pride—the source of withholding resources from the poor—we insist they have earned their situations. We need to be very careful when we are trying to tell someone else's story, particularly when we are using it to harm them or draw them into the margins of society. We should be wary of the stories we put onto other folk. As Christ does with the blind man,[24] Benjamin shatters the old doctrine that insisted that bad things happen because people sinned or made bad choices. He lets us know that our narratives will not relieve us of the responsibility of giving, serving, and loving. Ultimately, he introduces ideas of systemic violence toward the poor and insists that the stories we tell about the needy require a complete overhaul so that we can understand systems of violence toward the oppressed. That overhaul lies in a single phrase in verse 19, as poetic as it is powerful: "Are we not all beggars?"

We are each beggars before God. All our substance, even that which we inherited or earned through our own work, is not really ours. The first step toward accepting the call to upend systemic oppression is to face the truth of our own unworthiness. As scholar James Falcouner writes about this section, "Benjamin wants his people to understand that if their sins continue to be remitted, they will understand their relation to the beggar as a reflection of their relation to God and they will imitate Christ by remembering their own nothingness without God. As a result, they will deal charitably with

---

24. John 9:1–12

those who petition them for help and succor."[25] Maybe this is why Benjamin continued after he thought his talk had ended. He realized that he had only gotten the people halfway there: they understood their own dependence on God, but they did not yet understand what they needed to do with that truth.

Mosiah 4:22

Although Benjamin has already made clear the link between withholding our substance and creating a narrative that blames oppression on the oppressed, here he underscores the gravity of those narratives. Refusing to help the poor is one sin, judging that person is an additional sin. The stories that we tell about the poor are answered upon our own heads, leading to our condemnation.

Mosiah 4:23–24

Benjamin asks the people to live a higher law. Even if we do not have the ability to give, we need to imagine a world in which we have enough and, in that world, would be willing to give. That is an incredibly hard thing to ask of the poor and disenfranchised. But it speaks again to the importance of the narratives we tell. It is not just the act of giving that is important; it is the stories we tell about those around us. So even those who cannot give materially are encouraged to be looking around at one another and saying, "*I see you. I recognize your humanity. God loves you in the same way God loves me.*" This is a way to give spiritual sustenance, dignity, and respect. It is the story we all need to tell, whether we are rich or poor, whether we are giving to all who ask of us or just barely managing to survive.

---

25. James E. Falcouner *Mosiah: A Brief Theological Introduction*. Provo, UT: Neal A. Maxwell Institute, 2020, 79.

Mosiah 4:26–27

Guiltlessness before God requires imparting what we have to the poor, both spiritually and temporally. This is a radical idea. How we move in community, particularly with the hungry, the naked, and the sick, is closely tied to the state of our souls. The temporal and the spiritual are inextricably intertwined, both in the service that we render and our status before the divine. This is a terrifying and yet crucial verse to face honestly.

And yet, Benjamin also says we should not get so caught up in doing good that we forget to do it in wisdom. Truth, justice, and wisdom ought to work together. This is probably one of the most beautiful things said to people in caregiving work: you are not asked to do more than what you can. *You* are not the sacrifice here. God, Benjamin says, has a "wisdom and order" (v. 27) that does not require you to run faster or farther than you have strength.

How do we reconcile these verses which seem to simultaneously ask us to give up every bit of ourselves and also give us the space to engage in self care? Verse 27 should not be used as a loophole to avoid doing what Benjamin calls us to do. Not running faster than we have strength is not an excuse for apathy. But it is an invitation to do this work in conversation with God—the only being who can negotiate the tension on an individual basis. Benjamin does an incredible job in this chapter of speaking to a diversity of situations: he addresses the rich, the poor, the people burning themselves out in justice work, and those who create narratives to further marginalize people. Each person will find themselves in a different place in this sermon. Knowing what is needful and wise means participating in an ongoing and honest conversation with God. That means not being willfully blind to our own privilege, but also taking care of ourselves. We have to be watchful of the work we are doing and the stories we are telling because all of that is up for examination with the divine. It is a life-long, personal journey that can also move through a community, and it is one that starts with an awareness of our dependence on God.

Mosiah 4:29–30

Rather than attempting to list all the ways we can sin, Benjamin simply encourages the people to "watch yourselves" (v. 30). There are many ways to miss the mark with God, but Benjamin offers broad approaches to living while keeping in line with the gospel. By following the basic tenets he lays out, we can guard against many of the threats that come from leading a sinful life.

In addition to this textual moment, the Book of Mormon offers a number of times when a prophet asks us to take a spiritual inventory of our souls. God asks us to be deeply introspective and watchful in how we are living out the gospel. Benjamin names all the ways we may fail in that: through thoughts, our words, and our deeds. Consistently watching ourselves, considering our thoughts, the words we put out into the world, and the consequences of our actions, truly matters. We focus a great deal on our actions and our deeds, but how we think about other people, particularly those on the margins, deeply influences our other behaviors. Consider the narratives that we use about specific groups of people. Be willing to stay fiercely honest about the work you need to do. We need to be so intensely careful about the thoughts we have about other people and the words we use about them.

Benjamin finishes this first part of his sermon with a call to remembrance, a common theme of scripture. The work of remembrance is a vital part in our discipleship journey. We will spend the rest of our lives trying to remember. Humans tend to forget, tend to move on too quickly. The work of remembering is spiritual work. It is also a communal effort, not just for individuals. We perform rituals and traditions together as people of faith to remember our spiritual ancestors and what they sacrificed and what we may learn from their experiences.

Mosiah 5:1–5

At the beginning of chapter 5, there is this compelling moment where Benjamin checks in with his people and asks how they feel about what

he has said. It is his chance to get feedback and show that good prophetic work does not function in a single direction. He wants to know
how the people feel about his words, and he invites their response.
This is a healthy way to navigate doctrinal movements in the gospel.
Benjamin is closing the circle of learning. In response to his inquiry,
Benjamin gets this amazing response from the people, where they cry
out that they want to make a covenant with God. And it is this overwhelming call for entering into a covenant that precipitates the rest of
Benjamin's sermon in chapter 5. If he had not asked for the people's
response—if he had simply sent them on their way at the end of his
sermon—not only would we miss the people's testimony in verses
2–5, we also would not have the rest of the chapter, in which we find
some powerful proclamations.

The group shouts out their testimony in "one voice" (v. 2). There
is something particularly powerful in experiencing a vast movement
of the spirit as a collective. This experience binds this community
together and holds it together in times of deep hardship that will
follow in the coming chapters. They felt God together. We should not
underestimate what it means to have communal remembrance of the
movement of the spirit.

The people express a fundamental change and that they "have
no more disposition to do evil, but to do good continually" (v. 2).
They only want to do good, always. That is a move of God. Most of
us can only imagine what it feels like to have no inclination to do
evil, but only to do good continually. When we feel deeply changed,
our journey of conversion moves us down the path of doing good.[26]
That change happens not alone, but with "the infinite goodness of
God" (v. 3). A person who has experienced conversion sees them-

---

26. As Dallin H. Oaks said, "It is not even enough for us to be *convinced* of the gospel;
we must act and think so that we are *converted* by it. In contrast to the institutions
of the world, which teach us to *know* something, the gospel of Jesus Christ challenges us to *become* something." "The Challenge to Become," October 2000. https://
www.churchofjesuschrist.org/study/general-conference/2000/10/the-challenge-to-
become

selves through the goodness of God. This change that reorients them to do good continually occurs within the landscape of God, and they see that they themselves are good because of God. The people also share this line of spiritual maturity: they say they "could prophesy of all things" (v. 3). This is why the LDS Bible Dictionary says that a prophet "is anyone who has a testimony" of the gospel. Prophetic gifts are accessible to everyone who experiences conversion.

In verse 4, the people "rejoice with such exceedingly great joy." This underlines the intensity of the joy they experience through conversion. It is not just a regular rejoicing; it is a radical joy, surpassing the ability of their language to describe it. Disciples of God and those who fight for social justice face hard and endless work, commonly experiencing feelings of grief and hopelessness. This passage reminds us that it is not only possible, but also important, to have moments of rejoicing with great joy. We should name those moments and celebrate, not feel shame for the relief that they offer. Despite the world's darkness, there is also the offer of great joy. Populations in oppressive situations have always found ways to rejoice, whether through rituals of marriage and birth, the gathering of family, or the happiness that comes through music and dance. In fact, one of the tools of colonization is reducing a people and a place to a single story. For example, if we tell a dismal narrative of a place and its people, where everyone is backwards and in need, we fail to see the complexity of a people building lives that include beauty, healing, and meaning. Simplified stories of suffering reduce people to flat caricatures, making it easier to not see them as fully human. This strips God from them. At the time of king Benjamin's speech, the Nephites and the people of Zarahemla are in the midst of trying to unite their two peoples, forming a single government and language.[27] This speech illustrates an incredible moment of a shared spiritual experience and mutual rejoicing. It serves as a testimony of what the power of the good word of God will do.

---

27. Omni 1:18–19

Finally, the people state that because of their conversion and the joy that they feel, they want to enter into a covenant with God. This is the verse in which the shift of the first five chapters of Mosiah becomes clear. From this point, the Book of Mormon is no longer a story of a single family and their internal dynamics. As the Nephites unite with the people of Zarahemla and communally enter into covenant, the story zooms out. Instead of focusing solely on brothers and sons, we will see the sweeping chronicle of a covenant people that echoes that of the Israelites in the Old Testament. If we look for a hinge-point in that shift, it is here—the moment the people unite through a shared covenant.

As the people choose to move into covenant, there is also a shift in their relationship with God. The people say that they want to "be obedient to [God's] commandments in all things" (v. 5). The concept of obedience is sometimes difficult for seekers who are inclined to interrogate scripture. In this case, the desire for obedience comes from the people themselves. This is a movement of God's children saying, "*We want to be in covenant with you; we want to obey.*" If a person's children came to them and said, "*We want to be obedient to you,*" then that would signal a change in the typical parent-child relationship. It signals a maturing of the relationship. The Nephites' obedience is founded on a desire for a closeness with God, not on fear or conformity. They are ready for a different kind of relationship.

What effect does moving into covenant have upon a people? While we do not know exactly the language of the Nephites' covenant in this moment, the covenant described in Mosiah 18:8–10 gives us a good idea of what the people here likely promised to do. That baptismal covenant is with God, but it is also with one another—a commitment to the idea of expansive, beloved community. When someone weeps, we will weep. When someone needs comfort, we will be there. We hold all of this human experience together, and that is how we will witness God. This is what covenants do: they bind us to God and to one another. So in the context of social justice, covenantal work means that if one person is oppressed, we will be there with that person. It means saying, *"None of us are truly free until you are free because we are so tightly bound to one another."* The work of covenant helps us to see systems of oppression because we are all inextricably tied in the webs of humanity. We are not separate from one another's grief, mourning, and/or oppression. We are in this together.[28] This concept is underlined here by the way that this entire experience with king Benjamin's sermon happens communally: the Nephites listen, feel the spirit, respond, and covenant as a group.

Mosiah 5:7-14

The people reinvent themselves and their community as they enter into a collective, covenantal relationship. They are "spiritually begotten" (v. 7) of Christ, joining God's family as brothers and sisters who will care for one another. And it is "under this head that ye are made free" (v. 8). Through being bound to one another and covenanting with God, we find the true freedom that God offers. Your freedom is tied up in mine, which is tied up in yours, and the only way to freedom is to move into covenant and community together.[29]

Benjamin also makes clear that caring for one another in community is how we show obedience to God through his language in

---

28. Social justice advocates, such as Martin Luther King Jr. and Desmond Tutu, have long argued for this concept of interlocking interests. Tutu writes: "White people found that freedom was indeed indivisible. We had kept saying in the dark days of apartheid's oppression that white South Africans would never be truly free until we blacks were free as well. Many thought it was just another Tutu slogan, irresponsible as all his others had been. Today they were experiencing it as a reality. I used to refer to an intriguing old film, *The Defiant Ones*, in which Sidney Poitier was one of the stars. Two convicts escape from a chain gang. They are manacled together, the one white, the other black. They fall into a ditch with slippery sides. The one convict claws his way nearly to the top and out of the ditch but cannot make it because he is bound to his mate, who has been left at the bottom in the ditch. The only way they can make it is together as they strive up and up and up together and eventually make their way over the side wall and out." *No Future Without Forgiveness*. New York City: Doubleday Religious Publishing, 1999.
29. Cross reference v. 8 with Doctrine and Covenants 18:22–23.

verse 9, when he describes the "right hand of God" and the naming of Christ. This phrasing mirrors that of Matthew 25:35–40, in which Christ teaches that feeding, clothing, and caring for "the least of these" are how we serve Him. Just as the personhood or concept of Christ is fluid enough and big enough to cover all the weary, hungry, and imprisoned people in the world, so is the name of Christ boundless enough to identify all who serve those at the margins. Taking on the name of Christ through covenant means we take on others' burdens. If we are not rescuing one another in ways that seek for the liberation of everybody, then we are not fully moving toward the right hand of God.

Verses 9–14 focus on this concept of naming and taking on Christ's name. Names are important markers of identity in society. Most cultures signal the primal importance of the individual and family through names. We can imagine the chaos that would come from every person going by the same name. And yet, this is what Christ is promising: a single name that covers all who follow God. This radically communal idea requires us to think of ourselves less as individuals and more as part of a whole. This concept is particularly important for the descendants of Lehi and Sariah, people who have divided themselves in "any manner of -ites."[30] God tries to move these people into an understanding that they are to be one. Their salvation is directly tied to their ability to build Zion.

Mosiah 5:13–15

Here we have another moment in the Book of Mormon of combining justice, mercy, and wisdom in the being of God.[31] Wisdom balances out the tension between mercy and justice. Notice also that "power" (v. 15) is placed textually between wisdom and justice. Power does not exist on its own; it is held alongside wisdom, justice, and mercy.

---

30. 4 Nephi 1:17
31. See also Jacob 4:10

Although we may struggle to understand how to appropriately balance these traits, in scripture, justice and mercy seem to walk hand in hand. Ultimately, because justice offers comfort to the abused and oppressed, justice and mercy are inseparable.[32]

As chapter 5 ends, Benjamin finishes his sermon. These first five chapters of Mosiah form one of the most groundbreaking and rich sections of the Book of Mormon. Violence, slavery, rape, and other forms of oppression will quickly follow in the coming chapters of Mosiah. But this section, covering the conversion and communal covenant making, starts us off in deep goodness. It points us to the capacity for exceedingly great joy in a people who are willing to do good all the rest of their lives.

Mosiah 6:3

Benjamin chooses to not hold onto power or position. By voluntarily stepping down and facilitating the transition of power, he helps ensure that peace continues in Zarahemla. He recognizes that he has finished the work he was called to do and does not need to maintain his status as king. That ability to realize when to pass power to someone else is remarkable. Benjamin is a man who unites people politically, but also in ways of knowing God. He is a king who is truly possessed of prophetic gifts.

As Benjamin ends the meeting, he makes sure to create structures that will help people stay committed to their covenants. He seems to understand that humans, as a group, tend to wander and lose focus. Appointing priests and writing down names are actions intended to help the people recall what they promised to do.[33]

---

32. For further discussion on this, see the section on Jacob 6:10 in Volume 1 of this series.

33. The text describes this as "stir[ring] them up in remembrance." Being stirred up sometimes makes people uncomfortable. "Stirring the pot" is an accusation that someone is unnecessarily bringing up things that are difficult. While we should strive for peace, sometimes we also need to stir people up to remembrance.

Mosiah 6:5-7

Benjamin dies three years later (v. 5). We can only imagine the good he did in his retirement. Whenever the beautiful people of scripture pass on, it is good practice to notice. Grief and death are a part of their lives, as evidenced by the narrator taking note of them. Even though verse 5 is noted almost superficially, the verse contains great significance. This nation has lost one of its really good people, a person who moved deeply in community. We should notice that.

Benjamin's son, Mosiah, grows food and works the ground in order to avoid being a burden to the people (v. 7), just like his father. The text names Benjamin's death and describes the ways in which Mosiah is living into the ways Benjamin taught him to lead, and then immediately informs readers that there was peace for three years.

Mosiah 7:1

As we move into this section dealing with Ammon and the people of Noah, Limhi, and Alma, begin to notice how the people name the land. The section references the "land of Lehi-Nephi," but it is sometimes called simply the "Land of Nephi." Recognize the ways in which the naming of the land reflects people's attitudes toward it, its inhabitants, and the people in power.

Observe here that Mosiah sends out a group to look for Zeniff and the others who went up to Lehi-Nephi because the people "wearied him with their teasings." It seems that Mosiah was reluctant to engage in this mission, yet the people wore him down. He relents because the people will not stop bothering him, and that is not a bad thing. A big part of social justice work entails the constant petitioning to people in power, much like the parable of the widow with the unjust judge in Luke 18:1–8. It is the long-term work of exhausting people into doing what is right. This effort may create the conditions that make it easier to capitulate than to refuse. The Nephites are relentless in their pleading because they worry about the people who are being ignored because of their absence. Sometimes we have to weary our leadership to check on people.

Mosiah 7:2–4

The Book of Omni describes how the Nephites integrated with the existing inhabitants of Zarahemla. In many ways that integration seems complete: they share a government, religion, language, and land. And yet the text notes that Ammon is "a descendant of Zarahemla" (v. 3). He is not a Nephite. This tells us two things: first, that biology has receded into culture, but not so much that it goes unrecognized by the people or unnamed in the text. Second, that this distinction does not stop Ammon from being the leader of the group. Also, although he does not seem to be biologically related to Zeniff and his group, Ammon sees this work as a search for his brethren (v. 2).

Enough time has passed that the people in this group do not know how to reach the land of Nephi. They are wandering in the wilderness, led by a man who has never been to the land they are searching for.

Mosiah 7:7

The response of a traumatized community is to prioritize security. The people of Limhi assume an immediate threat because they are experiencing intense oppression from the Lamanites and have a history of maltreatment from their own priests and king Noah.[34] Limhi will regret this initial response and eventually spend time with Ammon sharing histories and discussing theology, but in the first moment, they do not ask for more information or act in moderation. Although Ammon and the Nephites are not the oppressors, Limhi's people react with a kind of aggressive defense because they experience so much constant threat. They do not recognize help or goodwill when they see it because their world has been so consistently dangerous.

---

34. Mosiah 11:3–6

This is important to understand about oppressed people: to assume the best in people can be a privilege. Someone who has experienced trauma will sometimes assume that someone is dangerous until proven otherwise because trust has not served them well.

In verse 11, we learn that Limhi came very close to putting Ammon and his group to death, which would have destroyed Limhi's opportunity to find freedom. Limhi acts against his own self-interest because of his deep-seated fear and sense of threat from every side. He reacts with violence because he is surrounded with violence. While we may not condone that reaction, we can understand how people who live with constant threat might act in defensive ways.

Mosiah 7:9

Notice how Limhi includes the land of Zarahemla as part of his introduction of himself. Understanding how people see the land as part of their selfhood is fundamentally important to appreciating the textures of identity in the Book of Mormon. Here, we learn several things about Limhi: first, multiple generations have passed away but Limhi knows his history and where his ancestors came from. These are people who tell the stories of their past. Second, Limhi describes the land of Nephi as "the land of their fathers." In the following pages, the record of Zeniff will make clear the danger of an inflexible and unyielding claim of ownership over land. That master narrative that prompted Zeniff to leave Zarahemla and return to take back the Land of Nephi continues to run down the generations, with harmful effects.

Mosiah 7:12–14

Unlike Limhi, Ammon has the capacity and strength to react with nonviolence and charity. Ammon has wandered in the wilderness for a long time, endured prison for two days, and then been threatened with death. When he finally has a chance to defend himself, the first thing he offers is a title of respect to his captor and an expression of gratitude for his life. Ammon is a gracious and humble person, although the only description we have had of him so far is that he is "a strong and mighty man."[35] Ammon says that he will "endeavor to speak with boldness" (v. 12), indicating that he knows how much danger he is presently in. In the face of violence, he responds with nonviolence. He even freely offers forgiveness, saying he knows that if Limhi had known who Ammon was, he "would not have suffered that [Ammon] should have worn these bands" (v. 13). There is incredible power in that. By offering a nonviolent response to brutality, Ammon challenges the response Limhi would have expected, de-escalating the conflict and earning Limhi's trust.

Unlike Limhi, Ammon does not share his particular ancestral lineage. He simply says that he is a descendant of Zarahemla, but he also claims the people of Zeniff as his brethren (v. 13). In his very introduction, Ammon is claiming Limhi's people as his brethren, although as a descendant of Zarahemla, Ammon does not have a biological connection to them. This is true community building because he sees brotherhood where no blood is shared.

Mosiah 7:15

Limhi says that they are "in bondage to the Lamanites" because of the tax they have to pay. Yet, keep in mind this "tax" is more of a tribute in contemporary understanding and definition. This is an economic oppression. The tying of bondage and tax is important to notice. Financial burdens that push people to the edge of survival are another form of bondage. It is not the kind of bondage that we think of when we talk about slavery, but it is a kind of oppression that keeps people in captivity. The system that Limhi describes in the following verses, with his people farming the land but keeping very little of the harvest, akin to post-Civil War sharecropping.

---

35. Mosiah 7:3

Mosiah 7:16

Ammon and his group journey into the wilderness to try and find their people. They wander for a significant time before finding Limhi and then spend days in a terrible prison. They have "suffered many things." The author names the things they have suffered: "hunger, thirst, and fatigue," and the response: a chance to eat, drink, and rest. Those things go together. Too often, we do not value the significance of fatigue and rest. People get tired, and that weariness is just as harmful to them as their hunger and thirst. Being tired is a kind of suffering, and it is a symptom of having been through the wilderness. To offer rest is a special kind of gift. There is a reason that Jesus said, "Come unto me, all ye that labor and are heavy laden, and I will give you rest."[36] Offering rest for those who suffer from exhaustion is just as important as offering food and drink.

This means that as we are offering food and drink to others, we should not forget the third piece of the trifecta. The food pantries and storehouses that work to relieve the suffering of hunger and thirst should also seek to give a respite for fatigue. How can we do better in offering rest?

Mosiah 7:18–19

The way Limhi speaks to his people has strong undertones of Black preachers. They are the words of a leader speaking to an oppressed and downcast people: lift up your heads and take comfort! You will not have to wait in vain any longer, but we need to have the courage to go on because "there remaineth an effectual struggle to be made" (v. 18). For those who labor against injustice, waiting can be particularly cruel. Reverend Martin Luther King Jr. wrote that "wait has almost always meant 'Never.'"[37] For a people whose strugglings

---

36. Matthew 11:28

37. Martin Luther King, Jr. *Letter from Birmingham Jail*. Penguin Modern. London, England: Penguin Classics, 1963.

have been in vain, hearing that they are about to begin "an effectual struggle" would be incredibly empowering and exciting. It is the restoration of hope, and as the Jesuit priest and liberation theologian Jon Sobrino is credited with saying, "Hope is the seed of liberation." People can continue to work for liberation if they believe that it will get them somewhere, that the struggle will have an impact.

Then Limhi asks the people to rejoice and put their trust in God. He invokes their Abrahamic lineage and the story of when God brought the children of Israel out of Egypt. This story of liberation has brought solace to many oppressed groups throughout history, including enslaved people in the United States and those working for civil rights during Jim Crow. Remembering the God who "brought the children of Israel out of the land of Egypt, and caused that they should walk through the Red Sea on dry ground" (v. 19) has inspired Black spirituals and sermons for centuries. It is beautiful to see those connections of how the Exodus story has been vital to oppressed people. The story gives people the strength to lift up their heads, to believe that they are facing "an effectual struggle."

Mosiah 7:20–21

Here we see the Old Testament's influence in Limhi's theology as he attributes the people's bondage to their own sins. Every time we read a verse like this, we need to hold it carefully, avoiding the conclusion that all bondage is due to the failings of the enslaved. Do we believe in a God who effectively approves of bondage for those who have made mistakes? Does that theology lead us to see ourselves, and all of humanity, as children of a loving God? If not, then we need to push against it.

If we remove divine approval from this narrative, we have a story of a people who asked to claim a land where people were already settled. Although the text reads as if this was a simple and peaceful transaction, there is an inherent violence to the forced removal of a people from their lands and homes.[38] Perhaps the results of the following generations, while tragic, were not so much a divine consequence as natural consequence: violence perpetuates violence. And Limhi's people did not deserve slavery; it is not what God wanted for them, but that was the result of their ancestors' actions. This generation suffers because of the choices of Zeniff's generation and how they claimed disputed land for themselves.

This interpretation of Limhi's people's suffering comes through in verse 21, as Limhi names Zeniff as the "over-zealous" ancestor whose decisions resulted in generational suffering. And yet, even as Limhi names Zeniff's mistakes, he does not quite get to a point of truly examining them. Overzealously taking other people's land is colonization. Limhi's strongest condemnation is for king Laman, although it seems that the leadership on both sides did terrible things.

Mosiah 7:22-23

Limhi describes the tax in so much detail, naming all the different forms that it takes. His words reveal how heavily the tribute weighs on the people. His question, "Is not this grievous to be borne?" (v 23) echoes with pain and frustration. This is how it feels for a people who are dealing with the burdens of exploitative and predatory financial practices.

Mormons sometimes interpret these verses as a condemnation of all taxes, arguing against social welfare programs because of the taxes required to fund them. Alternately, we need to read these verses through the lens of those who are financially on the margins in our society. Read Limhi's words through the eyes of someone forced to pay $20 for a bounced check. Or from someone who has to pay a fee for getting their lights turned back on after they could not afford their utility payment. Our society charges people in countless ways because

---

38. Mosiah 9:6–7

they are poor, breaking them down even further.[39] When Limhi asks "is this not grievous to be borne?" he is referencing a system that is structured to make poor people stay poor. These people have "great reason to mourn" (v. 23). They are facing financial trauma and exploitation.

Mosiah 7:26–27

The prophet that Limhi references here is Abinadi. Abinadi died not knowing if his martyrdom had any effect or long-term benefit. Yet beyond Alma and the people who followed him, there is Limhi, many years after Abinadi's death, citing Abinadi's testimony. Although Abinadi did not know whether he engaged in a vain or an effectual struggle, his influence rippled down through generations. This brings solace to those who dedicate their lives to a cause that demands enormous sacrifices. Limhi names Abinadi's testimony, passing it forward.

Mosiah 7:29–33

As in verse 20, we see Limhi's Old Testament theology explaining the causes for the people's oppression. Limhi knows the testimony of Abinadi and recognizes that his ancestors did something wrong. He has internalized this as their cross to bear because of God's will. If that is Limhi's truth for himself, we can understand that. However, we need to be careful to not read this in a universal way. There is great harm in believing that God will set people free at God's "own will and pleasure" (v. 33). That almost seems as if God enjoys people suffering. That idea can foster a hopelessness in people, because they are at the mercy of a capricious God who does not offer agency or grace.

---

39. Further reading should include Baradaran, Mehrsa. *How the Other Half Banks: Exclusion, Exploitation, and the Threat to Democracy*. Cambridge, MA: Harvard University Press, 2018.

Mosiah 8:1–3

One of the most beautiful themes of the book of Mosiah is the exchange of histories and stories. Limhi shares the story of Zeniff, Noah, and Limhi's people. Then Ammon tells them what has happened in Zarahemla and shares the words of king Benjamin. They exchange personal and communal history. Beloved community comes from telling our stories. Ammon has this deep desire to know the stories of the people who left Zarahemla. Recording our own and others' stories is a sacred work. This also underlines whose stories are not shared, like those of the Mulekites in Zarahemla. The Nephites take storytelling and record keeping seriously. They understand the importance of groups sharing their differing experiences. So the fact that the history of the Mulekites is completely absent from the record tells us a lot. We pay close attention when the master narrative overrides and silences other voices. For the authors of the Book of Mormon, there seems to be an intentionality about whose histories get to be told—whose voices are considered of enough value to be part of the record. We implore readers to take particular notice about who is present yet unheard.

Mosiah 8:5–6

Ammon and Limhi continue to exchange history as they read the plates together. We see this joining of people through the physical uniting of their records. They want to know the experiences of each other's people. History is such a deep part of beloved community that Limhi is eager for Ammon to translate the records of the Jaredites (v. 6). Limhi understands that he has been entrusted with a record and that protecting it and understanding it is a sacred work. This is a powerful compilation of different folks, joined together. In this way, text acts as a facilitator for building Zion. The Jaredites are completely unrelated and separate from the Nephites, yet they become part of their community through the Nephites' adoption of the record that the Jaredites left behind. Many years after their deaths, they are brought into community. This is a different way of thinking about the purpose of scripture: that the text exists to facilitate the breaking down of barriers between people. We sit in each other's histories and witness what is sacred in someone else's story. A crucial part of building Zion is the commitment to sitting down together and saying, *"Tell me your history. Here's mine. I know that we are bound up together."*

Mosiah 8:8–11

The material items that people carry with them in the Book of Mormon have extraordinary significance. Whether it is the Liahona, the sword of Laban, the brass plates, or the Urim and Thummim, the named things tell readers what the Nephites valued. Here, Limhi identifies the gold plates (v. 9), brass and copper breastplates (v. 10), and rusted swords (v. 11). Two of the three things Limhi names are items of war. The Nephites often have Laban's sword traveling with the plates.[40] What does it mean to have entire sets of armor and swords? What travels with scripture matters. It tells us what was most precious to them. Alongside almost every holy text in the Book of Mormon are weapons and articles of war. We should not be surprised that both the Nephites and Jaredites ultimately collapsed into violence. They held items of war too close to their hearts.[41]

Mosiah 8:12

Limhi specifically wants to know the cause of the Jaredites' destruction. For a nation that is barely surviving, this would be an immediate concern: *what happened here, and how do we avoid it?* It is certainly an understandable question, particularly for people who live in a subsistence society. But if you use that lens in examining a society, you will get a certain narrative focus. That focus seems to be how the entire

---

40. Doctrine and Covenants 17:1; Mosiah 1:16
41. Matthew 6:21

Book of Mormon is written. If the Book of Mormon was written with a focus on periods of peace, asking the questions, *"What did their families look like? How did they build relationships? How exactly did they care for the poor? What did a society free of hierarchy and living in covenant look like?"* it would be a very different text. The chosen narrative is through an angle of destruction and violence. That is not wrong, it is just one way of telling a story. Readers should be aware of that and think about why that is the chosen angle. That lens seems to be the focus of the Nephites, both in how they write their own text and what they look for in others' texts.

Mosiah 8:20–21

Wisdom has a female pronoun. This is in line with the Old Testament's rendering of divine wisdom, personified as Hokmaini. This gendered language specifically attributed to divinity is important to notice. Within one verse, God is referenced as "he" and also indirectly described as "she" (v. 20). God belongs with both of those pronouns and everywhere along the gender spectrum.

Mosiah 9:1

With the start of chapter 9 comes a change in narrator and a simultaneous jump back in time. While this transition is specifically noted in the text, these changes are not always clear. Notice when the narration changes because the shift in personality and social location is important. Also, while there are periods in the Book of Mormon when we do not know the narrator, we ought to pay particular attention when we do.

Zeniff tells us quite a bit about himself in his introduction. Notice that he starts off his record in a way that is almost identical to Nephi's: "I, Zeniff," followed by him naming his education and family history. Even if he is not the holder of the Nephites' records, he is familiar with their format. Through this language, he draws parallels between himself and Nephi, who also left his home and journeyed through the wilderness to find a promised land. Zeniff's direct comparison between himself and the great hero of his people's origin story is not coincidental.

Zeniff also describes being "taught in all the language of the Nephites," which differs from Nephi and Mosiah, who referenced "the language of our fathers."[42] Zeniff's identity is specifically intertwined with being Nephite, not being an Israelite or a descendant of Nephi. Notice also that he immediately refers to the "land of Nephi, or . . the land of our fathers' first inheritance." The naming of the land will shift for him in the coming verses, as he sometimes calls it the land of Nephi and sometimes the land of Lehi-Nephi. The former is more exclusive; the latter gives some land rights to the Lamanites by emphasizing their shared lineage. This is Zeniff's personal identity and how he sees his people and their division from the Lamanites. His perspective is complicated: despite his identification as a man of conscience who understands the Lamanites on some level, he repeatedly misjudges others and precipitates violence.

Finally, Zeniff describes the land of Nephi as "my fathers' *first* inheritance," (emphasis added) implying that there was another: the land of Zarahemla. Zeniff claims two inheritances of land, both of which, in some way, are shared with or were also given to other people. With Zeniff's account, we walk into a narrative deeply invested in who is telling the story and how this person sees language, land, and identity. More than other narrators, Zeniff moves away from ancestral lineage and toward a very localized ethnocentrism. He does not, for example, invoke the common language of "the god of Abraham, Isaac, and Jacob" as do some of the other Book of Mormon narrators.[43] A phrase like that would emphasize the shared ancestral history between the Nephites and the Lamanites. Zeniff's language is bound up in the Nephites as a separate and chosen people.

---

42. 1 Nephi 3:19; Mosiah 1:2
43. For example, Nephi in 1 Nephi 17:40; Ammon in Mosiah 7:19; or Alma in Alma 29:11

Not only does Zeniff give readers a clear sense of his worldview in this concise introduction, he also explains the intention of his group and his own remarkable change of heart. He writes that they went into this land with genocidal intentions, hoping to surprise the Lamanites and "destroy them." And yet, when Zeniff actually encounters the Lamanites during his time as a spy, his own prejudices about them begin to splinter and he no longer wants to follow the original mission. He set out on a military mission to wipe out a nation and occupy their land, but then he sees that there is "good among them." In the following verses, we will read about the complicated consequences of his change of heart, but it is essential to pause here and consider Zeniff's role as a powerful force in his people's history who, although he set out with hatred and violence in his heart, was capable of changing the narrative in his head. He defies his initial understanding of the Lamanites—which reflected the prejudices of the Nephite culture and which was strong enough to make him ready to participate in genocide—and opposes authority in order to stand for the humanity of this group that he recently hated.

Mosiah 9:2

Zeniff's disobedience to a military order prompts a civil battle within this Nephite group that has prepared to attack the Lamanites. The men divide themselves between Zeniff and the commander, inciting an incredibly bloody episode with family members fighting and killing one another. Zeniff works as a spy for a force created to commit genocide and occupy land. After witnessing the humanity of his enemy, he changes his position and goes up against his ranking officer. At least some of his compatriots, who were recently just as ready as he was to destroy the Lamanites, believe Zeniff's experience and turn against some of their closest kin.

This is not only Zeniff's story, but the origin story of the group that becomes the people of Noah. They had a leader whose life was saved through the deaths of friends and family. We will see the tendrils of this terrible episode of bloodshed and disregard for human life through the rest of these people's story. The people of Noah are founded on a conflict about the questions of *"Whose humanity is counted? Who is good enough to be free and safe? Whose life can be counted as mere casualties in a mission to control land and power? When is violence justified?"*

The greater part of this battalion dies in this internal struggle and the remainder return to Zarahemla to report what happened to the widows and children of the men they killed. They have to go back to their own people, possibly their own families, and share that they did not even make it to the land of Nephi; that the death and destruction of their group came at their own hands. It is a terrible, almost unimaginable task, and yet they seem committed to transparency and taking responsibility for their own actions.

Mosiah 9:3

Zeniff frankly shares many of his own weaknesses. He sees that he is overzealous and perhaps regrets how that created problems for him and the Nephites who go with him. He seems internally conflicted, aware now of the humanity of the Lamanites and yet greedy for the land he believes he is entitled to. As he returns to the land of Nephi, he notes that the people "were slow to remember the Lord our God." Ideas and language around remembrance play a crucial role in the coming narrative, so note in the following verses what stirs people to remembrance, what they remember, and the consequences of remembering or forgetting.

Mosiah 9:4

Zeniff's men pitch their tents in the exact place where they previously battled with their compatriots. The text does not tell us why they choose this same spot—perhaps it is a particularly good hiding spot or strategic in some other way. But their choice to return to the land haunted with the blood of their brethren is macabre and symbolically significant. Their choice reinforces the violence that underlies this entire story and points to a certain level of callousness in their willingness to stay in that place. What is Zeniff's mindset in this moment? It seems from the text that the group chooses this particular spot deliberately, even choosing to mention it in the record. The inherent violence displayed in that choice should make us wary of Zeniff, his values, and how he makes decisions.

Mosiah 9:5-9

Zeniff writes that his plan is to *"possess* the land in peace" (v. 5, emphasis added), a particularly provocative word in this moment. Previously, Zeniff referred to the "land of Nephi" (v. 1). That he now describes the land as "the land of Lehi-Nephi" (v. 6) indicates that he has truly made some kind of mental connection with the Lamanites. However, he never uses the phrase "the land of Laman," which is telling. Zeniff seems to believe that he can take control of the land without violence by appealing to the king of the Lamanites. However, given that this process involves removing people from their homes (v. 7), Zeniff's occupation of the land is inherently violent. The Lamanite king uproots his own people, forcing them to leave so that the Nephites can move in. This is a good way to create ripples of violence and resentment. The Lamanites who lost their homes do not appear to have had any choice or influence on this decision. People being evicted from their land, only to watch another people possess it, will not typically foster peace.[44]

As always, the land is another character in the Book of Mormon. The way it is treated, who lives in it, and how people reference it,

---

44. For a modern comparison, this looks like the 2005 order by the Israeli government for settlers to leave parts of the occupied West Bank. Israeli soldiers forcibly pulled people from their homes as they dismantled Israeli settlements. Although the land legally belonged to the Palestinians and the order was an effort to encourage peace, the images created resentment and anger within Israel. Although the intention was justice, the effect was an increase in violence.

all tell readers a great deal about the people involved in the text. Zeniff writes that the Nephites "possess" the land (v. 7), using a word commonly associated with land in the Book of Mormon, and which implies a kind of control or domination. Striving to possess land does not seem to turn out well for people in the Book of Mormon, although they do not stop attempting it.

Notice that Zeniff's people immediately begin to "repair the walls of the city" (v. 8). We don't know exactly the origin or purpose of these walls. Were they original to the time when the Nephites lived there? Were they part of the Lamanite city and in need of repair because of unreferenced violence in the removal of people from their homes? Regardless, the Nephites' decision to put resources into those walls is significant. It is important to notice when people build walls in holy text and ask what purpose those walls serve. Who is being kept out? What is the fear? A wall is never just a wall.

In addition to buildings and walls, the people invest in agriculture. The record lists the different kinds of seeds that they grew. Food culture is so crucial to people feeling secure, particularly when there is a mass movement of people. The text does not state whether the Nephites brought the seeds with them or whether they made use of the existing agricultural structure there. However, clearly their food pathways are intrinsic to their sense of "prosper[ing] in the land" (v. 9).

Mosiah 9:11

The Nephites' movement toward development and prosperity seems to trigger the Lamanites' response of wanting to regain control of the land. This story is familiar in scripture and in history. When the Israelites began to flourish in Egypt, the local people grew afraid of losing power and pushed them into slavery.[45]

We see this in modern times as well. In June 1921, a mob of white people destroyed Black Wall Street, a section of Tulsa, Oklahoma,

---

45. Exodus 1:1–11

where Black Americans had developed wealth and built a thriving community. A financially successful Black community felt like a threat that had to be destroyed with violence that killed more than 300 people.[46] In the Jim Crow South, many lynchings were to punish Black land owners. They acted as a tool to enforce power and limit the movement and opportunities of those who had begun to thrive. These stories feature a common narrative of an upper class that can be generous as long as the lower class stays in its station. When the under class displays a capacity to significantly grow in power, that generosity morphs into fear and violence. Those in power today are not immune to this dynamic. For example, much of the conversation about immigration policy in the United States is about how much power and influence the Latinx community has over American culture and whether their labor can continue to be exploited or whether they will demand a living wage.

Mosiah 9:12

Zeniff suddenly shifts the language of his narrative as the conflict with the Lamanites intensifies. As we have already observed, before leaving Zarahemla, Zeniff thought of the Lamanites as less than human. Spending time with them as a spy revealed to him the goodness of the Lamanites (v. 9). He became almost idealistic about them, believing that they would voluntarily give up their land and coexist in peace (v. 5). Now, he calls them "a lazy and an idolatrous people," and uses that description to explain why the Lamanites want to enslave Zeniff's people (v. 12). This type of language is familiar to the Nephites in regards to the Lamanites. It seems that as conflict with the Lamanites arises, Zeniff reverts to his latent prejudices rather than making the effort to overcome his cultural bias. However, within a generation, Zeniff's people will become wicked through the corrup-

---

46. Fain, Kimberly. "The Devastation of Black Wall Street." JSTOR Daily, July 5, 2017. https://daily.jstor.org/the-devastation-of-black-wall-street/.

tion of Zeniff's son, Noah.[47] Regardless of Zeniff's beliefs about the Lamanites, this kind of rotten society that he describes is not bound by ethnicity or culture.

Setting aside Zeniff's prejudices, his description of a structurally oppressive society is excellent. "That they might glut themselves with the labors of our hands; yea, that they might feast themselves upon the flocks of our fields" tell us exactly how financial bondage works. When leadership lives off the backs of the laborers, we should be very worried. Who gets rich while others do not get a living wage in our society? Oppression comes from an endless desire for more, even at the expense of others. Some people work, others live in gluttony. Some people care for the flocks, others feast on them. Zeniff describes an exploitive extraction, an imbalance in the power relationship that creates systemic oppression.

Mosiah 9:13–14

Here is the beginning of the shift from structural violence to overt violence. Notice that it literally begins on the margins, as the Lamanites attack the shepherds on the edge of the land (v. 14). The Lamanites choose to target the people who are poor and who live at a distance from the seat of power. In any conflict, this is the population group who will usually suffer first and most deeply.

Mosiah 9:17–18

This is the moment in which we see a critical shift in the language of war. Zeniff invokes the need to remember God, but he wraps it in violence. He returns to ancestral history and remembers how God delivered the Israelites and the Nephites from terrible circumstances in the past. But in this case, he claims that God not only delivers them, but helps them kill thousands of Lamanites in battle. This ties God

---

47. Mosiah 11:2

very closely to violence, as it prompts the people to remember God and that remembrance causes their brutal victory.

This theology will become a major theme of the Book of Mormon, and it deserves examination every time. God has always been a part of the narrative of war for every side involved. Does God take sides in war, helping to facilitate death? It is possible for believers to notice how God shows up in war without attributing victories to God. Those who sense God's presence in war may recognize the way God comforts those who suffer, gives hope to people in despair, and guides people to make better choices. But the idea of an all-loving God struggles to stand up against a narrative in which God assists some of God's children to massacre other children of God. A theology in which winning war indicates God's approval leads to some dark and ugly ideas about the history of the world.

One of the more effective ways to convince people to make the sacrifices inherent to war is religion, and yet it is rarely, if ever, the true cause of conflict. Religious differences between people in conflict can strengthen internal identity and make "otherizing" the opposition significantly easier. It can inspire people to believe that their cause is righteous, not just good. It is a powerful tool for those who are trying to instigate or exacerbate violence. When Zeniff writes that his people "were awakened to a remembrance of the deliverance of our fathers" (v. 17), readers should ask: Who awakened this remembrance? To what purpose? How did it motivate people and did those actions bring them closer to God?

Verse 18 spells out how this thinking works and how it plays out when used as theology. God hears the cries of the Nephites and answers their prayers. This leads them to go into battle with increased resolve. The result is the deaths of over 3,000 people. This is the equation that this theology creates. We should wrestle with and push back against that kind of addition.

Notice that, in the end, the results of Zeniff's people coming into the land of Lehi-Nephi are essentially the same as the original plan, before Zeniff rebelled and prompted the internal battle that killed a large number of Nephite soldiers at the beginning of this story (v. 1–2). So even though Zeniff's intentions in trying to avoid massacring the Lamanites were good, the outcome was the same. Zeniff saw good in the Lamanites and it changed his heart, prompting him to try to change. Yet his overzealousness and desire to possess land overcame his willingness to sacrifice something he wanted. In the end, his intentions mattered less than his actions and the unintended consequences that followed them. Wanting to do better is not enough.

Mosiah 9:19

Zeniff emphasizes three times ("I," "myself," and "mine own hands") that he helped bury the Lamanites. It is probable that he also dealt with the bodies of the Nephites who died in the internal battle of verse 2. In this short chapter, which covers approximately thirteen years, Zeniff enters as a soldier and spy, prompts a bloody battle within his own people, follows it with twelve years of a tentative peace, and then concludes with a raging war that kills over 3,000 people. This is a man who seems to leave a wake of death behind him. It is unsurprising that he writes of "great sorrow and lamentation."

Mosiah 10:1

Although Zeniff writes that the people "again began to possess the land in peace," it is clear that war and violence have become embedded in this society. Zeniff's language about possessing the land and the fact that he establishes himself as king indicates a worldview that revolves around power and ownership. Although he writes about establishing peace, true peace cannot be achieved while simultaneously mobilizing for war. Zeniff's "peace" is overlaid by engaging in and preparing for war and creating systems of rule, making it in effect simply a 22-year ceasefire.

Mosiah 10:5

For the first time, we read about the women who existed in this society. Zeniff did not mention before that women were present. Are
these Nephite women who came with Zeniff's soldiers? Or Lamanite
women who have married into Zeniff's people? Or another group
entirely? Significantly, the first time the account acknowledges the
presence of women is to state the kind of domestic labor that they did
"in order to clothe our nakedness." The women's existence in the narrative is inseparable from the work that they do for the men's bodies.

The importance of nakedness dates to the earliest Christian
scripture, with Adam and Eve feeling shame for their nakedness and
God making "coats of skins" to cover them.[48] Throughout the Bible
and Book of Mormon, a strong theme of nakedness denotes inferiority. Nakedness is a particularly complicated topic within Nephite
society. In verse 8, Zeniff describes the nakedness of the Lamanites
explicitly, writing that "they had their heads shaved that they were
naked; and they were girded with a leathern girdle about their loins."
For Zeniff, linen clothing is an important marker not just of culture,
but of righteousness. He closely ties the Lamanites' lack of clothing to their preparations for war, their readiness to engage in war.
So the women's role in Zeniff's account is to provide the physical
manifestation that separates the Nephites from the Lamanites. It is
their marker of cultural superiority, another proof of their supposed
enlightenment.

Mosiah 10:9

The wilderness served as a haven for Lehi's family when they left
Jerusalem[49] and for Nephi when he fled from his brothers after Lehi's
death.[50] In the Book of Mormon, wilderness can be understood as

---

48. Genesis 3:21
49. 1 Nephi 2:2
50. 2 Nephi 5:5

a place of both uncertainty and refuge, where people leave behind their "precious things"[51] and embark on a journey with God. In the coming chapters, the wilderness appears again and again as a place where individuals and communities go for safety or liberation. The wilderness plays such an important role in the Book of Mormon where readers are urged to track every time it appears in the text.

Mosiah 10:10

While writers in the Book of Mormon frequently invoke God in war, they do not often explain what they mean by it. What does it mean to have "strength of the Lord to battle"? Does it mean that God helped the Nephites kill more people? We should push back when people casually draw God into a narrative of bloodshed. What kind of theology follows from that kind of narrative? Are we willing to worship the God that our own stories describe? Every time God is tied to violence, questions can and should arise as to what the author is trying to do, what is implied, and whether we want to accept the logical outcomes that follow. Zeniff is a man whose life has been chiseled with violence, often of his own making.

Mosiah 10:12–19

Zeniff writes that the Lamanites believe in a narrative of ancestral victimhood—that Laman and Lemuel "were wronged" in Jerusalem, during the journey to the new land, and after they arrived (v. 12–13). There are two important points to make in this section. First, generational narratives play an important role in an individual's identity. The ways stories are passed down, whose stories are told and from what perspective, and what we know and don't know about our ancestors, affects how we interpret our lives today. Unaddressed trauma can continue rippling down through generations, as parents consciously tell their stories and unconsciously share their broken-

---

51. 1 Nephi 2:4

ness and dysfunction. This is, again, why narratives are important: whose stories are told and in what way will deeply affect the generations that follow.

Second, notice that Zeniff presents the Nephites' version of the Lamanites' narrative. This is not the Lamanite perspective; it is Zeniff's interpretation of their perspective.[52] The Book of Mormon does not share the story from the Lamanite point of view. Any time someone speaks for someone else's cultural narrative, there is an issue of implicit bias and a loss in the story, particularly if that person or culture is actively in conflict with the group for whom they speak. Zeniff introduces this section by writing that the Lamanites "were a wild, and ferocious, and a blood-thirsty people" (v. 12). Is there any chance that he will give an objective and nuanced account of their cultural narrative after that introduction? Zeniff is not actually trying to share the Lamanites' viewpoint; he is building a case against them while claiming to do otherwise. This is how prejudice and discrimination happen, through stolen stories that are infused with stereotypes and incomplete information, then passed along as fact. It is a kind of social violence that creates the foundation for justifying physical violence.[53] Indeed, as verse 19 makes clear, the purpose of this speech is to "stimulate" the Nephites "to go to battle."

---

52. Some scholars give Zeniff credit for at least attempting to address the claims of the Lamanite experience, which is something most Nephites never do. However, we feel this is an unjust, even risky interpretation of the text. A person in the dominant society cannot and should not attempt to represent themselves as the spokesperson for another culture, particularly one with which they are actively in conflict. Speaking on the Lamanites' behalf while simultaneously using xenophobic language to describe them is violent and aggressive behavior.

53. People claiming to be able to tell the narratives of a culture they overtly hate continues today. For example, after the September 11, 2001 attacks in the United States, it was not unusual to hear political commentators claim that Muslims were terrorists because their religion inherently encourages violence. In this case, rather than listening to the diversity of Muslim experiences and beliefs, critics flattened the community into a monolith, attached a single descriptive modifier, and claimed to know the cause for that description. This is what Zeniff does to the Lamanites.

Although Zeniff pretends to share the perspective of the Lamanites, he is actively working to increase the Nephites' hatred of them.

Zeniff's claim that Laman and Lemuel hated Nephi simply because Nephi was faithful and God loved him so much is essentially a strawman argument. The way he criticizes the Lamanites while pretending to share their perspective is neither clever nor subtle. Yet, it points to the fact that the entire text presents a single narrative of the origin story of the Nephites and the Lamanites. The Book of Mormon would be a very different book if it told Laman's and Lemuel's stories. We know the suffering that Nephi experienced, and we can believe in the truth of his account. But we can also believe that Laman and Lemuel's progeny were possibly wronged in ways that we do not understand and which Zeniff has no interest in understanding. We get only a hint of one way in which Laman and Lemuel felt victimized when Zeniff notes how Nephi took the plates with him when he fled into the wilderness (v. 16). While Nephi never documented his choice to take the plates, his brothers seem to have felt the loss.

Finally, Zeniff writes that the Lamanites taught their children to hate the Nephites and exact violence against them, claiming that the Lamanites have "an eternal hatred" (v. 17) toward them. Zeniff may be correct that the Lamanites have cultivated a culture of enmity toward the Nephites. What he does not see or chooses not to record is that the Nephites have done the same toward the Lamanites. Zeniff himself was a product of this: before encountering the Lamanites, he was ready to destroy them.[54] That kind of violent intent does not occur in a vacuum. It is born of a committed and deliberate effort to dehumanize another group of people. Zeniff can see how his personal interaction with the Lamanites changed his prejudices, but he does not acknowledge the culture that formed that hatred.

Additionally, "eternal" is a problematic word to pair with "hatred" (v. 17). Tying the two together does not allow for the hope of Christ's Second Coming, releasing us from the vile and fallen parts of this life.

---

54. Mosiah 9:1

Insisting that hate is eternal denies the power of God to cause evil to pass away. At times, hatred may seem never-ending. As is the case for the Nephites and Lamanites, it may be passed down through generations for hundreds of years. But God inhabits the eternal, and even hatred will fail with Christ's return and the establishment of Zion.

Mosiah 10:20–21

The violence described in these verses is shocking, even for the Book of Mormon. In an earlier battle, Zeniff's army counted over 3,000 deaths.[55] Here—a clearly brutal episode—they do not make an attempt to count. Yet, Zeniff immediately follows the description of the battle with the statement that the armies returned to their farms and life proceeded as normal (v. 21). He seems willing to compartmentalize the violence, stating it and then moving on as if it had no effect on the people. But humans are marked by that kind of engagement and witness to violence. Trauma at this scale in a society does not simply pass by. And while Zeniff's record ends, we know from the following chapters how unhealthy his society has grown. As Noah steps into power, a system of corruption and wickedness allows him to rule in unrighteousness. The violence that Zeniff dismisses so cavalierly will continue to reverberate through his kingdom, once again creating unintended consequences that Zeniff did not foresee.

Mosiah 11:1

At this point in the text, the narrator once again changes, this time without notice or explanation. Zeniff wrote chapters 9 and 10, and he introduced himself in the text. Here, without warning, we shift to a new author, presumably but not necessarily the same one who wrote chapters 1–8. An important signature of the Book of Mormon is the way the authors introduce themselves and give their social location. That being the case, we emphasize anytime the author goes

---

55. Mosiah 9:18

unnamed. While we know Mormon abridged this record, we do not know whose perspective this is. That means we cannot fully understand potential biases or whose voice is missing in the narrative. When the author is unnamed, it becomes easier for readers to interpret the text as omniscient and complete instead of as one person's record.

What we glean from the coming chapters is that the author had intimate knowledge of the inner workings of king Noah's throne room, including events that happened after Alma left,[56] so Alma could not be the sole author. The author also had the ability to recognize and record the corruption of religious and governmental authorities in fairly radical ways. Readers who wish the Book of Mormon included the voices of women may use biblical imagination here to create their own version of the author. Perhaps she was one of Noah's servants or concubines, quietly taking notes from the side and giving a record to Alma later.

Mosiah 11:2

Nephite men repeatedly commit the sin of having many wives and concubines. Jacob earlier in the text starkly condemned the Nephite men for their whoredoms and the damage it wrought within their families.[57] Yet, this damage recurs again. Here, the author names this problem first in a list of transgressions, although there is a multitude of other bad behaviors happening. Once again, the way the Nephite men think about and act toward women is foremost on the list of their sins. As scholar Joseph Spencer has noted, "The Book of Mormon undeniably presents a depressing picture of the situation for Nephite women."[58]

---

56. See Mosiah 17
57. Jacob 2:22–28
58. Joseph Spencer.*1st Nephi: A Brief Theological Introduction*. Provo, UT: Neal A. Maxwell Institute, 2020,104.

The author's assertion that Noah "did cause his people to commit sin" is interesting. Are those who occupy positions of leadership and power responsible for the sins of their people? Jacob appears to have believed so when he wrote that he called people to repentance in order to no longer bear the responsibility of their sins.[59] From the perspective of social justice, systems and laws that devalue humanity may encourage individuals to become agents of sin. For example, the American Fugitive Slave Act of 1850 stimulated a market and occupation in enforcing enslavement. The Nuremberg Laws prompted Gestapo officers to arrest and punish Germans who married Jews. Evil leaders have the power to create bad laws that will then encourage unjust and wrong behavior. Yet, the text seems to go further than that, stating that Noah *caused* the people to sin, not just that he passed power structures that encouraged it. Without knowing the details of this society, it seems possible that Noah went even further, perhaps using violence or coercion to more forcefully cause the people to do terrible things.

Mosiah 11:3–6

Probably more than any other section of the Book of Mormon, the Book of Mosiah explores concepts of fiscal violence. King Noah's story in particular looks at this theme through the lens of taxation. With Limhi's people, the burdensome tax came from the outside, as the Lamanites essentially enslaved the Nephites through weighty levies. With Noah, the fiscal violence is internal: a Nephite king harming his own people through harmful financial policies. The author finds it important to name all the items that have been taxed to emphasize the burden of Noah's taxes (v. 3). Yet rather than reading this as a broad indictment against taxes, it is important to note exactly where money is going in this society.

---

59. 2 Nephi 9:44

In Noah's financial system, money flows from the general public to the wealthy. This is not a system in which taxes exist in order to protect vulnerable populations. At certain times in the Book of Mormon, societies establish policies in which the rich give up their substance in order to care for the poor.[60] Noah's system acts in the opposite way, a system designed to allow the elites to profit from the laborers. Thus, king Noah's taxes are not unrighteous because all taxes are wrong, but rather because of the direction the money moves. Economic injustice has always been about policies that privilege the wealthy. When a tax exists to help the prosperous get rich off of others' poverty, that tax is both unjust and immoral. This is emphasized in verse 6, as the author states that "the people labor exceedingly to support iniquity." This is the culmination of a financial system built to oppress the workers and exalt the rulers. The people work hard but they do not profit from it. Instead, their labor flows to the wealthy and allows them to act with impunity. King Noah's financial structures are designed to force people to support the very system that oppresses them. Their work keeps him in power.

Noah's simultaneous corruption of the church and of the state (v. 5) offers a strict warning for us today. When we examine our own financial systems, we should ask the questions: who is working and who reaps the benefits of that work? In what direction do financial resources flow? Do marginalized people have to work in order to support an iniquitous system that keeps them in their place? If this is happening in our own financial policies, how can we begin to dismantle and change those laws?

Mosiah 11:8–12

The gold, brass, and copper that Noah taxes seem to go directly into ornamenting these elite buildings, making their very structure unrighteous. Buildings and monuments throughout history have

---

60. Examples include Alma 1:27 and 4 Nephi 1:3.

frequently been physical representations of the oppression used to construct them. Hundreds of thousands of people died while working to build the Great Wall of China. Many universities in the United States, such as Georgetown and University of North Carolina, were originally built by enslaved people. In addition to offering praise and prestige to whatever person or movement inspired them, these edifices are also representations of exploitation. Noah built his spacious palace and temple through materials taken from laborers. The temple—a building meant to be the holiest of spaces—came into being through fiscal violence and oppression. When the construction of a temple is laden in sin, it becomes a deep symbol of the values of those in power. Noah's commitment to physical reminders of his disregard for human value extends to the decoration of his palace, in which the priests sat above everyone else (v. 11). The author of this section of Mosiah clearly had close knowledge of the interior of the palace and an acute awareness of the king's hypocrisy and corruption.

Mosiah 11:14

While written in a separate time for a different situation, Jacob's sermon to the Nephite men perfectly addresses the sins of king Noah: a love of riches and the exploitation of women. According to Jacob, those two things are among the most grievous sins and will lead to the downfall of a nation.[61]

Mosiah 11:16–19

Martin Luther King Jr. said that "Hate begets hate; violence begets violence."[62] Any exercise of something makes it stronger. In this case, the Lamanites exercise their hatred. The Nephites respond with an

---

61. Jacob 2:34–35 and 3:3–4.

62. Martin Luther King, Jr. *Loving Your Enemies*. Sermon delivered at Dexter Avenue Baptist Church, Montgomery, AL, Nov. 17, 1957. https://kinginstitute.stanford.edu/king-papers/documents/loving-your-enemies-sermon-delivered-dexter-avenue-baptist-church

escalation of violence, with the consequences of death and glorification of bloodshed.

In Noah's kingdom, the laborers live on the economic margins of society. These are also the people whom the Lamanites initially attack, people "tending their flocks" (v. 16) on the edges of the land. Far too often, the same people who are overworked and oppressed by internal political systems also suffer the most from external forces. All forms of violence break most heavily on the backs of the vulnerable.

Notice that the author does not make any attempt to insert divine favor into this conflict. Neither side has any claim on righteousness as the Lamanites exercise hatred and the Nephites delight in the shedding blood. At root, these two groups' actions stem from the same sin of pride and dehumanization of others.

Mosiah 11:20–25

Abinadi's initial sermon to the Nephites is reminiscent of the Old Testament, with language about "a jealous God" (v. 22) and God allowing the unrighteous to "be smitten by their enemies" (v. 23). Abinadi even tells the people that "they shall be brought into bondage" (v. 23) and that God "will not hear their prayers" (v. 24). Should we understand Abinadi's words as a theology in which God allows slavery as a punishment for sin and refuses to listen to the prayers of certain people? This would clearly be a very problematic way of exegeting these verses.

When reading scripture, we are sometimes called to separate the universal and the particular. Certain stories and teachings are meant to have universal application: we read a story from scripture 2,000 years after it was written and we see how it continues to apply to us today. In other cases, a prophet's words are meant for that specific time and place. In this situation, Abinadi's sermon is for king Noah and the elites of the city engaging in these evil actions. That does not give us license to take the words and use them to justify slavery or claim that God always ignores the prayers of the unrighteous. This sermon is specific, not universal.

Mosiah 11:27–29

Noah built a luxurious temple and yet asks Abinadi who God is. The existence of the building, in itself, has no correlation with the maker's relationship with God. People and churches can have large and beautiful temples without giving them meaning. In fact, for Noah, God is fused with state power and exists to justify his own oppressive regime.[63]

The prevailing emotion in Noah's first response to Abinadi is one of extreme anger. Noah's intense and immediate desire to kill Abinadi stems from the same kind of fear that has led to the deaths of many of those who organize and agitate for change. Noah is angry because Abinadi might "stir up" the people—in other words, Abinadi might disrupt the status quo. Notice that Noah's excuse is that the people might engage in "contentions" (v. 28), as if the anger of the people is the problem and not the policies that are in place. Noah currently has the people under his control, and his defense for keeping it that way is that it superficially looks like peace. This tells us what happens to a community that is called to repent: it looks like contention and anger as people begin to move in changing structures. It looks like what civil rights leader John Lewis called "good trouble." An absence of conflict is not a good goal in itself, because that can simply hide the injustice and unrighteousness beneath. Disruptors may bring contention, but that's what is needed for real change.

Mosiah 12:1

After calling the people to repentance, Abinadi goes into hiding for two years. Dr. J. Kameron Carter claims that whether we are aware or not, we believe in a fugitive gospel, with a Savior who was cruci-

---

63. Joseph M. Spencer, *An Other Testament: On Typology*, 2nd ed. (Provo, UT: Neal A. Maxwell Institute, 2016), 142–45.

fied by a systematically oppressive government.[64] Abinadi serves as a fugitive prophet who spends years in disguise, hiding from authority. While the record does not give an account of this time, we can imagine that he tries to live his call as a prophet while also fleeing for his life and trying to protect himself. Abinadi is literally on the run for being a prophet. This parallels Lehi, who also had to escape the threat of his own people because he called them to repentance. While Lehi went into the wilderness and did not return to Jerusalem, other Biblical prophets acted similarly to Abinadi, leaving or hiding, and then returning after a time.[65] In scripture, prophets commonly move in and out of their communities in order to preserve their safety.

According to the account, God told Abinadi to return to the city and call people to repentance. Although "the people were blinded" because they "hardened their hearts," and had even tried to kill Abinadi already,[66] God still calls them "my people" (v. 1). God is angry with them and is ready to punish them, yet still they are God's people. And while they have done so many evil things, God still calls a prophet to walk among them and give his life to teach them. From this we can understand that 1) being called God's people does not imply righteousness or even specialness and 2) God values the worth of even the most sinful people.

Mosiah 12:3–8

Of all the Book of Mormon prophets, Abinadi is the closest to an Old Testament prophet in terms of his preaching style. He vividly describes the bad things that will happen to the people, acted out against them by an angry God. He sounds like Jeremiah, Ezekiel, or Isaiah in the way he narrates God. After giving the list of ways God will punish the people, he summarizes by telling them that God "will utterly destroy them

---

64. J. Kameron Carter. *Dietrich Bonhoeffer course,* Lecture at Duke Divinity School, Spring 2015.
65. Examples include Elijah, John the Baptist, Moses, and Jesus.
66. Mosiah 11:29

from off the face of the earth" (v. 8). And yet, here he deviates from the ways of the Old Testament prophets as he tells them that a record will outlive the people. He explicitly states that those that follow will learn from the mistakes of earlier people and the record will help those people make better choices. An interesting theme of the Book of Mormon is that creating a record will bring others to God, even if your own people die out, by bringing peace and hope to others.[67] Part of the work of the Book of Mormon is to help people not repeat the great failures of the Nephites and the Lamanites. The records are preserved, in part, as a cautionary tale, and not always as a template to follow.

The text gives clear and specific lists of what the Nephites did under king Noah to warrant God's wrath: they treated women as commodities and made wealth into an idol.[68] Along with their long-standing hatred of the Lamanites, these are recurring problems for the Nephites. The Book of Mormon makes clear what happens to a society where people do not treasure their wives and children. We know what happens to communities that choose not to let go of their hatred for another group of people. The record tells us what happens to a civilization where violence and war are the strongest organizing forces. This is a sacred text that tells us explicitly, again and again: we are a people who are going to be destroyed, but we will leave you a record so that you do better. One of the purposes of the Book of Mormon is to call us to repentance and to learn from the Nephite civilization.

Mosiah 12:9–16

The people bind Abinadi and deliver him to the corrupt government. The community turns on the prophet and lets the political institution do the work of killing him. This is a heartbreaking betrayal for

---

67. For example, Enos' "soul did rest" after God covenants with him that the Lamanites will eventually have the Nephites' records in Enos 1:17. Moroni wrote about his words being for the Lamanites in Moroni 1:4.
68. Mosiah 11:2–6.

Abinadi. According to the people, Abinadi's offense is that he "prophesied evil" about the people and warned of the fragility of the king's life (v. 9–10). Notice particularly what the people say as they appeal to power to intercede for them against someone who has publicly spoken about what is wrong in their society: "we are guiltless, and thou, O king, hast not sinned" (v. 14). Abinadi spoke the truth of the evil that has permeated this society and they want to punish him in an effort to maintain the fiction of their own innocence. If they can preserve that narrative, then they do not have to take on responsibility for changing anything.

When injustice and unrighteous things happen, who claims that there is nothing wrong and that they have no culpability? A strong tie exists between the ability to perpetuate an evil system and the narrative of innocence. For example, in the case of structural racism, people will say, "*I am not at fault, I am not a racist, those things are not my fault.*" This lynchpin perpetuates the status quo by allowing every individual person to reject responsibility for it. We have to be honest with ourselves and be accountable to truth because the prophetic will often incriminate every one of us and ask us to push back against accepted power structures. If we do not see how we are complicit in those structures, if we insist that we are guiltless and so are our political and ecclesiastical leaders, then we do not work for justice. The people of king Noah may not see their own sin, but it is imperative that we see it. Our heeding ensures that Abinadi's prophecies were not in vain.

As evidence of their innocence, Noah's people employ ideas of prosperity gospel. When they state that they "are strong" and that Noah "hast prospered in the land" (v. 15), they are saying that they are privileged and that there is no way that they could ever be not privileged. Their wealth and strength must mean God favors them. Abinadi counters by stating they will lose their measures of identity and what they value—strength and wealth. The people do not believe that can happen because they are blinded by their own privilege. This is the threat of internalizing prosperity gospel: you believe that the good things around you are indicative of God's approval of your current state, which means that as long as you do not change, you will always have those good things.

Finally, the people tell king Noah to "do with [Abinadi] as seemeth thee good" (v. 16). They do not ask him to do what *is* good, but rather what *seems good* to Noah. Problems arise when authorities and systems do what they see as good, not what *is* good. The people here have ceded any kind of moral authority to their political leader. This is the final way that they attempt to maintain their own guiltlessness: the moral imperative is for Noah to do what seems good, not for them to insist on what is good.

Mosiah 12:19–37

The priests interrogate Abinadi in order to "cross him" (v. 19). Not every question is designed to elicit truth, or is asked with good intentions, which is why Jesus often used parables. Be wary of those who weaponize questions. Yet, Abinadi answers "boldly" (v. 19), which is why he is such a compelling character in the Book of Mormon. Abinadi goes straight up against the authority that simultaneously occupies the seat of religious and governmental power, and he confounds them. He speaks truth to those who wield every earthly weapon in his society, and they cannot cross him. He almost seems to revel in doing this, as he taunts them with questions about their authority. In verse 25 he asks, "Are you priests, and pretend to teach this people, and to understand the spirit of prophesying, and yet desire to know of me what these things mean?" He repeatedly underscores the gap in their social stations, making clear the meaninglessness of those titles of power.

Abinadi identifies two ways in which the priests have erred: in corrupting the legal systems and in "perverting the ways of the Lord" (v. 26), which is even worse. The priests "have not applied [their] hearts to understanding" (v. 27). They appointed themselves spiritual leaders without doing the work required. They have not wrestled with scripture and engaged in a dialogue with God so that they could step into the responsibilities that come with religious power. As the priests begin to answer Abinadi's questions, they respond on the defensive. Standing alone and defenseless in front of a council of people with immense privilege, Abinadi is the one with real power. Through nonviolent confrontation, Abinadi shows that status and wealth mean nothing without God.

Readers are invited to sink into the question Abinadi asks, because it is useful for any person or organization that wants to do God's work: If you teach the law, why do you not keep it? Do we truly live the laws that we teach? Have they penetrated our hearts and transformed how we act? Abinadi uses these questions specifically to call out the religious leaders of his society. The priests are no good if they do not live the words they teach. The priests exemplify misusing scripture for their own ends, interpreting Isaiah as they wish in order to justify the oppressive regime they embody.[69]

Mosiah 13:1–4

One of those tools that the powerful use when faced with a threat to their privilege is to question the agitators' sanity. Noah and the priests go into this confrontation intending to trick Abinadi into giving them a reason to accuse him. When they cannot do that, Noah dismisses him as mad (v. 1). Abinadi emphasizes this charge in verse 4, saying that Noah has accused him of insanity "because I have spoken the word of God." Throughout history, when ideas and individuals have become too much of a threat to institutional power, they get simply dismissed as insane. Truth-tellers frequently have to face charges against their mental health in their efforts for justice.

In introducing his last, defiant speech, Abinadi makes clear that he is the person with true power in the room. They will not stop him before his task is done. And when he finishes, they can do what they

---

69. Spencer, *An Other Testament*, 142–45.

want, but ultimately it is on his terms. This is the striking power of nonviolent resistance: by voluntarily offering up his life to his cause, Abinadi markedly underscores the limits of his enemy's power. Even if they kill him, they do not control him. They cannot stop his ideas and his words from spreading. Nonviolence is one of the powerful tools against oppressors because it removes their ability to control fear.[70] Abinadi does not fear death and so his enemies have no power over him.

Mosiah 13:8

We do not often think of wonder, amazement, and anger coexisting as feelings together. Normally the response to wonder and amazement is a feeling of humility or awe. Abinadi's words provoked an introspective response from the priests: this is the wonder and amazement. Yet, the result is a conviction of their behavior, prompting shame and, finally, anger. This is not a healthy guilt or remorse, motivating them to better behavior. It is a festering shame which turns them away from God and toward violence. Feeling anger along with wonder and amazement indicates hard-heartedness, a signifier that one has reached a place of being beyond the goodness of God's word. The divine still feels powerful, but it no longer prompts repentance; it pushes the person toward a vicious anger. When Laman and Lemuel were still willing to listen and repent, Nephi could teach them. It is when they became "past feeling" that they responded with anger and brutality.[71]

---

70. "Nonviolent struggle both requires and tends to produce a loss (or greater control) of fear of the government and its violent repression. That abandonment or control of fear is a key element in destroying the power of the dictators over the general population." Gene Sharpe. *From Dictatorship to Democracy*. Boston: Albert Einstein Institution, 2003.

71. 1 Nephi 17:45–48

Mosiah 13:12-14:12

Theologically and rhetorically, Abinadi acts as a bridge between the Old and New Testaments. He invokes the story of Moses and the Ten Commandments while looking forward to Jesus and the higher law. He warns of destruction, but also offers the intercession of Christ. He beautifully ties it together: if you know the Law of Moses, you know the commandments. If you know the prophets, then you know there is a Messiah coming. And if you know that, you should know that he will be oppressed and afflicted. The emotional peak of Abinadi's sermon comes as he describes Christ. Of all the scriptures to reference, Abinadi chooses Isaiah 53, which emphasizes that the Messiah will come forth in the margins of society: "he is despised and rejected of men; a man of sorrow, and acquainted with grief" (14:3). Particularly for an audience like Noah and his priests, this is a radical sermon. Abinadi places Jesus at the point of the oppressed, as a person of sorrows. In the halls of religious and governmental power, Abinadi bears testimony of a God who will know grief. After starting his sermon with warning of plagues and damnation, he ends with a Christ who is "oppressed" and "afflicted" (14:7). What is extraordinary about Abinadi is that as a prisoner, with his life at stake, he tells the most powerful men in the land, "You will find the Messiah in prison" (14:8).

Mosiah 15:5-8

Imagine what it means for Abinadi, a man betrayed by his own people and facing execution, to know that the Savior would "be mocked, and scourged, and cast out, and disowned by his people" (v. 5). Like Christ, Abinadi faces the voluntary surrender of his life, "the will of the Son being swallowed up in the will of the Father" (v. 7). Of all the testimonies of the Book of Mormon, this one is striking in how personal and immediate it is for the speaker. We can only imagine what it means for Abinadi, in this moment, to speak of how "God breaketh the bands of death" (v. 8).

Mosiah 15:9

After having experienced this extraordinary suffering, Jesus will "ascend into heaven, having the bowels of mercy; being filled with compassion towards the children of men" and "having redeemed them, and satisfied the demands of justice." What does it mean to believe in God who not only knows pain and grief, but who emerges from it with bowels of mercy *and* having satisfied justice? If we are trying to be like Jesus, it means moving toward justice, answering the demands of justice, while having mercy and compassion. It is not simply balancing mercy and justice, but realizing that one of the works of justice is to create space for mercy and compassion. Mercy is a by-product of justice work done well; they are inseparably linked. Satisfying the demands of justice allowed Christ's bowels to be filled with mercy.

Even after warning Noah and the priests of their coming destruction, Abinadi offers a strikingly generous theology in these verses. He teaches them about the God who opens up the way for their repentance. Abinadi names their failings and sins, but then explains how Jesus has built a way for them to come back. He does not simply call them out, but instead teaches them: here is who God is; this is what Jesus' suffering means for you. Even as justice will inevitably move forward, compassion and mercy can come in its wake.

Mosiah 15:10–19

This discourse about God's seed is beautiful. It is slightly different from Alma's sermon about the word being like a seed in Alma 32. Here, the "heirs of the kingdom of God" (v. 11) are the seed of God, pointing to the potential of humanity to grow into the divinity within them. Who are God's children? The question leads to an inclusive theology because it nods at the expansive embrace of God.

The prophets publish peace and "good tidings of good" (v.14). Abinadi says that prophets publish peace through calling people to repentance. This is the good tidings of a God who moves in justice but also mercy and compassion: there is rest waiting for you because we speak of a Christ who has suffered all things and is "the founder of peace" (v. 18).

Mosiah 15:25

This sentence, formed in just seven simple words, marks one of the most important doctrinal principles of the Book of Mormon. Children have eternal life. No other explanation is needed; no qualification is appropriate. Do not try to condemn children. This is good tidings indeed.

Mosiah 15:26–27

Here Abinadi returns to tougher rhetoric, reminding his audience that they ought to fear and tremble. He needs them shaken because even God "cannot deny justice when it has its claim" (v. 27). Abinadi recognizes Christ's "bowels of mercy" (v. 9) while insisting that if we do not want to change and repent, if we are not willing to love God and one another, then God will not deny justice. God stands between us and justice, but not if we do not desire it. This theology offers so much mercy and compassion, but it is consistently couched in understanding that the claims of justice are real.

Mosiah 15:28–31

Once again, Abinadi balances out his warnings with beautiful, inclusive language about a loving God. Every group of people will have the opportunity to hear God's word, and we will sing together in Zion.[72] The phrase "they shall see eye to eye" emphasizes equality

---

72. This idea of Zion as a global choir was the foundation for Jeffrey R. Holland's April 2017 General Conference talk: "Brothers and sisters, we live in a mortal world with many songs we cannot or do not yet sing. But I plead with each one of us to stay permanently and faithfully in the choir, where we will be able to savor forever that most precious anthem of all—'the song of redeeming love.' Fortunately, the seats for this particular number are limitless. There is room for those who speak different languages, celebrate diverse cultures, and live in a host of locations. There is room

among people as they stand on a footing that allows them to look one another in the eyes (v. 29). Abinadi goes on, stating that God comforts even "the waste places," and promises that the land will be healed (v. 30). The invitation to "break forth into joy" is hard to resist. Once more underlining that God's promises are universal, Abinadi reminds us that "*all* the ends of the earth shall see the salvation of our God" (v. 31, emphasis added). Noah and the priests' use of these verses to justify their system of taxes and extravagant living[73] make Abinadi's interpretation all the more radically joyful.

Mosiah 16:1–2

Notice that the consequence of disobeying God is to "be cast out" (v 2). Being cast out means no longer having the option or opportunity to be part of the community. This starkly contrasts with the description of Zion and a joyful worldwide choir at the end of chapter 15. The other side means losing Zion, to be forced out of community. This is one of the claims of justice: if you sin against God through the mistreatment of others, you cannot expect to continue to have the joy of community. Abinadi does not mince words in his description of what being cast out looks like: it is a moment of weeping and wailing and gnashing of teeth. It is one of the greatest losses we can experience.

---

for the single, for the married, for large families, and for the childless. There is room for those who once had questions regarding their faith and room for those who still do. There is room for those with differing sexual attractions. In short, there is a place for everyone who loves God and honors His commandments as the inviolable measuring rod for personal behavior, for if love of God is the melody of our shared song, surely our common quest to obey Him is the indispensable harmony in it. With divine imperatives of love and faith, repentance and compassion, honesty and forgiveness, there is room in this choir for all who wish to be there." "Songs Sung and Unsung," April 2017. https://www.churchofjesuschrist.org/study/general-conference/2017/04/songs-sung-and-unsung

73. Mosiah 11:8–12

Mosiah 16:3

Using the phrase "our first parents" as a way to reference Adam and Eve is simultaneously familial and egalitarian. It is a thoughtful way of describing them, a title uniquely used in the Book of Mormon. While scripture frequently references only Adam, ignoring Eve altogether, this title inclusively connects readers to ancestral legacy.

Mosiah 16:7–9

Although Abinadi speaks to Noah and the priests more than a hundred years before the birth of Christ, he references the resurrection as if it has already happened. His powerful, prophetic way of speaking shares a hermeneutical quality with other Old Testament-era prophets, such as Isaiah and Lehi. We also see it in other prophets, such as Martin Luther King Jr. and Joseph Smith, where they spoke of the future as if it was the present. For them, time seems to have had less meaning. They could own the blessings of something, even if they did not live to see it in their mortal lives. Abinadi was able to live into the manifestation of the conquering of death long before Christ lived. Martin Luther King Jr. seemed able to celebrate an end of racism, an idea not only far beyond the end of his life and seemingly also beyond ours.

The language of these particular verses has long held special significance for worshippers in varying Christian denominations: "[T]here could have been no resurrection. But *there is* a resurrection, therefore the grave hath no victory, and the sting of death is swallowed up in Christ" (v. 7–8, emphasis added). When people suffer in life and feel surrounded by death, the idea that death has no sting, that death does not have the final word, is an extraordinary promise. God "is the light and the life of the world; yea, a light that is endless," who promises future healing for those who grieve and struggle today. While this language offers comfort for everyone, it holds special promise to those who are most oppressed. It overturns everything in mortality: everything that is hurtful and wrong is washed away, and God stands ready with profound and endless light. For Abinadi, a man walking toward his death as he begins to conclude his sermon, these ideas must have been particularly strengthening.

Mosiah 16:12

Working for social justice in any field demands a degree of selflessness and effort to respect the humanity of all humans. Living a life of carnal wills and desires inhibits our ability to move in community. Repentance, or being willing to accept "the arms of mercy" extended toward us, is the way that we check our tendency to center our own desires and will.

Mosiah 16:14–15

With the last words of his sermon, Abinadi tells the priests how to teach the gospel. This is, at its core, an Easter sermon: he shares a message of hope through redemption. The fact that Abinadi chooses those hopeful words while preaching to a community that has gone so far down a path of wickedness shows how much faith he has in God's extended arms of mercy. He tries to share that hope with the priests, to give them the motivation to do better. At the very end, he addresses the clergy one more time. For any of us who teach the gospel in some capacity, this message is crucial: if you're going to do anything, teach people that redemption comes through Christ. Give them that hope.

Mosiah 17:1–3

As Abinadi faces his death, "there was one among them" (v. 2) who responds to his words and takes action. This is how social justice and the prophetic work: it requires great risk, and it should light a fire. It means a person proclaims truth, even when facing the possibility of death, because she has faith that truth will start a movement that will fight for the oppressed.

The author notes that "Abinadi had testified against them" (v. 2). In a church context, we usually think of testimonies as a way of proclaiming what we believe to be true. The language in this verse indicates that spiritual testimonies, like legal testimonies, can also be used as a witness against people. Nephi also taught that the testimonies of the oppressed could be used as evidence against the wicked in the last days.[74] It is therefore imperative that we listen carefully to those testimonies today, not just the ones that affirm our own faith, but the ones that call us to see others in new and more complete ways and to repent of our past actions.

In verse 2, we get a little bit of information about this responsive listener, Alma: he is a descendant of Nephi, he is young, he believes in Abinadi's words, and he already knows about the iniquity Abinadi preached against. Something in him previously had a sense that things were wrong in his community. Since we do not yet have a first-hand account by Alma, this is essentially the introduction of Alma's social location. Readers can use this information as the events around Alma unfold and he begins to preach his understanding of the gospel.

Abinadi's words move Alma from someone who passively observes a problem to someone who becomes actively engaged in the cause. Immediately, Alma puts his own life in danger for this cause, pleading with the authorities to grant Abinadi clemency. Disregarding the risk, Alma speaks truth to power and advocates on behalf of the prophetic. His first appeal to Noah is to let go of anger, a common responses to a call to repentance. Many times in social justice work, people respond with anger or even explicit violence. That kind of wrath stems from a rejection of any kind of questioning or confrontation of their power and privilege. For Noah, the anger is so intense that it spills over from Abinadi onto Alma, forcing Alma to "be cast out" and run for his life (v. 3).

---

74. 2 Nephi 26:3

Mosiah 17:5–10

Abinadi returns to prison for three days before he is brought back to the court where Noah says, "Abinadi, we have found an accusation against thee" (v. 7). The wording of this statement tells us so much about Noah and the kind of government he has created. He has *found* an accusation. The justice system exists, in this society, to uphold the power of the ruling class. However, Abinadi refuses to retract his words, choosing instead to reiterate two of his most important points: First, through nonviolent activism, he has taken away their power because he has no fear of them. He draws a clear line around the limits of their authority through his willingness to accept death. Second, he emphasizes that his testimony will act as evidence against them. Abinadi takes the idea of testimony to a new standard by explaining that others' testimonies are not just for edification, but also for conviction.

Mosiah 17:11–12

Although Noah is ready to release Abinadi, the priests convince him to kill the prophet, using Noah's pride to convince him. Here, the church leaders are complicit in the death of the prophet, the man calling for repentance. As believers, we too have to be watchful that those who we follow are not operating in ways that work to silence testimony.

The priests can convince Noah of what he should do because of his pride and anger. They deliberately stir up those feelings of wrath, knowing that he will act out in violence. Anger can be used righteously, as Jesus used it to cleanse the temple, but be wary of it. If we are in the habit of employing anger in a decision, there is a need to carefully examine what kind of choices we make while in that period of anger and how much time we spend there.

Mosiah 17:15–20

Abinadi preaches again of a God of compassion and mercy, but also of a God of justice. In this moment, it becomes clear how testimonies stand as witnesses against people. Abinadi tells the oppressors that they cannot keep doing evil work and think that God will not exact vengeance on behalf of those who have suffered harm because of their sin. This is an excellent example of why God cannot encompass mercy without also embracing justice.

Abinadi's final words, "O God, receive my soul" (v. 19), are followed by an editorial commentary about Abinadi's death: "[H]aving been put to death because he would not deny the commandments of God, having sealed the truth of his words by his death" (v .20). These words sound like the words of many martyrs of just causes, whether it is Táhirih Qurrat al-ʿAyn or Joseph Smith. What does it mean to seal truth with your death? Truth does not require blood to stand. Perhaps it simply indicates a perceived threat if someone would kill a truth-teller for their work. It is not that truth requires a martyr, but that in truly terrible situations, death is often the outcome of someone speaking out.

At the moment of his death, we should take a moment to honor Abinadi. While we do not know much about his life or who he was, the events of the following chapters would never have happened without Abinadi's work. He died without knowing exactly what effect his sacrifices would have, yet the record of his words affected innumerable journeys with God. This is why every time there is a shift in the text with a new author or prophet, it provides an opportunity to reflect on the contributions and sacrifices of our spiritual ancestors. We can mourn and grieve that Abinadi had to seal his truth with his death. And then we can begin to walk with Alma on his journey of living the truth that Abinadi preached.

Mosiah 18:1

Alma does three things after going into hiding: he repents of his own sins, records the words of Abinadi,[75] and begins to preach to others. In this moment of changing his way of engaging with the community, he first spends time on self-examination and reflects on how he needs to change. This is critical. Too often those who work in social justice move straight from learning the truth to calling others out. Alma does not skip the step of meditating on the beam in his own eye. He works on his own transformation while holding close the words of the prophet, then leans into those words by sharing them with others.

Alma experienced a mighty change as he became converted. The accounts of both Alma the Elder and Alma the Younger are amazing because these are prophets who are open about their history of wickedness before they experience a change in heart. Readers do not get to witness that kind of spiritual maturation and changing of a life with most prophets. Both father and son spent many years in close relationship with the church, surrounded by church leadership, but explain how they had to repent and choose God.

Mosiah 18:4

Reading through the lens of how the land shapes the Book of Mormon gives this verse additional depth. We do not know for sure which king named this land, although it seems likely to be Noah. The area is "called Mormon . . . being in the borders of the land having been infested, by times or at seasons, by wild beasts." This is where the people go to find refuge from the king. They leave their homes and become a displaced people because of the danger they face due to their belief in the gospel. They move to a borderland, a liminal space geographically and spiritually, a dangerous place that is also a safe

---

75. Mosiah 17:4

haven. Institutional power has labeled the land as threatening, but the greater peril to the people comes from that institutional power.

People going into the wilderness as part of their spiritual journey serves as an important theme of the Book of Mormon. The wilderness may change—for Lehi, it was a desert; for Alma, it is a forest—but the threat remains the same. There is a peril that comes with the wilderness for the people of this era. Time and again, people simultaneously risk their lives and seek shelter at the borders. This theme of displacement, wilderness, and borders can serve as a metaphor about spiritual journeys, but it can also be taken literally, prompting readers to think about populations today who flee their homes because of violence and walk into the wilderness in a desperate attempt to find refuge.

Mosiah 18:7-11

Alma describes a striking part about the baptismal covenant: it is not just a relationship between an individual and Christ. Communitarian and social justice elements are intrinsic to baptism. Verses 8 and 9 ask if we are "willing to bear one another's burdens, that they may be light" and "mourn with those that mourn; yea, and comfort those that stand in need of comfort." The language is of a people being inextricably tied to one another in order to be called God's people. A person may seek to come into the fold of God because of their belief, but that is not enough. Discipleship requires sharing our burdens as a community. Individual salvation depends on joining and building Zion. These verses are some of the most important in the Book of Mormon because of how they encapsulate the way that the individual and community are inseparable in Mormon theology.

If there was anyone in the Book of Mormon who would preach the importance of "stand[ing] as a witness of God at all times and in all things, and in all places that ye may be in, even until death" (v. 9), it would be Alma, the student of Abinadi. He learned from someone who would not recant his testimony in the face of death. Alma also faced the threat of violence and held fast to his beliefs. So for Alma, these words are not just theoretical. There are real risks involved in building Zion and testifying of God.

In verse 11, the people "clapped their hands for joy, and exclaimed: This is the desire of our hearts." Clapping can be reverent. Shouting can be an appropriate response to a sacred, holy moment. This excitement reflects hearing deep truth and having it elicit a response of pure joy. Both hushed silence and joyful noise can be holy.

The responsibility to mourn with others and bear one another's burdens may create very different responses in people. For some, it may feel like a sober responsibility, a call to take on something heavier than they are sure they can bear. For others, like Alma's people, it may be a moment of gladness as they realize that they will have a companionship as they mourn and struggle. Our social locations may affect our initial responses to this call, with those who have had more privilege feeling more keenly the weight of taking on others' burdens. Alma's people, who have been hunted and had to hide and feel completely isolated in their struggles, recognize the ultimate joy in the promise of community.

Mosiah 18:12–29

Alma's baptismal cry expresses a desire to "do this work with holiness of heart" (v. 12). The baptismal covenant calls us to work. This is not a passive experience, in which a person is saved simply by accepting Jesus into their lives. It also requires acceptance of the responsibilities that come with it, including bearing one another's burdens. Given his life experiences, Alma understands the problems that come from an anemic church. In the following verses, he is ready to get to work and build a church that looks very different from what he previously experienced.

When Alma organizes a new church, his personal experiences get reflected in how he teaches the priests. He is wary of false doctrine, so he encourages focus on the fundamentals of the gospel (v. 19–20). He came from a hierarchical society centered around the most privileged members, so he emphasizes unity and equality (v. 21). Alma consistently works to build a church that emphasizes community, from the way he teaches the people about baptism (v. 8–9) to his exhortation that the priests "have their hearts knit together in unity and in love one towards another" (v. 21). Alma also tells the priests that they must "labor with their own hands for their support" (v. 24) so that they do not become a burden on the people. Noah exploited labor for the benefit of a small upper class. Alma teaches a gospel that counters oppression, insisting that the leaders work alongside the people, as all labor is equal.

These verses, followed by verses 27–29, lay out how to build a society that counters privilege. First, everyone labors together and all labor is valued. Second, whatever extra abundance people have is meted out to those who have less. While Noah heavily taxed the people in order to sustain the wealth of elites, Alma describes a society in which resources move from those who have more to those who have less. The Christian community that Alma imagines has an equitable economy, one that ministers to "*every* needy, naked soul" (v. 28, emphasis added), not just those deemed worthy in some way.

Having escaped from the plutocratic regime of Noah, Alma wants to build a society focused on caring for one another through love and material support. Being knit with unity and love means people are bound to one another, recognizing that each person matters. They care for one another emotionally by bearing one another's burdens. They also tend to other's temporal needs, sharing their abundance and looking after the poor. Christ also cared for people's bodies and souls together as he taught and healed. Spiritual work that tries to separate those two things misses something. Caring for bodies and souls together is how Alma's people become "the children of God" (v. 22).

Mosiah 18:31–34

Once again, the Book of Mormon tells us that borders matter. What is happening at the borders of your land geographically, spiritually, and culturally? What is happening at the margins, where two places meet? At these borders, the people build a church completely revolutionary to the older institutions of power. The king did not know about the forming church because it occurred at the borders. If those with power build a society in which people go to the fringes for safety, then they will be taken by surprise by what happens there. Borders are blind spots for governmental or religious powers when they focus only on their own maintenance instead of caring for the oppressed. The gospel can move in new and vibrant ways at the margins because these places are often ignored by institutional powers. This is why revolutionary theology oft times comes from the borders, literally and figuratively.

The king sends an army to "destroy" the believers in the wilderness. Alma's group numbers fewer than 500 people, including women and children (v. 35). Yet, the king sees threat and rebellion. Here, the gospel at the border looks to those in power like an act of rebellion against the state. The threat to Noah is the organization of a society that counters the structures of power he has so carefully cultivated. Alma's church jeopardizes Noah's government because of its insistence on equality.

In a moment that mirrors the story of Lehi's family, Alma's people have to flee into the deeper wilderness because they are following God's commandments (v. 34). The violence they face comes because of their choice to defy the laws, and their choice to gather together puts them at risk. Repeatedly in the Book of Mormon, obedience to God puts people in great danger. While we would like to believe that doing what God asks would result in increased safety and an ability to guard our privilege, this is not the case for the people in this book. For people in the Book of Mormon and in the Bible, a faith journey is riddled with risk. The prophets are clear that journeying with God has never been without pain, turmoil, and the forsaking of privilege. It is never easy. This book asks us to grapple with important questions, such as, "What do we choose to do when we take actions that are right and good in God's eyes and still end up in places of suffering or distress?"

This chapter ends with Alma's people on the move. They take their tents—just as Lehi's family did—and they depart in a hurry. This is a story of people building a radically egalitarian society at the borders and living in tents. They move from the borders into the wilderness, even further into the wild. Running for their lives because of their faith and devotion to God, they will carve out a new community.

Mosiah 19:1–2

Harm and violence haunt this chapter. It begins with king Noah's army searching for their own people—a group of families living in tents—in an effort to destroy them. As the army returns, some of Noah's citizens on the homefront revolt against the king. While the text does not give exact reasons for this shift in the populace, it seems likely that Alma's preaching, the departure of their neighbors, and the king's order to kill civilians, may have played a role. It appears that Noah ordered something so terrible that he sparked resistance, even from the people who did not follow Alma. This society was founded after Zeniff revolted against leadership and prompted bloodshed within families,[76] so its history has been wound up in internal violence for generations. This legacy of brutality has perhaps made the population more sensitive to orders of death to families (maybe even to members of their own families who have departed).

---

76. Mosiah 9:2

Mosiah 19:4

This verse introduces readers to Gideon, who reappears in the text multiple times and in complicated ways. His minor character plays many major roles. Here, he is described as "a strong man and an enemy to the king," and yet we also know that he did not choose to go with Alma. So he may or may not be a believer at this time, but he has a moral compass and a commitment to justice.

This section of Mosiah 9–22 includes some of the most complex characters in the Book of Mormon. While the Book of Mormon sometimes depicts people as caricatures of good and evil, these chapters feature more nuance. It is not clear whether Zeniff or Gideon are good or bad men—they seem to each make good and bad decisions in morally murky situations. The narrator allows Zeniff and Gideon to remain complex.

Mosiah 19:9

Once again, the wilderness becomes a place of refuge. In this case, Noah himself seeks safety in the land which he recently attacked with his own soldiers. While their stories differ in timing and threat, everyone in this community eventually finds the wilderness safer than their own homes. For both those who followed Alma and those who stayed with Noah, the wilderness becomes safer than their city.

Consider times and places in which humans have found the wilderness safer than civilization. Escaped slaves ran toward the dangers of the wilderness rather than living with the hazards of the plantation. Refugees often escape to rugged mountains, jungles, perilous waterways, or deserts rather than stay with the threats that face them at home. When wilderness is safer than someone's homeland, it signals something deeply troubling because that wilderness is not safe; it is simply *safer* than the alternative. Public policy, civil society, and individuals can work to realize the level of threat that prompts people to seek refuge in the wilderness.

The coming verses and chapters reference women and children multiple times, noteworthy for a text that rarely recognizes women and children. Almost every time, women and children get rhetorically linked as an entity, while men go into a different category. We pay particular attention to when women and children are separated from the men and when they are rhetorically placed together. What does it mean when women are paired with children and removed from men? The language used gives evidence of how the men in that moment think about familial commitment and the importance of women and children in that society. It reflects cultural and religious norms of who has value and who is vulnerable. The way the text speaks of women and children tells readers about social hierarchy as clearly as the actions the men take.

Mosiah 19:10–15

King Noah tells the men to "leave their wives and their children, and flee before the Lamanites," who are waging an attack (v. 11). The group splits into two: the men who follow Noah's order and abandon their families and those who "would not leave them, but had rather stay and perish with them" (v. 12). At first glance, it would seem that the men have separated themselves out into good and evil. It is true that the men who follow Noah are clearly immoral and they do terrible, evil things in the coming chapters. Yet the men who stayed also do terrible things, as we will read in verses 13–15. So while we have these two groups of men who make a very different choice in a crucial moment, ultimately the women and children are sacrificed in both cases. They are at the center of how we read this story.

The men who stayed with their families face the Lamanites and "caused that their fair daughters should stand forth and plead with the Lamanites that they would not slay them" (v. 13). The Lamanites "were charmed with the beauty of their women" (v. 14) and "took them captives and carried them back to the land of Nephi" (v. 15). While the text obfuscates, all signs point to rape. In the middle of a war, young women were sent out to charm soldiers, who then carried them away as prisoners. It seems unlikely that these girls merely had to stand there and look beautiful. Men "carrying" women places seems to be a euphemism for rape, made clear in Mosiah 20:5 when the Noahite priests carry the Lamanite daughters into the wilderness. These men, the ones who were supposed to be better than the others because they stayed with their families, sent their daughters into a different kind of slaughter.

The Book of Mormon does not usually skirt its way around violence. Murder and war are often explicitly described and detailed. Yet these verses use language that glosses over and hides what happens to these young women and girls. It allows readers to not fully face the violence of this story and the Nephites' deeply misogynistic society. We cannot know the author's intentions, but this lack of focus on the tragedy of this moment carries an additional layer of heartbreak for readers today.

Mosiah 19:18–24

Gideon reenters the scene, intent on finding and killing Noah. Gideon sends men into the wilderness to hunt down the king and his followers, except that when they find them, they are no longer with Noah or his priests. The men who had abandoned their wives and children turned on the king and burned him to death. The priests ran away. All the men in these verses have a deep sense of blood lust and rage. The men who went with Noah seem to experience regret and guilt for what they did and they act on that through murder. At no point do they confront their own actions and their complicity in deserting their families. They killed the man they had followed when he told them to again act in cowardice and selfishness. This is an incredibly violent society.

Mosiah 19:22–29

In verses 22–24, the men tell one another what happened to the other group. Fully three times, the men who followed Noah recount how they turned against the king (v. 20, 23, and 24). The men of Gideon tell of how the Lamanites spared them and how they must now pay a tribute (v. 22). At no point do the men of Gideon report that they sacrificed their daughters to the Lamanites. That part of the story, it appears, is not worth mentioning. The text remains silent about the reactions of the women and children as the men who abandoned them reintegrate into society. There is nothing about the conversations that happened or how families dealt with the violence these husbands and fathers enacted in a crisis. The men simply walk back into the community.

Two sets of mothers and wives exist in this society now, and the text ignores both. No verse describes the mothers who watched as their daughters were forced to "charm" the Lamanite soldiers. No record exists from the perspective of the abandoned women and children. These men, every one of them, have perpetrated violence on their families. And their reaction, when they come back together, is not to confront what they have done, but to boast about the death of the king and how they escaped the Lamanites. They even hold a "ceremony" to celebrate before they "returned to the land of Nephi, rejoicing" (v. 24). Although the text does not directly confront it, these stories make clear the ways in which sexism destroys families and communities.

The text never returns to the Nephite daughters who were sacrificed to the Lamanites in order to usher in two years of "peace" among the people (v. 27). We cannot know whether this omission stems from shame over what happened or simply a lack of interest. Either way, those daughters are never mentioned again.

Verse 28 once again underlines the role that the wilderness plays as a refuge in the Book of Mormon. Limhi's people are not truly experiencing a period of peace; they are prisoners and slaves to the Lamanites, to the point where Lamanite soldiers surround them and keep them from the wilderness. As dangerous as the wilderness might be, the Lamanites understand that it could be more attractive than remaining in a civilization that oppresses and binds people.

Mosiah 20:1–5

Once again, a group of young women appear in an account of sexual assault. While the text brushes past them, a social justice reading centers them in the narrative, keeping their experiences foremost in understanding the story. This is another heartbreaking incident where young women are pawns of powerful men, some of whom abuse them and others of whom use them as an excuse for war.

The gathering of these young women is initially quite beautiful. They have a place where they go to be happy together, where they can sing and dance. This tells readers that the Lamanite women had carved out a space in their world where they could celebrate together without men. That makes that space somewhat sacred because they have intentionally set resources aside to be merry together. The fact that Noah's priests attack them there, in that space, is particularly painful. Consider times and spaces in our world today in which violence has deliberately entered at a site created as a safe harbor for oppressed people. It is the girls in Chibok, Nigeria, attending school when Boko Haram terrorists, opposed to female education, kidnapped them. It is the Charleston Nine, where Black churches have served as a central nurturing space in American Black neighborhoods, when a racist man went to murder people. It is the people at the Pulse nightclub in Orlando, as gay bars have functioned as safe spaces for queer communities, when a man went to shoot as many people as he could. These are places where people at the margins have gone to find safety and fellowship and which become the sites of heartrending violence. When men bring rape and murder to those sacred spaces, it is particularly horrendous because the compounded violence strips people of their faith in a place where they can find community and happiness.

Do not miss how verses 3–5 lay out the mindset of the priests. They did not return to their wives and children because of the shame they felt because of what they had done (v. 3). These men abandoned their families in a crisis. They ought to feel guilt, as should the other men who followed king Noah but then returned to the land of Nephi without confronting what they did. The priests also felt fear because they worried that the Nephites would kill them. Powerful men feeling shame and fear can be a very dangerous thing. Rather than feeling guilt that pushes them toward repentance, their shame and fear prompts the priests to lash out in violence toward vulnerable women.

The priests "laid and watched" (v. 4) the Lamanite girls, deliberately placing themselves where they could wait until "there were but few of them gathered together" (v. 5). This is predatory violence. The daughters "gathered together to dance" and the men "came forth out of their secret places and took them and carried them" away (v. 5). Notice that the language is the same as when the Lamanites took the Nephite daughters in the previous chapter.[77] The men carry off the women, but what happens to the women? The text is not explicit, but there's something very wrong about women not walking on their own feet. That action of carrying, particularly in conjunction with captive women and powerful men, tells readers a great deal more about what's happening underneath the surface.

Mosiah 20:6

The rage of the men in these chapters is striking. They are more eager to attack one another than they are to follow truth or secure safety for their daughters. For both the Lamanites and the Nephites, the value of the young women seems to lie in the status they lend to the men. The Lamanites' choice to leap to false conclusions and use them to justify a war reveals how they think about human life.

Notice that the king of the Lamanites goes unnamed in these verses. The story references him repeatedly, but always with the awkward use of his title rather than a name. The Book of Mormon uses naming to signal who matters in the text. It humanizes or

---

77. Mosiah 19:15

dehumanizes people. Here, the author would rather say "king of the Lamanites" over and over again than give him a name.

Mosiah 20:11

The text states that Limhi's people win the battle because "they fought for their lives, and for their wives, and for their children." This reasoning seems illogical, as the Lamanites are literally fighting for their daughters. While it is true that the Nephites fight to protect their lives and their families, the conflict began because of the Lamanites' anger about harm done to their children. This is a good example of how the text's explanations for victory in battle do not always hold up under examination. A strict scrutiny is applied when the book offers interpretations of why a person or group triumphs in violence.

Mosiah 20:15

This war is founded on anger and assumption. A failure to communicate leads to impulsive violence, and many people die. These events undermine the previous chapter's claim that the two years preceding this war were a period of "continual peace."[78] True peace does not exist when communication is so poor that war can erupt this quickly and easily. Just because people are not actively killing one another does not mean that peace is present. The actions the Lamanites take and the speed with which they start a war indicate the presence of many underlying structural problems.

Mosiah 20:17–18

Gideon steps in again, acting now as king Limhi's captain. He protests strongly against searching the people, although readers do not get an explanation of why he feels so strongly about this issue. Would

---

78. Mosiah 19:29

a search be violent? Is he worried about what would be found? How does Gideon know so accurately and confidently who did this terrible thing? Gideon's knowledge on this topic and the strength of his opinions prompt some interesting questions about him, about Limhi, and about this society.

Mosiah 20:22

Gideon states that "it is better that we should be in bondage than that we should lose our lives." While that may seem like a universal conclusion, history says otherwise. Many people have chosen death over life, as Frederick Douglass—a previously enslaved person—famously said, "Better even to die free than to live slaves."[79] This is not to say that one conclusion is better than another, but to underline a real, actual decision oppressed people have had to make. The question of whether it is better to die than stay in bondage is a hard and devastating choice. Note that Limhi's people agree with Gideon and take the route of slavery over death because it will impact the latter decisions that they make and the way they speak. For instance, when Limhi first speaks with Ammon, he offers his people as slaves to the Nephites if Ammon will help free them from the Lamanites.[80] These are people who have had to make hard decisions between terrible options. They live lives where freedom is not one of their choices, and bondage is part of their narrative all the time.

Mosiah 20:25-26

Finally, people in this story take actions to de-escalate the conflict. The Nephites go out to meet the Lamanites without weapons. The Lamanite king bows down before his own people and pleads for the

79. Frederick Douglass. *Men of Color, To Arms!* Speech given in Rochester, NY, March 2, 1863. https://www.blackpast.org/african-american-history/1863-frederick-douglass-men-color-arms/
80. Mosiah 7:15

lives of the Nephites. Take note of the consequences of the Nephites' choice to spare the life of the king and talk with him about his actions and motivations. Rather than reacting with increased violence, they choose to have a conversation with their adversary. That leads to increased knowledge, which helps both sides realize their shared values and common goals. The Nephites take a risk in their desire for peace, the king then makes himself vulnerable, and that is how everyone finally sets down their weapons and ends the war. The choices of peace, like the choices of violence, have ripple effects far greater than we can anticipate.

Mosiah 21:1–3

Chapters 21 and 22 deal with people subjected to literal bondage and how their liberation occurs. These are important verses for anyone interested in social justice and the literal and figurative binding of oppressed people.

The Lamanites made a pact to not kill Limhi's people. However, this did not stop them from enacting violence in other ways. Although verse 1 says the people lived in peace, verse 2 undermines that claim, saying that only days after the bloody battle, the Lamanites began to attack the Nephites at the border. The borders around the land of Nephi hold almost all the important events of these chapters. While Alma's people previously sought refuge at the borders,[81] now the borders have become a dangerous space for the Nephites. As in Mosiah 9:14, the Lamanites choose to focus their primary attacks on those who are at the margins or edges of the land.

Verse 3 catalogs the real oppression Limhi's people endure. They experience slavery, or an indentured servitude so violent it is akin to slavery. Any kind of rhetoric comparing people to animals—in this case, the Lamanites began to "drive [the Nephites] as they would a dumb ass"—is a red flag signaling slavery or ethnic cleansing.

---

81. Mosiah 18:4

Mosiah 21:4

The text posits that violence and subjugation happened so that "the word of the Lord might be fulfilled." This is an interesting and problematic theology. Readers do not need to decide absolutely whether that is true or not. But be wary. Pause over any text that teaches the merits of oppression and slavery or claims that ever God wills them. If taken to its logical ends, that theology can go down many bad roads. Sometimes writers of the Book of Mormon have a tendency to move God into the deep violence of the narrative. Be careful with those verses and consider the motivations and experiences of the author. Think about what kind of God you believe in.

Mosiah 21:5–8, 12

Fully acknowledge the destruction and death that occurs in these too-brief verses. It begins with the people so wretched in their situation that they beg Limhi to start a war (v. 5–6). This is an oppressed people driven to the risk of bloodshed. Then, after many deaths and failure in battle (v. 9), they desperately return again to war, only to face defeat again. After all their loss and grief, they go to battle a third time and lose again (v. 12). Readers should imagine what it would feel like to believe that their only option of improving their situation might be through a doomed war. The Nephites cannot help themselves; they believe their only choice is to fight their way out. They experience the kind of hopelessness that prompts a person to believe that putting her life on the line is the only answer. Like those who followed Nat Turner into rebellion,[82] knowing that they would likely die, they were unable to continue to live in slavery.

---

82. Nat Turner was an enslaved person living in Southampton County, Virginia, who organized a rebellion in August, 1831. The rebellion lasted four days before being suppressed. Nat Turner and his followers, along with many other enslaved and free Black people living in the area, were executed.

Mosiah 21:9–11

"There was a great mourning and lamentation among the people of Limhi" (v. 9). Mourning and lamentation are separate things. Mourning shows deep sorrow while lamentation is a spiritual practice, where God plays a role in the expression of grief. Sometimes, during periods of seemingly unbearable sadness, a person simply mourns. God is not in it and the person just needs to sink into deep sadness. At other times, they can lament and speak to God about their grief. Mourning and lamenting can occur together or separately.

Note who in society gets mourned. In these verses, the community grieves for the men lost in battle. The women, who also likely faced death and violence during these numerous battles, go unrecognized. We did not get this kind of record of mourning and lamentation when the Nephite women were carried away by the Lamanites. When the Lamanite daughters were kidnapped by Noah's priests, they responded with anger and revenge. This society never gives any acknowledgement of what happens to women's bodies in war, nor do they see that wound as a cause for mourning and lamentation. While they recognize the men's lives lost in battle, they do not identify the other sacrifices that have been made in this conflict.

The community uses the widow's grief as an excuse to engage in repeated battle. Widows are people who normally have very little power or influence, and the loss of their husbands will push them further onto the margins. They have many reasons to fear for their future. As their sadness pairs with fear, it erupts into anger. Although the circumstances and outcomes are very different, this is not unlike the priests of king Noah, who felt fear and shame and expressed it with brutality.[83] Often, violence poses as a visible house built on a hidden foundation of fear, shame, and sadness.

---

83. Mosiah 20:3–5

Mosiah 21:13–14

The people "did humble themselves even to the dust, subjecting themselves to the yoke of bondage, submitting themselves to be smitten, and to be driven to and fro, and burdened, according to the desires of their enemies" (v. 13). As a social justice reader of the text, there is the need to interrogate this depiction of humility. This problematic description equates humility with one's spirit and humanity being broken. Humility does not require people to endure abuse, nor does it prevent folk from standing up for themselves. Humility does not require submitting to bondage and letting go of any sense of human dignity. It is not about becoming so beaten down that you accept violence.

Readers can scrutinize this definition of humility as it pertains to the scriptures in which God blesses the humble. Unfortunately, people in religious leadership throughout history have wielded religious power to tell their followers that this kind of self-abnegation is the kind of humility God wants. As an example, apply this scripture to enslaved people on a plantation, and imagine how an overseer could weaponize these words to tell the laborers that God wanted them to accept their situation uncomplainingly and not fight against it. Imagine how an abusive man could convince his wife that she should submit quietly to her husband. Reading the text for the least of these means centering the people on the margins and being aware of how scripture might affect them.

Believers who support social justice can carefully consider verses like this and put a stop to practices that ask people to break themselves in the name of faith. Telling people that they must silently accept abuse weaponizes and fouls the sacred principle of humility. Divine humility counters pride and prompts people to be generous and grateful. It should never be confused, particularly in a religious forum, with being beaten down. Those two very different definitions of humility should not be used interchangeably.

Mosiah 21:15

The Book of Mormon allows readers to notice the extraordinary ways prophets and writers name God. This text reflects innumerable personal, individual journeys with the divine. In this verse, the author states, "the Lord was slow to hear their cry because of their iniquities." This does not mean that anytime prayers seem to go unanswered we can fault the seeker's insufficient humility. This moment is a singular, particular experience, interpreted through the lens of the author. Adding a "because" to any statement about God not listening to certain prayers is dangerous. It can lead to a theology where people justify disasters or tragedies because they believe God intervenes to help the righteous. Any instance of people explaining oppression or violence by putting God's name on it can be a sign of perilous doctrine.

Even simply calling God "slow," without giving a reason for it, enters tricky territory. Unfortunately or fortunately, we do not always know the mind of God. To suppose God's intentions and/or the meaning of God's timeline can run us into risky, if not perilous, theological territory. We do not know the mind of God. Consider the lesson of Job and his friends. When Eliphaz, Bildad, and Zophar were willing to simply sit with Job in his grief, there was no problem. But when they started to question Job, asking him what he did to earn God's wrath, and then tried to explain God's intentions behind Job's suffering, they betrayed their friendship and offended God.[84] Sometimes our silence is better than coming up with reasons for why bad things happen or explaining why God does not intervene.

Mosiah 21:16

Lack of food and the inability to meet basic needs drives people to desperation. The first thing to note in this verse: when the people do a little bit better, they no longer "suffer with hunger." This is likely

---

84. Job 42:7

the underlying reason for why they returned to battle the Lamanites repeatedly. Hunger and violence are closely intertwined—in this case, slavery drove hunger and hunger encouraged war. The desperation evoked from sites of hunger and poverty creates particular forms of violence.

Mosiah 21:17

This has become a community of widows. So many men died in the wars that a significant portion of the population can no longer support themselves, even with increased prosperity. In response, king Limhi *commanded* the men to care for the widows and children. This was not optional charity. The government-instituted program ensured that the most vulnerable people had a safety net. And for this community in particular, it is revolutionary. These same men abandoned their families with king Noah or offered their daughters to the Lamanites. For them to now give up their own substance to protect women and children signals a shift in values. It reframes society as directed toward serving the most vulnerable rather than giving free rein to the most powerful.

The widows of this kingdom are particularly vulnerable because of the structures of society that seemingly gave power and resources to men, making women dependent on husbands. When the men die in large numbers, the society goes into a crisis of potential starvation. This new law helps to alleviate some of that problem, but it does not address the underlying issue of women in this society having so little power to protect themselves.

Laws and miracles that protect unsafe populations is a thread that runs throughout sacred texts. The deuteronomical law spelled out how to care for unmarried women and children.[85] Elijah cared for the widow and her son, making sure that they had enough food for the

---

85. Deuteronomy 14:29

rest of their lives.[86] One of Jesus' first miracles was precipicated by compassion for the widow of Nain.[87] For Mormons, it is worth noting that none of these scriptural examples of supporting widows, including this one from Mosiah, required the men to marry the women.[88] Limhi's edict allows the widows to live independently with financial support from their society.

Mosiah 21:20–23

The priests sneak into a land made up mostly of women and children who are essentially enslaved to the Lamanites, then steal food from these people close to starvation. These priests continue to be a vile scourge on this community. They continue to inflict violence of all kinds in their willingness to sacrifice others—particularly women and girls—for their own interests. Noah's choice to install selfish, amoral people in positions of power has consequences that ripple out past his own death.

Limhi captured Ammon and his friends and put them in prison because of the actions of the priests (v. 23). They did not communicate or ask questions, much like the Lamanites attacking the Nephites when they thought the Nephites had taken the Lamanites' daughters. It is an immediate, emotional response, born out of trauma. These people respond in brutal ways because of the suffering they have experienced. These are good examples of how violence perpetuates and escalates violence. Ammon did nothing wrong, yet he becomes a casualty of the trauma of the Nephites. When people who have been seriously harmed react in fierce ways to new threats, they often unintentionally hurt innocent people around them. The aphorism "*hurt people hurt people*" runs throughout the Book of Mormon, on both an individual and societal level.

---

86. 1 Kings 17:15–16

87. Luke 7:11–17

88. The idea that men need to marry women in order to financially support them is a common folklore justification for Mormon polygamy, as the early LDS Church had a significant number of widows and orphans.

Mosiah 21:26–28

In a search for Zarahemla, Limhi's people instead find a "land which was covered in bones" (v. 26). From this place, they retrieve a record. Ammon tells Limhi that king Mosiah can translate the record, which fills Limhi with joy. They do not need evidence that they are connected to the destroyed civilization to care deeply about the record. They simply want to know others' narratives, to be able to add others' records to their own. This is a wonderful example of the excitement we should feel upon encountering the stories of other people, especially those that are different from our own. The gift of such stories is a case for rejoicing.

Mosiah 21:29–31

As Ammon and his friends learn about the history of Limhi's people, they are "filled with sorrow" (v. 29) for many reasons. They grieve for the deaths of people in war. They mourn for the evil that Noah and his priests had caused. They are saddened by the death of Abinadi, even though they never met him. They grieve that they do not know what happened to Alma and his people. Most striking is Ammon's sadness directed toward people he never knew. He appears to be not biologically related to them, as they are descended from Nephi, and he is a descendant of Zarahemla.[89] And yet, he grieves for them. Their people become his people, and he feels their suffering in his soul.

Story sharing holds sacred power: Ammon does not need to experience something personally for him to feel the sorrow or joy of what happened. Through listening to stories, the struggles of Limhi's people become his struggles. Their relief becomes his. The people knit their hearts together in unity. When the text says that Ammon and his friends miss Alma and his people, and "would have gladly joined with them" (v. 31), it signals how the records have brought people together and worked to build beloved community. This is a moment of records

---

89. Mosiah 7:3

colliding, and the way that Ammon and his brethren open their hearts and feel the emotions of what happened to other people is the beginning of building Zion. Ammon and Limhi are about to create a plan for liberating the people, but before they do that, they take the time to tell their stories. Before the risk and bravery of snatching freedom, they sink into one another's histories. The beginning of liberation is sharing stories. It means taking the time to mourn for the past and recognize what went wrong. In Limhi's case, they say: we murdered a prophet. Our priests did terrible things. Part of our people are gone because of their faith, and we mourn their loss. As they say those things, Ammon and his brethren listen and let themselves be flooded with the power of it. *Then* they are ready to form a plan for freedom.

Mosiah 21:33-34

Since Ammon declines to baptize Limhi's people, they choose to not form a church. They have faith, they have created a good community, and they want to make their commitment formal. But they cannot, because they do not feel that they have authority. This is similar to the early Saints in Ghana, who read the Book of Mormon and wanted to be baptized, but were excluded from the Church for fourteen years because of the priesthood and temple ban.[90] The continued faith in face of separation from the church organization is strikingly beautiful and moving. Yet, a shadow gets cast over the story as good people cannot participate in important faith rituals. The people of Limhi suffer from feeling unempowered over their own spiritual lives. They are already serving God and one another; they are just waiting for someone to formalize it. That wait causes grief.

---

90. Elizabeth Maki. "A People Prepared." The Church of Jesus Christ of Latter-day Saints, April 2013. https://history.churchofjesuschrist.org/article/ghana-pioneer-jwb-johnson

Mosiah 21:36

Liberation becomes a study of all the people. They have been bound physically and ecclesiastically, but now emancipation has become their entire focus. The text now moves them from a place of waiting to one of action and anticipation for the many ways that they will be set free.

Mosiah 22:1

This verse tells readers how much this kingdom has changed in how it values people. Ammon and king Limhi consult with the people to make a plan. They gather *all* the people together so "that they might have the voice of the people concerning the matter." Under king Noah, the society centered the king and the most powerful men around him. Limhi has flipped that on its head: now he listens to everyone and includes them in the decision-making process, giving power to the people. The shift is further emphasized by the fact that most of the people left in this community are women and children. This signals a radical shift for a society that once left those women and children to die at the hands of the Lamanites. Now, everyone is brought into the conversation of how to achieve freedom. That is true liberation.

Mosiah 22:6–7

Notice the language in the description of this plan: "Behold the back pass, through the back wall, on the back side of the city" (v. 6) and then through "the secret pass" on the left side (v. 7) and into the wilderness to freedom. Freedom moves through the back ways. It goes through the secret pass, not where it can be seen. Freedom takes the traditionally less-favored, left-hand side. And it leads to the wilderness. This detail of their route is not necessary to the text. But the symbolism, for those who plan their own routes of social justice, is crucial to recognize.

Mosiah 22:14

Mosiah receives Limhi's people with joy. He receives their records with joy. This is the beautiful moment when all the records come together: Ether and Zeniff have found a home in Zarahemla and Alma's record is about to join them. Their gathering is spiritual as well as physical. Pause and appreciate this moment of holiness, when the records are brought together with joy.

Mosiah 22:15–16

The Lamanites pursue Limhi's people into the wilderness, but cannot follow them, and get lost in the wilderness. Limhi's group was made up of a large number of women and children, "their flocks and their herds" (v. 11) and "all their gold, and silver, and their precious things, which they could carry, and also their provisions" (v. 12). This was a stealth mission. Tracking that many people and animals laden down with precious things and provisions should not be exceptionally difficult, particularly for soldiers. Large groups like this cannot simply disappear. The text even seems to acknowledge this just a few verses later, in Mosiah 23:1–2, which describes God's intervention to stop soldiers from overtaking Alma's people. So while we often unfavorably compare Limhi's story to Alma's, pointing to the use of alcohol and trickery in the first case and divine intervention in the second, that misses the miracle of Limhi's people. Their story is closer to that of the Israelites leaving Egypt, as an entire people found refuge from pursuing soldiers. Although the author does not seem to see God as a part of this, it does not mean God was not there. God is so frequently at the center of stories of abolition. Hope gives us the ability to see God here, with Limhi's people, even if they did not see it themselves. Part of the work of these chapters in which we can compare and contrast Limhi and Alma is to recognize the myriad of ways that God shows up in people's lives. The beauty of having these stories of Limhi and Alma given back to back is that their parallel stories of exodus, bondage, and escape weave in the divine in very different ways. We can restore God to the narrative and see that God does not work in only one way, but in every individual path toward liberation.

Mosiah 23:1–5

The story of the flight of Alma's people out of the land of Nephi and into the wilderness, their capture by the Lamanites and Amulon, and their escape to Zarahemla, is full of contradictions about how God moves with people. At one point, God warns Alma and they elude Noah's priests. At another, God allows Alma's people to suffer. Readers may feel confusion about why God seems so inconsistent. This text gives insight into a textured, complicated journey with God, a God who at times will rescue and at other times hold back, then turn again and perform a miracle. This is important for anyone trying to understand the many ways that God moves with people who struggle.

Always notice what people in the Book of Mormon take with them when they flee. In some cases, they take only food and tents.[91] In others, they take provisions, gold and silver, and herds of animals.[92] Here, Alma's people take their flocks and grain. This gives readers a little bit of insight into the severity of the situation and the time the people have to plan. It offers readers a chance to reflect on what they would take with them in a crisis, and to consider what refugees and immigrants take with them today.

In the Book of Mormon, tents signal times of transition, often tinged with danger. Tents underscore home's impermanence and often belong to people who have to move quickly. Alma's people transition rapidly from pitching tents to erecting buildings, reflecting a desire to settle a new nation. They immediately establish themselves and work to make the wilderness their own.

91. 1 Nephi 2:4
92. Mosiah 22:11–12

Mosiah 23:6–10

Compare Alma's rejection of the throne to Nephi's choice to decline it in 2 Nephi 5:18–19. Nephi appears to have temporarily ruled over the people until his brothers sought to kill him. After that, even though he leaves and forms his own nation, he no longer desires the seat of power. Alma's explanation is a little different. Alma fears a kingship because he believes that no one should ever be thought of as more important than another, which is inherent to the concept of royalty. Alma's experiences with king Noah taught him that having a king meant the threat of a society divided into class and hierarchy. Nephi and Alma come to the same conclusion, but their way of reasoning is filtered through their personal experiences. How violence broke differently on these men deeply influences the way they see power.

Alma wants the people to clearly remember what bad leadership can do. He does not turn away from the evil that happened in his community or from his complicity in those events. In fact, he emphasizes the pain of realizing the harm he caused and of his own repentance process. Alma also links the "many things which were abominable in the sight of the Lord" (v. 9) with the social hierarchies that came with Noah's rule. His government aimed to provide extreme luxury and privilege to a small ruling class, even if that meant enacting violence against the rest of the population. When a system is built on that idea, abominable things happen. In the case of Noah, the taxes that moved wealth from the people to the priests and king, and the terrible ways they treated women,[93] were the product of a government rooted in "esteem[ing] one flesh above another" (v. 7).

Mosiah 23:12–14

In these verses, Alma lays out a theology of oppression through bad leadership. Noah's people were led into iniquity through evil political powers, through laws and policies. Their participation in

---

93. Mosiah 11:2–3

sinful actions was a form of bondage. Alma is saying that political policies and laws matter in an individual way. They have spiritual outcomes, not just physical ones. When our own government makes us complicit in sin through bad leadership, we are spiritually bound. Because of this, Alma is extremely skeptical of too much power in leadership. He encourages the people to exercise caution in choosing their teachers. Given Alma's experiences of abuse at the hands of government and church leaders, his suspicion is well-founded. He wants proof before he trusts anyone to exercise power. That is typical of someone who has been harmed by unjust systems.

Mosiah 23:15

Alma, a survivor of trauma and violence, lays out a theology stemming from "sore repentance" (v. 9) that is built on a love ethic and the principle that no one is more valuable than another. He emphasizes this message over and over again. This is what he taught about the baptismal covenant.[94] Alma's extraordinary and exciting prophetic teachings reflect his personal experiences of violence and liberation. He finds healing through faith and community after suffering harm from an oppressive government and church. He wants a community that values human life and cares for each person and mourns one another's griefs. He makes sure that his people do not do all the work of getting free simply to recreate what bound them before. His teachings focus on building a better life in which the gospel is deeply tied to respect for human dignity and beloved community.

Mosiah 23:21–24

One frustration about the book of Mosiah is that at times readers do not know the author. Unlike much of the rest of the Book of Mormon, where interpretations can be placed in the context of the writer's life experiences, Mosiah's authors insert their views anonymously. The

---

94. Mosiah 18:8–10

book is also filtered through Mormon, adding the very likely possibility that certain sections are his commentary. These verses are an important example of that problem. It is theological conjecture to claim that Alma's people suffered because God wanted to test and chasten them. It may help readers feel better about terrible things happening in the world, but it describes a God who actively sends people trials in order to see what they do.

The author of these verses—Mormon or someone else—seems to be trying to make sense of this story. But the story offers no simple, easily gleaned moral. Rather, it invites questions: Why do righteous people come into bondage? Why does God save them from Noah's army, then let them be captured by the Lamanites? It is okay to not have good answers to these questions. We do not know why God lets people suffer or why God chooses at certain times to deliver them. We can wrestle with that without coming to any clear conclusions. In these verses, the author seems unwilling to let those questions sit unanswered. He or she constructs a theology that gives answers, that allows him/her to set those questions down. These verses tell the reader more about the author than they do about God. He or she is struggling to make sense of the text, and readers can offer grace for that space, even as we give ourselves the liberty to interpret the story in our own way and with our own understanding of the nature of God.

Mosiah 23:27–29

Alma makes a prophetic pronouncement to his people that God will deliver them, but emancipation does not happen immediately. The ultimate liberation takes a long time to happen, but it is preceded by a series of small deliverances. Salvation takes many different forms for these people.

They "hushed their fears, and began to cry unto the Lord that he would soften the hearts of the Lamanites" (v. 28). Consider the power and the challenge of hushing one's fears enough that a person is capable of praying for their oppressor's heart to be softened. Harriet Tubman said that for a long period, she prayed for her master's heart to be changed. Once she realized God would not answer those prayers, she started praying that he would die.[95] Alma's people's initial inclination is to pray for the people overtly harming them.

At this moment, Alma's people face the exact same threat as Noah's people: they are fleeing from the Lamanite army. Yet, compare the actions of the men following Alma to the men who followed Noah. Those who followed Noah either abandoned their wives and children[96] or they offered up their daughters to Lamanites.[97] This community is different. They stay unified as a group and the men pray not just for their own protection, but also for the women and children. When they go to negotiate with the Lamanites, they do not send their daughters in their stead. Alma and other men go and "deliver themselves up into their hands" (v. 29). Particularly in comparison to the other stories in this section, this narrative is curiously devoid of violence. Alma does not sacrifice the most vulnerable people in his group, but he also does not fight. His is a path of nonviolent diplomacy and resistance. The community stays safe as a result, united in their care for one another.

Mosiah 23:33–35

Amulon's men send women out to face the Lamanite army. This differs starkly from Alma's people in verses 27–29, who kept their family group together. These women facing down the army are the same ones that Noah's priests assaulted and kidnapped.[98] They are now put in the position of begging their former community for the lives of the men who attacked them. The situation of these women is

---

95. Sarah Hopkins Bradford. *Scenes in the Life of Harriet Tubman*. Freeport, NY: Books for Libraries Press, 1971. 14–15.

96. Mosiah 19:11–12

97. Mosiah 19:13–14

98. Mosiah 20:5

horrific. Amulon—a former priest of king Noah—and the other men ultimately not only get away with their lives, but join with the Lamanites and become powerful players in their clan. The text says that the men live "because of their wives" (v. 34). Survivors of rape and abduction become the reason that their assailants live. It is their bodies and pleading that create compassion on behalf of their rapists. Amulon offers them up, not knowing what the Lamanites will do to these women, willingly sacrificing them to protect himself. Given what we know about Amulon and his men, his actions are unsurprising. These men committed whoredoms under king Noah. They abandoned their wives and children when the Lamanite army attacked. They lay in wait to assault young women. The entire arc of the story of these priests is based around their complete disregard for the lives of women.

As the former priests of Noah join with the Lamanites, consider how that melding reflects on prior events. The Lamanites attacked Limhi's people because they believed Limhi's people had kidnapped their daughters. Yet, with clear evidence that Amulon's men kidnapped the young women, they bring the men into their community and make Amulon "a king and ruler."[99] This makes the Lamanites' explanation for war suspicious. The Lamanites did not attack Limhi because they valued the lives of their daughters. They only value the power and status that those lives can potentially offer.

Mosiah 23:37–39

The Lamanites betray Alma and then occupy the land of Helam, eventually enslaving Alma and his people. While reading the account of Amulon and Alma, remember that both men used to be priests for king Noah. For Alma, that makes this situation particularly painful. He went through the process of repentance and fled from his former life, probably coming to believe that he had moved on from it. But then this figure from Alma's past returns, bringing with him

---

99. Mosiah 23:39

violence toward all of Alma's people. For Alma, it might have felt like his repentance efforts were futile, that he would never be able to escape the consequences of his poor choices. Sometimes a journey of liberation from sin or other burdens will feel long and hopeless.

One important sign of the Lamanites' intentions is that they bring their families to come live in the land of Helam. When colonizers bring their families, it is not temporary. The soldiers are creating settlements and building structures of oppression. Throughout history, when colonizing forces bring their families, they signal a higher commitment to take possession of a land, often subjugating people in the process. This is a tragic distortion of the sanctity of families.

Mosiah 24:1–7

Interestingly, the Lamanites do not just occupy the land of Helam through force. They also set up the former priests of Noah as "teachers" over the people. This is, in effect, a recreation of the system under Noah, with the same people being put in positions where they wield power to oppress people through being close to the king. Amulon and the former priests are so skilled at manipulation that they begin to influence the Lamanites, spreading their language and culture. They do not teach the Lamanites about God or the commandments, but they teach the Lamanites to keep a record, which is how the Lamanites begin to become very rich (v. 6–7). Language and literacy are cornerstones of a culture and economy. That is why oppressed people are often denied an education or the ability to keep records. Amulon understood, as do other tyrants, the power inherent in language and books.

Mosiah 24:8

Amulon teaches his children to persecute the children of Alma. Oppression is learned. The older generation teaches the younger generation the tools of oppression, and it becomes a familial legacy.

Recognizing how injustice has passed through generations is part of doing family history.

Mosiah 24:10–12

The Lamanites respond to the cries of Alma's people by outlawing prayer. Colonizers commonly attempt to regulate spiritual practices. But the line to focus on is in verse 12: the people "did pour out their hearts to [God]; and he did know the thoughts of their hearts." The Lamanites believe they can exercise power through cutting off the Nephites' access to the divine. They do not understand the limits of their own power. Marginalized people will find ways to reach God, and God still hears them, no matter what human structures exist to try to stop that connection. While attempting to cut people off from communication with God is deeply violent, it lacks the domination that the Lamanites believe it has. Again, this is the power of nonviolent resistance: it rejects the power of the ruling class, claiming for itself a power that is beyond laws and restrictions.

Mosiah 24:13–16

When Alma's people covenanted to "bear one another's burdens, that they may be light,"[100] they probably did not imagine that they would soon be literally carrying around burdens and that those burdens would become light through their faith. They are living into that promise of a shared community and, in response, God is there with them, helping make the burdens light.

Alma's people do not have a Gideon to come up with a plan of escape. Instead, "the voice of the Lord came unto *them*" telling them to prepare to leave (v. 13, emphasis added). This is a collective revelation for a people who have become truly unified. These people suffer together, make decisions together, and receive inspiration on their lib-

---

100. Mosiah 18:8

eration together. They have made real progress toward building Zion. They get ready, believing in God's promise that something will happen.

Mosiah 24:20

Alma's people return to pitching tents in the wilderness. The text specifically states that they escaped through a valley, which rhetorically is not unlike Limhi's people taking "the back pass, through the back wall, on the back side of the city."[101] It is almost identical to Nephi's prayer as he fled from his brothers that he might "walk in the path of the low valley."[102] Again and again, people find safety in unexpected and lowly places in the Book of Mormon: the wilderness, the valley, the back way. These may not be flashy miracles, but they reveal how God takes people into unexpected places to liberate them.

Mosiah 24:22

"*All* their men and *all* their women and *all* their children" give thanks and praise to God (emphasis added). The text underscores the inclusivity of this community, how deeply they have rejected king Noah's way of dividing men from women and children, and how they have built a society that works and worships together. They remained true and faithful to one another.

Mosiah 24:25

Just as with Limhi's people, Mosiah receives Alma's people "with joy." The people of Zarahemla consistently welcome outsiders. In the following chapter, Alma's people, Limhi's people, and Mosiah's people will come together and share their stories. They are an incredible example of how we should welcome strangers seeking refuge in a new land. Imagine if, like the Nephites, we could receive people with joy. If we welcomed them and asked them to share their stories of exodus to

---

101. Mosiah 22:6
102. 2 Nephi 4:32

the wilderness, their experiences with pitching tents and fleeing from violence, their knowledge of how God brought them over waters and through valleys. And imagine if we said to them: *we grieve for the sadness of your story. We rejoice in your safety. You are one of us now.* This would make story sharing a spiritual practice, a communal move toward God. It is unsurprising that this happens in Zarahemla, with a people who have recently experienced collective conversion.[103] Through a wide variety of experiences, the different groups in this society have deeply learned the lesson of beloved community.

Mosiah 25:5–6

Mosiah gathers all the people, including the people of Zarahemla, Nephi, Limhi, and Alma, together to read the records of Zeniff and Alma. He wants to ensure that everyone hears this important account so that they can sink into the history of their fellow brothers and sisters. Mosiah understands that to build a community together, they need to understand what the others have been through and what their ancestors lived through. This is how personal narratives become sacred text. Readers can watch the evolution of scripture as Mosiah's people take Alma's and Limhi's records and literally combine them with their own records. This is the extraordinary power of our stories and the stories of our ancestors: they are an important tool in understanding one another and a crucial part of building Zion.

Mosiah 25:7–11

As the people listen to the records, they are caught between a number of intense emotions. They feel wonder and amazement at all that happened. They feel intense joy for the liberation of their new friends. They grieve for the people who died, people they never knew. They are grateful to God for saving people and worry about the sins of the Lamanites. For these people, joy and sorrow are so tightly

---

103. Mosiah 5:2–5

bound together that they are unsure of even how to react, whether they should celebrate or weep. So often the human journey reflects this complexity, with lives so full of miracles and grief that it is hard to pull them apart. While we sometimes think of joy and sorrow as polarized emotions, they are actually sisters in the human journey with the divine. The Nephites do not attempt to separate them. They allow themselves to be overwhelmed with the grief and goodness, amazed by what happened.

We should try to approach scripture with this same kind of wonder and amazement, the same perplexity of how to feel, letting tears mix with our joy. It is also the way we should approach one another's stories and family histories, feeling them deep in our bones and letting the complex emotions wash over us. Cultivating the sensitivity to weep and honor people we have never met is one of the great spiritual works we can do. We should strive to read scripture and history with a capacity to feel true joy intermingled with sorrow.

Mosiah 25:12

The children that Noah's priests abandoned as they fled from the Lamanites finally find out what happened to their fathers. Up to this point, they only knew that their fathers had left them and had disappeared. Now they know about the thieving, stealing, kidnapping, and enslaving. They no longer want to be associated with their fathers, so they rename themselves, ending any lingering connection with those men. As with any renaming in scripture, this is a pivotal moment for these children. When the descendants of Nephi, Jacob, and Joseph took on the name of "Nephites," it became a new identity, a way of severing themselves from their shared past with the Lamanites. Similarly, these children renounce their biological fathers and take on the name Nephi, adopting themselves into the community and forming new families.

Mosiah 25:13

How did the land of Zarahemla become a kingdom that could only be ruled by the descendants of Nephi? Who created that rule? When the Nephites arrived in Zarahemla, there was already an existing government, language, and functioning society. Now the ethnic identity of the people of Zarahemla disappears and the land can only be passed to the ruling Nephite family. Although this is a period of peace as the people rejoice in reunification, readers should recognize how issues of power and identity play out here. The culture, name, and identity of the original people of Zarahemla entirely disappears under the strength of the Nephite society. Although they arrived as guests, the Nephites now seem to control every level of power in Zarahemla.

Mosiah 25:15–16

Alma's record recognized God and miracles more than Limhi's. The way Limhi narrated his people's story, their escape hinged on Gideon's ideas, the power of alcohol, and luck. Because Limhi's people tell their story in that way, readers sometimes assume that the story is complete, as originally told, and that God was absent from Limhi's people's experiences. But here, Alma teaches Limhi's people to reframe their story as a miraculous one. Although Limhi's people may not have seen it originally, God was with them in their bondage and in their liberation. Alma teaches the people how to tie theology and narrative together. The capacity to see and recognize God is a crucial part of faith.

Mosiah 25:17–18

Limhi and his people enter into baptism. This is the third mass conversion in the book of Mosiah, two of which Alma led.[104] The book of Mosiah fundamentally explores principles of community: what

---

104. Mosiah 5:5–7 and 26:10–11

makes a healthy or unhealthy community, what kind of leadership helps people reach their potential, how the values of a community point to who it privileges and protects, and how conversion can transform a community.

Mosiah 25:24

God blesses the Nephites, and they prosper in the land. This verse ties those blessings to two things: the Nephites "were called the people of God," and "the Lord did pour out his Spirit upon them." Importantly, both of those are relationship-based. Being blessed and prospering in the land does not necessarily mean gaining material wealth. Here, it references becoming a beloved community, unified with a common purpose of following God and feeling God's Spirit poured out on them. This mirrors the two greatest commandments, which are to love God and to love our neighbor.[105] This verse helps readers understand the right way of associating blessings with commandments: as the people loved God and one another, they built a community that could be called "the people of God," and they received God's Spirit.

Mosiah 26:7–14

As the number of dissenters grows, the church faces a problem. The people bring the skeptics to the priests, the priests go to Alma, Alma goes to Mosiah, and Mosiah hands them back to Alma. Despite a great deal of evidence that this group has done wrong (v. 9), the entire leadership hesitates about what to do in response. The text repeats that Alma is "troubled" (v. 10 and 13) and Mosiah refuses to play any role in the issue. These verses exemplify how difficult it is for a church to deal with sin. It is good that the priests, Alma, and Mosiah all hesitate to act in this moment because intentionality and care are crucial when weighing these issues. The text states that

---

105. Matthew 22:36–40

Alma actually "feared that he should do wrong" (v. 13) in this case. That kind of slow reaction and deliberation should act as a model for many kinds of difficult decisions in the church.[106]

Mosiah 26:15–32

God's answer to Alma's prayer begins with a long introduction. It reiterates God's relationship with Alma, God assuring Alma of his place, and God reminding him of God's willingness to care for the people. The first five verses of this response use the word "bless" seven times. The blessings all focus on faith and the works of faith. Alma and his people are blessed for their faith in the words of Abinadi and Alma. They are blessed through their baptism and taking on the name of God. Alma is blessed for organizing a church and for praying for direction. The faith is the blessing. The blessing does not need to look like wealth or prosperity or any other gift. Having faith and acting on that faith are blessings to us. Verse 17 makes this clear: "they shall be my people." God names them and claims them. God will establish that God has been with the faithful and seen them for who they are and carried them in their suffering.

Starting in verse 22, God references the people who need to repent. It starts with loving language, punctuated with teachings of repentance and forgiveness. Verse 22 tells Alma that God will "freely forgive," and verses 28–29 remind him that God will forgive people again and again, and that the people need to forgive one another as well. God makes clear that people must repent and that God's judgment is real, yet also encircles those words with teachings about the

---

106. When Alma consults God on the issue, the text says that "he had poured out his whole soul to God" (v. 14). Cross-reference this with Enos 1:9, when Enos pours out his "whole soul" in prayer for the welfare of his people, the Nephites. In both cases, the person giving the prayer reaches a particular communion with God when he prays for his community. They can pray with their whole souls because their souls have become whole through their love and concern for others around them.

gift of forgiveness. The language of judgment in these verses consistently gets counterbalanced by repentance and forgiveness.

Finally, God tells Alma that unrepentant transgressors "shall not be numbered among my people" (v. 32). This is the result of doing horrible things: God cannot call you into community. This mirrors the introduction to this sermon, where God reminded Alma that the blessing of faith is to carry the name of God and be called the people of God. Taken as a whole, God's response to Alma teaches that people can always come back, even when they have left the community and sinned against God. Repentance is always available.

Mosiah 26:37

Although readers routinely assume that "prospering in the land" means gaining wealth, most would not think that "to have peace and to prosper exceedingly in the affairs of the church" means the church became rich. In this context, prospering would seem to mean a healthy community with people caring for one another and obeying God. Prospering does not necessarily mean material gain, and reading the text with multiple possible definitions of the word can significantly change the messages readers take away.

Mosiah 26:38–39

Paul used the term "fellow laborers" to describe the people who helped him teach and lead the church. Importantly, he included women in that term, asking men to "help those women which labored with me in the gospel . . . and with my other fellow laborers, whose names are in the book of life."[107] Although the text does not specifically name women as those who acted as Alma's fellow laborers, the term in verse 38 seems unusual enough that readers should assume that it is meant to include all genders.

---

107. Phillippians 4:3

The leaders and fellow laborers "did admonish their brethren; and they were also admonished, every one by the word of God" (v. 39). This community shows commitment to a lack of hierarchy, constantly pushing back against what they experienced under king Noah. Everyone can admonish anyone for their sins. No one is above the need to repent and become better. They labor together.

Mosiah 27:3–5

Once again, Alma focuses on the problems created by social hierarchies and inequality. Alma reminds the people repeatedly to not value one person over another: "there should be no persecutions among them" (v. 3), they should work for equality, they "should let no pride nor haughtiness disturb their peace; and that every man should esteem his neighbor as himself" (v. 4). He also reiterates that teachers and priests ought to work for themselves and not take advantage of the people. Any community, including a church community, that does not strictly follow the injunction to not persecute one another will never be able to reach Zion. It is worth examining the communities to which we belong and considering how we can follow Alma's counsel in these verses. Are our people living into a radical call for equality? How does that translate into our treatment of queer folk, single parents, people who are poor or recently incarcerated, or immigrants? What kind of hierarchies do people face at church, and what can we do to break them down? Alma's insistence on this point seems to stem from his previous life as a priest of king Noah. He remains committed to a pure, simple gospel that treats everyone as equal. His experiences reveal the dangers of haughtiness and discrimination.

Verses 4 and 5 emphasize the importance of everyone working to support themselves, but with an important caveat. Alma goes out of his way to emphasize that all people, including leaders, should work, but adds, "in all cases save it were in sickness, or in much want; and doing these things, they did abound in the grace of God" (v. 4). Those who are sick or poor warrant an exception. Those are the people who receive help from their community. In Noah's society, social support went to the elites in society, with disastrous results. In Alma's church, everyone works to care for themselves and for the most marginalized. And in doing so, they did "abound in the grace of God" (v. 5). This is an extraordinary phrase. Alma's people learn to move into an abundance mindset, one in which they manage their finances so that they can care for the poor and sick. God's grace then steps in, making what they have sufficient for all.

Mosiah 27:7-9

This is one of the times that the Book of Mormon specifically names prosperity as having lots of people and money. Because of the unknown authorship of the book of Mosiah, readers are left to wonder who made this commentary. Without the context of the authorship, it is difficult to understand the intent of this verse.

Yet, verse 7's commentary about prosperity seems undermined by the surrounding verses. Verse 5 focuses on the importance of labor, care for the poor, and grace of God. Verse 7 says simply that God blesses the Nephites with wealth. And then in verse 9, the text states that dissension becomes "a great hindrance to the prosperity of the church of God." This is a very different definition of prosperity than the one given in verse 7. Verse 9 ties prosperity to "the hearts of the people," not to wealth. Verse 5 offers an economic structure focused on caring for others, not on wealth. Verse 9 links prosperity to an internal or spiritual state, not just a quantity of people or wealth. Together, verses 5 and 9 question the reductionist theology of verse 7.

Mosiah 27:11-17

As with the shouting angel of 1 Nephi 11, God speaks to Alma through a loud messenger. The spirit can speak through a "still small voice,"[108] or through "a voice of thunder" (v. 11) that shakes the earth. Do not assume that reverence requires quiet, and do not judge those who worship loudly. God speaks in diverse ways.

After crying out and causing Alma to fall to the earth, the angel asks a series of questions in verse 15. Angels in the Book of Mormon ask rhetorical questions.[109] They move in ways that are powerful but different from other scripture, such as Psalms. For those who study angels, the Book of Mormon adds to the landscape of understanding the work of angels. They do not merely show visions, but are also fiercely committed to asking questions and challenging people to do better. They shout at and knock people over. When in our lives have we beheld angels? Readers engaging with the questions of angels in the Book of Mormon should use them as a spiritual practice. Read their questions personally. Answer them as journal entries to examine one's own relationship with God. Examine them closely and consider the questions in verse 15: "Can you dispute the power of God?" "Doth not my voice shake the earth?" "Can ye not behold me before you?"

Mosiah 27:23-24

Given that the angel appeared to Alma because of the prayers of the Nephites,[110] it seems appropriate that Alma addresses his first testimony to the community that has been fasting and praying on his behalf. Like his conversion, Alma's discipleship will go on to be deeply tied to communal experiences. The angel seems to understand community as a spiritual entry point for Alma when he tells

---

108. 1 Kings 19:11–13
109. For example, 1 Nephi 3:29
110. Mosiah 27:14

Alma to remember his ancestry and what God did for his people.[111] Alma's call is to the Nephites. The Nephites prayed for him, and he will remember and testify to his people. His prophetic call will be embedded in community for the rest of his life.

Mosiah 27:25–26

These verses deserve recognition for their inclusivity. They specifically include all people when referencing mankind: "men and women, *all* nations, kindred, tongues, and people" (v. 25, emphasis added). Naming different social barriers—nations, families, tongues, groups of people—emphasizes the inclusivity of God. None of those divisions matter. Every single one must be born again.

Think carefully about the concept of birthing and what it means to be reborn. Birth requires a womb. Therefore, to be born of the spirit would require the spirit to have a womb. Until we repent and follow God, we are waiting in a womb, waiting for spiritual birth. This is particularly gendered language, tied closely to God and the Spirit.

Mosiah 27:28–29

The verb "snatch" that Alma repeats here is such a vivid one, almost violent in nature. Some people will feel as if God has snatched them from sin, as a parent would grab a toddler running toward a car. It is a jerking, harsh movement. Alma uses it twice here, reminding readers that God can snatch us from parts of our journey when we head in the wrong way, particularly those parts that are unjust and harmful to our communities.

Usually the phrase "eternal torment" (v. 29) conjures up ideas of life after death. Instead, Alma uses it to describe something he experienced in mortality, something that ended when he repented. Alma's torment was not from literal demons torturing him, but from

---

111. Mosiah 27:16

his internal state. The choices he made were in themselves an eternal torment until God snatched him back. Not all torment is posthumous. Hell may come one day, but Alma tells us that destroying one's own community and harming the people around you through luring them away from the love of God is a Hell in itself.

Mosiah 27:32–33

After this extraordinary epiphany and conversion, Alma and the sons of Mosiah begin their ministry. This verse portrays an accurate idea of the reality of ministry, preparing readers for Alma's tribulation and persecution. Working with the divine and working for those on the margins will, inevitably, lead to times of "being smitten" by unbelievers (v. 32). Yet, Alma and the sons of Mosiah offer consolation through the church in response (v. 33). Alma's ministry depicts a time of struggle for the faithful. Choosing to follow God in this place and time puts people in danger of persecution and means that they will need consolation.

Mosiah 27:35

Before the sons of Mosiah leave, they travel around Zarahemla to repair the damage they have done. The text emphasizes the energy they put into this effort: "*zealously striving* to repair *all* the injuries which they had done" (emphasis added), including confessing and replacing old narratives with new ones. Social justice, particularly within a church, sometimes looks like zealously repairing the wrongs of the past. It is the church collectively asking: What have we done to harm other people? And once we become cognizant of that harm, then we work hard to mend it. Disciples cannot disregard the injuries they may have caused, even unintentional harms. The impact of what the church has done to people's testimonies matters. The sons of Mosiah were part of the church, and yet they harmed other members of the church. When they awoke to what they had done, they did not move on until they had done the healing work of repairing those injuries. This exemplifies the importance of apologizing and making amends within the church.

Mosiah 28:1–3

All of Mosiah's sons reject Mosiah's path of monarchy and instead ask to walk into enemy territory in order to preach the gospel. Although Mosiah did not travel to or live in the land of Nephi, he has read the records of what happened there and welcomed the people who fled from that land. Readers can imagine how terrified he might feel allowing his sons to go to a place haunted by so much suffering. This Mosiah is the grandson of the Mosiah who allowed Zeniff to return to the land of Nephi. This decision must have weighed heavily on him, as shown by his choice to ask God for direction on the matter.[112] Yet, Mosiah's willingness to let them go has enormous implications for the Lamanite and Nephite societies. Their ministry shifts the entire political structure, fundamentally changing the relationship between the peoples, and bringing countless people to God. Their work is a priceless gift.

The sons of Mosiah think about the Lamanites in complex ways at this point. On the one hand, they see the humanity of the Lamanites and refer to them as their "brethren" (v. 1), which, considering the recent history between the people, is remarkable. On the other hand, they maintain some of their own prejudice, evidenced by their desire to "convince [the Lamanites] of the iniquity of their fathers" and "cure them of their hatred toward the Nephites" (v. 2). The sons of Mosiah do not quite yet see the role the Nephites have played in the conflict, or face their own potential hatred toward the Lamanites. Yet, their idea of tying preaching the gospel to curing hatred is intriguing. How would missionary work tightly entwined with curing hatred look? What if missionaries felt a solemn responsibility to heal enmity between themselves and other people? Curing hatred

---

112. Mosiah 28:6

requires internal and external work, and that kind of conflict will not end with only one side changing. These verses show how missionary work can heal relationships and how the gospel offers an opportunity to cure hatred.

Mosiah 28:12–18

The Nephites care so much about what happened to this unknown society that the text says "they were desirous beyond measure" (v. 12). Through their interest in records, these people consistently make clear their interest and concern for others, including groups who are biologically unconnected to them. It appears that they simply want to know the history and, when they learn it, they feel it deeply. Reading the account of the Jaredites causes the Nephites "to mourn exceedingly, yea, they were filled with sorrow; nevertheless it gave them much knowledge, in the which they did rejoice" (v. 18). Once again, reading the stories of scripture prompts the people to feel the sister emotions of sorrow and joy together. They grieve for what happened to the Jaredites while feeling gratitude for what they have learned. Moving in sacred text and in the stories of one another will feel like a sorrow and a lament. But it will also offer the gift of knowledge, and that process of learning is a cause for rejoicing. The way the Nephites hunger for others' records, then experience them so personally and deeply, offers a template for how we should engage with the Book of Mormon and with the stories and histories of one another. Sitting with someone else's narrative, listening and reading eagerly and then allowing the emotion to overwhelm us, has the potential to fundamentally alter us. The Nephites feel gratitude for the knowledge they have gained because it offers them opportunities to change. They do not read and move on; they internalize and consider how they can improve. This is the sacred nature of history: as the Nephites grieve for people they never knew, they also rejoice because they have learned how they can make better choices than they have in the past.

Mosiah uses "two stones" (v. 13) which Joseph Smith would later describe as the Urim and Thummim[113] to translate the record of the Jaredites. In the Book of Mormon, God repeatedly gives the prophets physical tools to help them find guidance or inspiration. There is a kind of materialism to the role of a prophet, one that is passed down to Joseph Smith. This use of items is unusual or unknown in the Bible. It shows how God speaks to people in a wide variety of ways, including ways that may seem foreign or inappropriate to people who have not experienced them. Becoming aware of the ways in which our own faith leaders have communicated with God in unconventional ways can help us empathize with people who worship or receive inspiration in ways different from our own.

Mosiah 29:1

Mosiah takes this moment of peace and transition to consider a new form of government. The text spends time on this question, with Mosiah in dialogue with the people about potential pitfalls of various government structures and all the people considering what kind of society they want to build. Throughout this chapter, notice how often Mosiah returns to the people to ask for their opinions and desires. They collaboratively reimagine their government, realigning the community to be fairer and more just. Their thoughtful decisions about powder structures reflect the kind of society they want to build. They repeatedly say to one another, *"This is what we do not want. How do we choose structures that help prevent that?"* And then they use their historical records to inform their decisions. Ultimately, they seek a society that emphasizes fairness, peace, justice, equality, and democracy.

---

113. Joseph Smith History 1:35

Mosiah 29:7-9

Mosiah strongly discourages the people from continuing a monarchy. He levels two arguments against it: the first clearly references what he has learned from the book of Ether—kings invite contention. Until this point, Nephite history has not seen a moment when an heir to the throne returns and fights with the person currently in power. Yet, this is one of the narrative themes of the Jaredites and, ultimately, a foundational part of their destruction. This moment shows that Mosiah did not just read the records, he internalized them. He has learned from them and wants to do better.

In verse 9, Mosiah gives his second reason: he frankly admits that his son has not always been a great person or made good choices. Mosiah realizes that, although he has reformed, Aaron may return to his previous ways. This is a beautifully honest look at his own child. He sees that his sons have agency and autonomy, and he accepts that they will not always make the decisions that he wants. To admit that publicly seems like a vulnerable move, yet he does it to shield his people. Mosiah gives up his son's potential claims to power for the good of the community. This exemplifies Mosiah learning from Zeniff and Noah, the ancestors of some of the people in this society. In both these arguments, Mosiah shows how he has learned from others' stories in order to act wisely and promote peace.

Mosiah 29:17

The book of Mosiah repeatedly emphasizes the potential for evil governments and leaders to cause corruption and sin among the people. The human instinct to justify oneself and condemn others means that readers of this section, and particularly this verse, believe the "wicked king" to be their political opponent. On one level, this seems to indicate that we should refrain from mixing politics and scripture, since anyone can use scripture to solidify their own political beliefs and attack others. Yet, womanist theologians posit the impossibility of that goal, noting that the personal is political, and that divorcing religion from politics does not allow for a full moral examination of racism and sexism. Accepting that theology and politics are inseparable means accepting that people will reach completely different political conclusions from reading the same text, and this is simply a reflection of their values and moral framework.

This chapter powerfully engages questions of how people construct moral governments and the ways in which social structures affect people personally. Mosiah repeatedly encourages the people to be wise and consider how their own leadership might ultimately harm them. Do our laws keep people in a form of bondage? Do our leaders encourage iniquity? Do our policies affirm human dignity? Regardless of the answers we eventually reach, having a dialogue about the potential evils of our laws is a worthwhile task.

Mosiah 29:21–23

Those who are interested in connecting scripture to contemporary issues of inequality and violence may find value in reading holy text with a newspaper in hand. This practice reveals connections between God's words about ancient problems and the appearance of those same issues in our world today.[114] Mosiah explicitly describes "an iniquitous king" (v. 21) and its consequences to a society. His list perfectly outlines a threat that is both eternal and immediate to current events. While Mosiah may have been thinking specifically of king Noah in these verses, reading them alongside today's newspaper will continue to reveal their truth.

Mosiah 29:26

This verse calls for inclusive government. Mosiah's endorsement of democracy works only with the caveat that *everyone* must be a part of "the voice of the people." Partial democracy, when some voices are

---

114. William C. Turner. *Preaching into Social Crisis* course, Lecture at Duke Divinity School, Spring 2016.

suppressed, routinely "desire[s] that which is not right." And while majority rule may work generally, Mosiah admits that, while "not common," sometimes the voice of the people may choose poorly. In Zarahemla during this time, people live under principles of human dignity, justice, and peace. This is the context most likely to ensure that "the voice of the people" chooses wisely.

Mosiah 29:32

In order for the land to be a land of liberty, in which "every man may enjoy his rights and privileges alike," inequality cannot exist. Inequality inherently destroys freedom. This verse comes in the midst of Mosiah's discourse about structures of government and how they may cause people to commit iniquity. Equality and liberty must go hand in hand, as equality gives people the capacity to exercise freedom. Mosiah invokes "rights and privileges" as the franchise of all people, which is broader than solely endorsing rights. Rights belong in a legal category and focus on survival, while privileges pertain to a social category that allows for life to be comfortable. Mosiah ties rights and privileges together while simultaneously predicating them on equality.[115]

---

115. Rev. Dr. Martin Luther King said, "In a sense we've come to our nation's capital to cash a check. When the architects of our republic wrote the magnificent words of the Constitution and the Declaration of Independence, they were signing a promissory note to which every American was to fall heir. This note was a promise that all men, yes, black men as well as white men, would be guaranteed the 'unalienable Rights' of 'Life, Liberty and the pursuit of Happiness.' It is obvious today that America has defaulted on this promissory note, insofar as her citizens of color are concerned. Instead of honoring this sacred obligation, America has given the Negro people a bad check, a check which has come back marked 'insufficient funds.'
"But we refuse to believe that the bank of justice is bankrupt. We refuse to believe that there are insufficient funds in the great vaults of opportunity of this nation. And so, we've come to cash this check, a check that will give us upon demand the riches of freedom and the security of justice." Martin Luther King, Jr. "I Have a Dream." Speech presented at the March on Washington for Jobs and Freedom, Washington, D.C., August 1968. https://avalon.law.yale.edu/20th_century/mlk01.asp.

Mosiah 29:38–39

The people listen to Mosiah and heed his counsel about their govern-ment. Their culture values listening and learning. They adapt and change with new information and stories. Led by Mosiah, this society idealisti-cally chooses greater equality over stability and continuity. Importantly, this shift does not immediately create a utopian society. Within the first five years of the new system of judges, violence and schisms overwhelm the Nephite nation. That does not mean that their choice was wrong; it means that expanding equality and freedom is a process, not an event.

One possible reason for the new government's weakness lies hid-den in verse 38: "every *man* should have an equal chance throughout all the land" (emphasis added). This chapter of Mosiah uses par-ticularly gendered language, referring to men repeatedly without reference to women. Possibly, this use of man and men is intended to include women. The nature of scripture requires women to guess at when they are included or excluded. But it is also possible, even likely, that only men received these new rights and privileges to vote. In that case, the Nephites would not have listened to the voice of all the people, but only a portion of them, corrupting their new attempt at democracy. The new reign of the judges is an improvement on the monarchy, but with limits. The hope of every unfinished democracy is that by anchoring itself to the ideals of liberty and equality, rights and privileges will continue to expand.

Mosiah 29:40

As Mosiah's life comes to a close, the people's deep love and respect for him is abundantly evident. He led by welcoming strangers, unit-ing diverse people, expanding equality and justice, and establishing peace. He did his best to reimagine a better life for his people. He freed them from "all manner of bondage," not just literal slavery, but all the various forms of oppression that keep people from full and comfortable lives. Mosiah cared about the quality of life of his people and worked for those on the margins. No wonder his people "did esteem him, yea, exceedingly, beyond measure."

ALMA

Alma 1:1

The text never explains why Alma the Younger and the sons of Mosiah chose very different ministerial paths. Possibly Alma the Elder could not face the prospect of his son returning to the Land of Nephi to teach the Lamanites. Mosiah, who had not experienced the trauma at the hands of the Lamanites that Alma the Elder lived through, might have had different feelings. It is also possible that Alma the Younger follows in his father's footsteps of ministering to those within the church. Rather than evangelizing abroad, Alma the Younger's path leads him to confront and reform the failings within his own people, just as his father did. Regardless of the reasons, it is worth noting the differences between the paths that the young men choose. They all live into their callings, although those all look very different.

Verse 1 says that Mosiah died, "having warred a good warfare." This curious eulogy commemorates a man who never went to battle and ushered in a period of peace for his people. Two things to observe here: first, the use of the word "good" to modify "warfare." Calling warfare good, in any way, is an interesting linguistic choice that creates some tension. Second, note the ways the text subtly normalizes violent language. The Book of Mormon contains an enormous amount of information about battles, death, and war strategy. Mormon, a general for almost all of his life, likely had something to do with this as the editor of the text. But war-saturated language and metaphors that invoke violence like this, in addition to the many overt descriptions of war in these scriptures, compound to affect how readers engage with the Book of Mormon.

Alma 1:2

Even though Mosiah prayerfully and thoughtfully created this new form of government, things start to go awry in the very first year of its implementation. Even with the best of intentions and good people striving to build something that will increase equality and justice, major problems arise almost immediately. Although one of the lessons from the book of Mosiah was that poor systems create bad outcomes, the reign of the judges will reveal that better systems can still produce poor results. The human element, a constant in any structure, means that sin, inequality, and injustice will grow up through any society. The work of the righteous is to try to make things better, to fight against hopelessness, and to understand that "the arc of the moral universe is long but it bends toward justice."[1]

Alma 1:3-6

As is common for those wishing to confuse the faithful, Nehor mixes good theology and truth with bad theology and lies. His description of a God who offers love and redemption, and his invitation to rejoice with gratitude, are good and worthy. Yet he mixes those tendrils of truth with corrupted ideas: "that every priest and teacher ought to become popular" (v. 3) and not work, and that God extends a "cheap grace"[2] devoid of laws or requirements.

---

1. Martin Luther King, Jr. *Remaining Awake Through a Great Revolution.* Speech given at the National Cathedral, Washington, DC, March 11, 1968.
2. Dietrich Bonhoeffer describes the concept of cheap grace as "the preaching of forgiveness without requiring repentance, baptism without church discipline, Communion without confession, absolution without personal confession. Cheap grace

As Nehor's popularity grows, the people give him money (v. 5) and he begins "to wear very costly apparel" as well as establish his own church (v. 6). Compare this to the beginning of Alma's church: a community in the wilderness, pursued by those in power, acting out their faith in defiance of the dangers they faced. When looking at a church, consider its orientation toward those in positions of power and those on the margins. Examine the church's origin story and how it chooses to tell that narrative. Its foundational roots will bear fruits reflecting core values.

Alma 1:7–9

While Nehor is large and strong (v. 2), Gideon is elderly and frail. Gideon's ability to preach to and contradict Nehor's teachings enrages Nehor, prompting him to physically assault and then kill Gideon. Gideon dies a victim to a religious dispute that turned violent. Significantly, while Gideon was prone to rash and violent actions earlier in his life, his confrontation with Nehor appears to be limited to words until Nehor attacks. Alma describes Gideon as "a righteous man, yea, a man who has done much good among this people."[3] He was a community hero for the ways he helped Limhi's people, and his death is a tragedy for the Nephites. This story exemplifies the very real danger of letting any kind of violence infiltrate religious conversations.

Alma 1:12

Although the concept of priestcraft is not unique to the Book of Mormon, the Old or New Testaments do not use the word. Across the canon of scripture, the Book of Mormon seems to struggle with the problem of priestcraft most frequently, from Noah's priests to Nehor to Korihor. Priestcraft surfaces throughout the text, from Nephi

---

is grace without discipleship, grace without the cross, grace without Jesus Christ, living and incarnate." *The Cost of Discipleship*. New York: Touchstone, 1995.

3. Alma 1:13

defining it as when "men preach and set themselves up for a light unto the world, that they may get gain and praise of the world; but they seek not the welfare of Zion,"[4] to warnings in 3 Nephi of priest-craft wreaking destruction on saints in the latter days.[5] Priestcraft, like pride and ethnonationalism, is one of the great social ills of the Book of Mormon. This story, and particularly the description it gives of priestcraft, therefore warrants close examination.

Chapter 1 narrates priestcraft in the following ways: first, Nehor preaches to the people "that which he termed to be the word of God."[6] Nehor uses God for his own purposes, turning preaching into an idol. Second, he claims that priests and teachers should enjoy the kind of popularity and financial support from the people that allows Nehor to dress in expensive clothing. Nehor makes pride into a vir-tue and consumption into an ideal. Third, even after Nehor's death, priestcraft spreads through Zarahemla because of the "many who loved the vain things of the world, and they went forth preaching false doctrines; and this they did for the sake of riches and honor."[7]

Nehor succeeded in adulterating the role of a pastor through teaching a gospel of unbridled inclusivity. His warped approach mimics the inclusivity of the gospel of Jesus Christ but is ultimately so broad and lacking in nuance that it damages people's relation-ship with God. He pairs kernels of truth ("the Lord had created all [people]") with a complete absence of accountability and respon-sibility. By offering universal acceptance of any kind of behavior, Nehor attracted people to his church, succeeding in his ultimate goal of enriching himself.

---

4. 2 Nephi 26:29
5. 3 Nephi 30:2
6. Alma 1:3
7. Alma 1:16

Alma 1:13–14

In addition to the local laws dispensing justice, Alma also underlines the need for divine justice. Again, although we generally hold mercy and justice as ideals in tension, true justice is a form of mercy for the victim. Without it, Alma says, Gideon's blood "would come upon us for vengeance" (v. 13). This is why there cannot be peace without justice.

Alma 1:15

The text seems to go out of its way to avoid naming Nehor until this point in the story, naming him only after it has eulogized Gideon and explained the damage Nehor enacted. This linguistic/narrative choice exemplifies how to maintain focus on the victim rather than on the perpetrator. Through naming Gideon immediately, the text shows respect and gratitude for his life. Through waiting to name Nehor—and then doing so only once—it subtly reduces "the man who slew [Gideon]."[8] The Book of Mormon consistently uses the power of naming to reveal who the society honors and reveres.

Nehor "suffered an ignominious death" on the hill after being forced to confess the falseness of his teachings. This disturbing description implies some kind of torture or shaming in his death. While the text is vague enough that readers are left without clarity regarding exactly what happened to this man, it is apparent that the Nephites enacted some pretty awful kind of violence. It also seems to have been done in anger, as a reaction to the tragedy of Gideon's death, rather than out of a sense of fairness. While the text skates around this event, readers should pause and take note, because whatever happened on the hill Manti is troubling.

---

8. Alma 1:10

Alma 1:20–22

The persecution of the faithful begins with words. The words are, in themselves, a form of persecution, even without bodily harm or structural oppression. Because the harm is not visual, it's easy to fail to understand that language can be abusive. The text says that the perpetrators persecuted people *"because* of their humility; *because* they were not proud in their own eyes, and *because* they did impart the word of God . . . without money and without price" (v. 20, emphasis added). Humility is a worthy and important virtue, but those enacting violence warp it into a weakness to target and mock. A common tool of abusers is to identify the best parts of people, then to reduce that trait into a vulnerable point of ridicule.

Though this theocratic society has rigid laws based on a religious code, they uphold a policy of not persecuting one another, including anyone outside of the church. Although the text describes this as "a strict law" (v. 20), the policy specifically applies to members of the church. This is a powerful example of the majority enacting protections for the minority, even a minority that vocally opposes them. They have also defined persecution broadly, including verbal abuse as an offense. These policies should prompt readers to consider what kind of language they employ, particularly toward those who are not part of the modern church.

Notwithstanding the policy of avoiding any kind of persecution or retaliation, the conflict escalates. Verbal violence is consistently the foundation of physical violence. Some members of the church, because of pride and the persecution they endure, begin to fight their adversaries "with their fists" (v. 22). These three verses broadly examine the personal events in verses 7–9: religious beliefs lead to contention, which intensifies into overt violence. How can the faithful engage with nonbelievers, even those who deliberately provoke others? This chapter offers two examples—one individual and one societal—of the tragedies that result from religious contention.

Alma 1:25–28

These verses are some of the most radical and important in the Book of Mormon. A fundamental shift occurs in the people, transforming how they engage with the church and with one another. It begins with a description of their faith and their patience, a marked change from verse 22, in which people had begun physically fighting one another. This poor behavior caused grief and "affliction" in verse 3, which is a profound, telling response that the most faithful feel toward their church and their fellow members engaging in violence. Then, they set aside deliberate time. The priests and the people "left their labor" (v. 26) to preach and listen to the word of God before returning to their work. The text emphasizes the equality of this community, with no hierarchy or division between the teachers and the learners. This is what a church should be for people. The community is reminiscent of the time of the Montgomery bus boycotts, in which Black people would gather in their churches and listen to Martin Luther King and other preachers encourage them and give them strength. Gathering renewed their ability to walk or carpool to work, lending them patience and resolve in the face of persecution. A community of faith can be the saving grace in social justice work that feels hopeless or never ending. It can refill and renew people to continue doing what they know is right, particularly when they are living in oppression.

The text also offers the beautiful caveat: while all the people labored, they did so "according to [their] strength" (v. 26). They are all expected to work, but they do not all have to do the same thing. They offer grace to anyone who, for whatever reason, cannot do the same labor. When everyone labors with the strength they have, there is no grinding expectation for someone to work beyond their capacity.

The result is an extraordinary step toward Zion. They care for "the poor, and the needy, and the sick, and the afflicted" (v. 27), through living simply and emphasizing equality and dignity. In difficult circumstances, the church succeeds in cultivating a sense of communal peace and interconnectedness. It is what a church ought to be: a refilling station so that people can have the courage to press on. It allows them to do the good work of caring for the poor and needy.

These verses tell readers what church can and ought to be for the persecuted and for the most marginalized in society. They explain to readers how a church can establish peace in the midst of persecution. The role of a church is to sustain people, to renew them so that they can live in ways that are holy and generous despite their suffering.

Alma 1:29–31

The church enters a period of prosperity, but without pride. It has found internal peace in the midst of persecution. Perhaps the persecution they face externally helps prevent them from following the typical pattern of pride the Nephite society repeats so often in the Book of Mormon. Instead, they use their prosperity to care for the naked, hungry, thirsty, sick, and those who "had not been nourished" (v. 30), a beautifully encompassing phrase. The text emphasizes the inclusivity of their generosity, saying, "they were liberal unto *all*, both old and young, both bond and free, both male and female, whether out of the church or in the church, having no respect to persons as to those who stood in need" (v. 30, emphasis added). This extraordinary example shows people able to gain wealth without it leading to their spiritual decline. Instead, their riches allow them to do more good in the world, to elevate the human condition, and to build community. We rarely see this combination of wealth, liberality, and inclusivity. They do not even draw a line around the membership of the church: they care for everyone. They are no respecter of persons when it comes to need.

The key sentence in this chapter comes in verse 31: "And thus they did prosper." By giving away their wealth, they prospered. This calls into question our frequent assumptions about prosperity gospel. Rather than viewing wealthy people as righteous, or that if people are righteous, they will inevitably be wealthy, the author seems to point to an important mechanism: these people prosper in persecution, but their prosperity comes from giving away their abundance to anyone, regardless of their identity. It is their radical, inclusive giving that leads to their prosperity. Rather than an individual prosperity, in which a few people hoard extreme wealth, this church has embraced a communal prosperity, one in which everyone has enough to live comfortably if they share.

Alma 2:1

Once again, the text goes out of its way to not name Nehor, using a roundabout way of referencing him that invokes the name Gideon instead. While it feels somewhat awkward, this beautifully refuses to give power to someone who has become famous for the violence they have done. This approach subtly reclaims the narrative power, making it a form of nonviolent resistance. Perhaps his name has become a curse.[9]

Alma 2:10–14

The moment that the followers of Amlici begin calling themselves by a different name, they "take up arms" to try to subjugate the Nephites. Once again, the Book of Mormon returns to the theme of separating and labeling people and the process of a society descending into violence. This division of people does not involve the Lamanites in any way, thus serving as a useful comparison. In this conflict, the narrator structures the rupture around spiritual and political decisions. There is no language about skin color, clothing, or the nature of the Amlicites, similar to the treatment shown to the Nephites throughout the Book of Mormon.[10] The text situates this conflict as one about issues, not about human identity. And even as the struggle descends into war,

---

9. An example: in 2015, some referred to Dylann Roof as "the man who killed nine Black saints in their own church," or "the murderer of the Charleston Nine." This centers the victims of the violence instead of the perpetrator.
10. Such as in Mosiah 10:12

the narrator sees them as one people, fighting against "their brethren" (v. 14). That kind of familial connection goes unrecognized in conflicts between the Nephites and the Lamanites, despite their shared lineage.

Alma 2:18–19

Every time the text places God in the role of enabling or encouraging more death, readers should pause. In this case, we cannot identify the writer, making analysis of perspective and motivations impossible. Perhaps the author is right and God was involved in this battle. But consider what kind of theology that leads to and think carefully about what that says about the nature of God. The text claims here that God not only protects the Nephites, but helps them kill the Amlicites. The slaughter was so great that more than 19,000 people died. Is God in that? Does God step onto the battlefield in order to facilitate more death? These theological questions in the Book of Mormon can push us to ponder these questions for ourselves.

Alma 2:20

Please do not miss the language of this verse, as the narrator takes pains to emphasize and repeat the name of Gideon. Remember that the land acts as a character in the Book of Mormon, and it tells its own story. This conflict started because of the man who killed Gideon. The Nephites are pitching their tents again, this time in a valley. Strategically, a valley is not a good place for a military to encamp. But Nehor died on a mountain, and the Nephites went to the valley. As Lehi left Jerusalem, he traveled through the valley of Lemuel. Nephi walked in the "low valley."[11] Alma's people pitched their tents in a valley as they fled from the Lamanites.[12] Although it does not logically make sense, God's people go to the valley for safety in the Book of Mormon. They seek sanctuary in the lowest, most humble places, where they pitch their tents.

---

11. 2 Nephi 4:32
12. Mosiah 24:20

Alma 2:22

The men sent out to watch the Amlicites' camp play a minor role in this story and are never mentioned again in the Book of Mormon, and yet, all four soldiers get named in this verse. There is no reason for the reader to need to know their names; they appear in this single episodic moment and then disappear. We are left to wonder why they are named, while important women who play major roles go unnamed and unidentified. The choice of who gets named in the Book of Mormon indicates who has power and authority in Nephite society. The entire Book of Mormon names only six women. Only three of those women—Sariah, Abish, and Isabel—are from the Book of Mormon. The other three—Eve, Sarah, and Mary—are from the Bible. Four men who appear for a single instant, in contrast, get named in this one verse. We pay attention to the ways in which the Nephites overlooked and disempowered women.

Alma 2:25

The Lamanites and Amlicites join together to attack the Nephites. Again, notice the lack of parallelism in how the Nephites name the people and things that run from the danger. They flee with "their flocks, and their wives, and their children" and "except we make haste [the Lamanites will] obtain possession of our city, and our fathers, and our wives, and our children be slain." First, the men are the active subjects, with everything else put in relationship to them. Second, Women are only named as wives, not as sisters, daughters, or mothers. Flocks, wives, and children are listed together as kinds of wealth. Third, fathers, wives, and children are named, but no mothers are mentioned. Their rhetoric tells readers what they value. Wives and children have a lower priority than men, and elderly mothers or single women have no value worth mentioning at all. This disturbing verse indicates what the Nephites value, and in what order.

Alma 2:29

This verse contains the first account since Nephi of a Book of Mormon prophet killing someone. Alma the Younger is the chief judge, the prophet, and a warrior. He fights alongside his people in battle and kills Amlici as they fight face to face. Although Jacob described Nephi fighting for his people,[13] he never gave this level of detail about the violence. Having a prophet going to war and killing someone marks an important shift. And while the Book of Mormon repeatedly claims God's favor for the winners of battles, this is a singular time in which a prophet prays for God's help in combat. Although his plea is for protection, the result is that he has the strength to kill someone. This kind of pivoting toward a theology of violence is an important moment in the text.

Alma 2:34–3:3

This is an incredibly violent section of scripture. As the dominance of the battle shifts, the Nephites pursue the Lamanites and slaughter them. The Nephites even use the bodies of the Lamanites to form a bridge in order to cross the river and continue the battle. The violent language makes the scene clear: the Lamanites are "slain and driven, until they were scattered" (v. 37) in the wilderness, where they die from their injuries and the attacks of wild beasts. This denotes an intensely bloodthirsty moment, with no room for mercy as the Lamanites flee. The book declines to give a death toll, but as the previous battle counted over 13,000 deaths,[14] readers can assume that this was higher.

The land speaks as a character twice in these verses. First, the text explicitly describes how the Nephites dumped innumerable bodies into the River Sidon (v. 37 and v. 3). While the Nephites bury the bodies of their own dead (v. 1), they do not afford the bodies

---

13. Jacob 1:10
14. Alma 2:19

of the Lamanites the same dignity. Second, the Nephites chase the Lamanites into the wilderness, where the wild beasts destroy them and "their bones . . . have been heaped up on the earth" (v. 38). Both the wilderness and the river are filled with the bones of the dead. The wilderness has traditionally been a place of transition and sanctuary for those fleeing for their lives in the Book of Mormon. This story shows a disturbing perversion of that theme, as it becomes a site of mass death. The River Sidon also has strong symbolic meaning, which will be explored further in the section on Alma 4:4.

When the Nephites finish the battle, what do they return to? Their land, then their houses, then their wives and children. Not their families, just their wives and children. Again, the listing order indicates the societal values: first the land and houses, then the women and children. That rhetorical choice is a doctrinal and cultural move. The way the author repeatedly does this in these chapters points to a fundamental problem in the Nephite society at this time.

Alma 3:2 is one of the few times the Book of Mormon acknowledges the deaths of women and children in war. Yet, even at this moment, they get listed among an inventory of destroyed property. When the Book of Mormon numbers the deaths of soldiers, it does not simultaneously describe the loss of land and crops. The loss of men is a loss in itself. But when women and children die in battle, they are part of a list of property. The book frequently pairs women and children with possessions, but this is particularly jarring when done in reference to their deaths.

Alma 3:4–7

Here, the author digs up the worst, most destructive parts of Nephi's theology, adopting it and building upon it in even greater detail. Up to this point, the prophets of the Book of Mormon have not directly invoked Nephi's racist words in their writings. This section reawakens those words, strengthening them and solidifying their role in the Nephite society and, in turn, the modern church. That is the danger of a bad exegesis: it pulls dangerous theology up through the centuries, influencing how people understand God today.

We do not know the author of this section, but we do know the context. This passage gets written in the wake of one of the bloodiest, most graphic battles in the Book of Mormon. Countless people died, including women and children. The incredible violence acts as a foundation for these words. Crucially, it is the same kind of heartbreaking brutality that Nephi had just lived through when he originally wrote his own racist theology about the Lamanites. It is not coincidental that the author directly invokes Nephi's words (v. 14–17). While not excusing embedding scripture with harm, understanding the author's state of grief can help readers understand the verses differently. In moments of distress, humans tend to look at the menu of available doctrine and apply what feels soothing and comforting. The Nephites have suffered through a terrible war, but also engaged in the slaughter of people who fled for their lives.[15] They killed not only Lamanites, who have been divided from the Nephites for centuries at this point, but also the Amlicites, who were recently part of their own people. Thus, the author seeks to do three things with these verses: first, mentally separate the Amlicites from the Nephites and connect them to the Lamanites. Second, dehumanize the new Amlicite/Lamanite group. Third, justify the Nephites' violence.

Verse 4 begins the work of the first goal. Pointing to how the Amlicites marked themselves as Lamanites allows the Nephites to no longer think of the Amlicites as part of their own people.[16] They have

---

15. Alma 2:35–36

16. Some scholars interpret the self-marking of the Amlicites as a way to defend the Book of Mormon against charges of racism. We find this explanation unsatisfying and ultimately dangerous in the way it disregards the long history of constructing the Book of Mormon as racist.

Jared Hickman convincingly argues that the Amlicites' marking is perhaps not specifically a racial act, but that ultimately the entire episode should be considered within the racialized context of the rest of the book. "The Book of Mormon as Amerindian Apocalypse." *American Literature* Vol. 86 No. 3 (2014), 429–461.

been turned into "the other," a faceless enemy, part of a group that the Lamanites have been fighting for over four centuries. The second intention becomes clear in that linkage with the Lamanites, as the author describes "shorn" heads of the Lamanites and their lack of clothes (v. 5). The implication of cultural superiority is clear. Finally, the dehumanization of the Amlicites/Lamanites works to further the third goal: justify violence against them. This is a well-worn pattern within ethnic violence when the goals of warfare demand a change in the definition of race or ethnicity.

In periods of particular struggle or trauma, humans tend to look at scripture and doctrine and choose to apply what is most satisfying in that moment. Following the suffering of this war and this period of mourning, when the Nephites must face the consequences of engaging in a war that killed so many people, it must be tempting to reach for doctrine that allows them to justify their actions. Reaching for Nephi's words and interpreting them through the lens of anger, division, and hatred, allows the Nephites to perhaps feel slightly better about filling the River Sidon with bodies and also gives them an outlet for their grief at the deaths of their own loved ones. It's a self-soothing, yet violent, way of weaponizing scripture and theology.

Alma 3:8–10

Verses 8–10 contain anti-miscegenation and are some of the most distressing of this section. Anti-miscegenation laws exist in segregated societies to keep people from learning to love one another. If people can be kept from intermingling, joining together, and creating families, white supremacists retain one of their most potent weapons. Preventing intermarriage stops people from forming close relationships, which is the strongest force for pushing people to do their internal work of renouncing racism. Here, the text makes the purpose of "the mark" explicit: to keep people separated. Is that the work of God? This is a very serious moment of theology. Do readers believe in a God who marks groups of people in order to keep them from intermingling? Do readers believe that creating loving families is a pathway to being swept up in destruction? This is the narrative the author puts forward at this moment.

At certain points in the Book of Mormon, speakers indicate that the Lamanite men treat their wives better than the Nephite men treat theirs.[17] And yet, the Nephites are threatened with destruction if they intermarry with the Lamanites. If the Nephite women were to become aware of the conditions of the Lamanite women's lives, they might want to choose a better life for themselves. However, this doctrine of anti-miscegenation keeps them bound to their current system. This structural violence gives the ideological foundation a path to overt physical violence.

Alma 3:11–12

The author states that the records of the Nephites have been kept and are true, of "their people, and also of the people of the Lamanites" (v. 12). This should raise a red flag. It is not possible to hold a record for another people and claim its universal veracity. It is one thing to submit your own records and maintain their correctness for yourself. It is another to state that they are also the truth of other folk, separate from you, who have had experiences completely different from your own. This text entirely lacks the Lamanites' narrative. In fact, it overtly and repeatedly condemns them, and yet the author presumes to claim it as their truth. This is a misguided move, one which leaves no space for the Lamanites to tell their own story for themselves. Taking this action with a religious text is theological violence. One group cannot hold the records of another's truth. We need to leave space for everyone to speak for themselves.

---

17. For example, Jacob 2:35

Alma 3:14–17

These verses invoke and quote Nephi at one of the lowest points in his life. The author takes what Nephi said in trauma and reawakens it 400 years later. Instead of containing the damage, the author spreads it to a new generation and helps pass it down again to subsequent generations. This is why everyone needs to use caution when exegeting scripture. The author could have interpreted Nephi's racist words in a way that stopped the spread of destructive theology. Instead, he amplified it, choosing to pick up something centuries old, that already caused deep harm, and resurrect it. Nephi's words have already consistently moved as tendrils through the Nephite culture, encouraging prejudice and exacerbating conflicts. The author only makes those problems worse. As readers, we can see how the Nephites passed down that damage from generation to generation. And we can choose to exegete scripture differently. We can read holy text differently from the author of Alma. We can say that the trauma and hatred stops with us, and we will not teach our children that Nephi's racist rhetoric was right.

Alma 3:18–19

We have abundant evidence of how bad humans are at deciding who has been blessed or cursed and who has not. The scriptures, including the Book of Mormon, are full of stories of righteous people suffering. Avoid naming who God can bless and for what; avoid naming who God curses and for what. God is too big for that.

Alma 3:24–27

For a brief period, there is a measure of peace in the land. But in the first five years of the Nephites' new society, built on idealism for a new kind of government, tens of thousands of people died in violent conflict. There is a real need for grief here, both for the suffering and the deaths, and for the damage to the brightness of hope that brought about the reign of judges.

Alma 4:2-3

The war took a terrible toll on this community. They have lost people, animals, and food. They suffer the aftermath of war: "every soul had cause to mourn" (v. 3). It prompts them to consider whether their sufferings are because of their unrighteousness, believing that God is punishing them in order to change their ways. Yet, Alma 1:25-33 spends significant time describing how just and righteous they were. That period of time was only two or three years before this, but now the people recognize their need to repent. Did the Nephite society change that significantly over those couple of years? Or was it always more complex than the earlier account described?

Notice that although the Nephites recognize their wickedness in this moment, there is no connection to the color of their skin or their culture. When the Lamanites are wicked, the text links that behavior to dark skin, a cursed mark, a lack of clothing, or their shorn heads. When the Nephites sin, they simply need to repent. They allow themselves the privilege of their unrighteousness being separate from their group identity, but do not give others the same privilege. That is a sign of an unjust society.

Alma 4:4-5

They establish the church through baptizing people in the waters of Sidon, the same body of water that they recently filled with bodies killed in war. First the Nephites crossed Sidon by building a bridge of dead Lamanites in order to pursue them in war.[18] Then they dumped innumerable other bodies of Lamanites and Amlicites in the river as the Nephites recovered.[19] Now, just a year later, they baptize people in that same river. A year after the Nephites "establish the church more fully" (v. 4), the church begins to collapse under pride and cru-

---

18. Alma 2:34
19. Alma 3:3

elty.[20] Yet, they never question whether making a site of bloodshed into a holy place is a good idea. They have not faced their role in the terrible violence that happened at the river and how it may have affected them.

This could be seen as the land speaking as a character. Just as Zeniff returned to camp on the hill where he led a coup and killed his brethren,[21] the Nephites utilize a place without recognizing the violence that has become a part of the history there. Readers should not miss the symbolism of rebuilding a church on the foundation of a battle that ripped apart the Nephite community. Neither should it surprise us that, just a year later, the church begins to disintegrate. Their choice of where and how to build their church points to the Nephites' unwillingness to confront their own role in the terrible violence that occurred at the River Sidon.

Alma 4:6–8

Just a few years earlier, the Nephites enjoyed "prosperous circum-stances," yet continued to care for the poor, avoiding pride, and loving their neighbors.[22] In that time, the Nephites used power dif-ferently than they do in this section. The most significant change between the righteous society from a few years before and this one now is their willingness to protect the vulnerable. Wealth and priv-ilege frequently act as corruptive forces, but it is possible to wield them for goodness. The distinction lies in the individual actions and social policies about hospitality, welfare, and common social goods. A society that seeks to build wealth as part of an effort to establish hierarchies and exclusive groups is fundamentally different from one which builds wealth in order to make life comfortable for as many people as possible.

---

20. Alma 4:6–8
21. Mosiah 9:2–4
22. Alma 1:29–30

Alma 4:9

The pride among the people of the church "*exceed* the pride of those who did not belong to the church of God" (emphasis added). The church no longer does the work of the gospel. It allows corrupting forces to affect it to the point that unbelievers sin less than believers. It should not surprise readers, given the racist doctrines of Alma 3 that came right before this moment of devastation within the church. Pride in the form of nationalism or classism—both exhibited within the church in this period—rapidly corrodes church community. It spurs people to believe that they are separate and chosen, held to a different standard than others. It sets them free to enact violence against others because of their belief in their own entitlement and others' status as unworthy. When even church leaders teach that God requires separate and distinct groups,[23] it bolsters the human tendency toward pride and hatred of others. When wealth and social power are added into that situation, there is no hope for humility and charity. The church sets itself on a downward spiral. It cannot do the work of protecting the marginalized when it is othering people and elevating itself as more righteous and worthy of God's love. This stretch of time—from founding a church in a location of deep violence, to teaching ethnic nationalism, to taking pride in wealth—is a template for how to do bad theology and destructive religion. This is when religion does harm.

Alma 4:10

Instead of doing the work of the gospel, the church becomes "a great stumbling-block" to those outside of the church. When the church becomes mired in ethnonationalism, classism, pride, and contention, it is unsurprising that people would resist associating with it. This is important because we tend to think of missionary work as going out and saving others, not realizing that doing internal work, making the

---

23. Alma 3:15

church the best version of itself, is one of the greatest acts of missionary work we can do. When a church has not confronted and repented of the ugliest parts of itself, it will struggle to attract people to join.

The text says that the church "began to fail in its progress," which is an extremely gentle way of describing what happened. And yet even the author does not fully examine the problem. By saying that the failure of the church is others not wanting to join, the text implicitly describes the problem as one of people not converting. But that is not the real problem of the church. The church declines because its members are not living the gospel. The church is failing, whether or not people continue to be baptized. Regardless of the status of church growth, the membership fails to live into their covenants. The inability of the church to attract people is not surprising, but it is not the true marker of failure.

Alma 4:11–13

The church becomes so terrible that it leads others into iniquity. Notice the emphasis on the problems of inequality in this society. After slaughtering people in war, resurrecting destructive theology, and idolizing wealth, there is no doubt that "great inequality" is tearing apart these people. When a church embraces a doctrine that allows people to demean and degrade an entire neighboring civilization, members then turn their backs on the poor and downtrodden. This society is deeply divided down lines of charity and humility, with one group rejecting the least of these and others making great sacrifices to care for them.

Alma 4:15–20

Alma boldly chooses to leave his political office just a few years into this new government and become a full-time prophet. He walks away from power because "the Spirit of the Lord did not fail him" (v. 15), not because he is being sanctioned or punished in any way. This is God telling him to leave politics and do the work on the ground.

Alma selects a wise man to be the new judge and gives up his ability to enforce laws or judge people, a decision that will prompt some to defy and mock him later.[24] Sometimes, God asks people to step back or limit their workload. Sometimes God asks people to walk away from positions of power or prestige. Others may assume that this is a failing or rebuke, but it is simply following God's call.

At the formation of the reign of judges, the Nephites felt inspired by their new system of government. They believed God had directed them to do away with the monarchy and make these steps toward greater equality. Yet, these first eight years have been mostly disastrous. Rather than questioning whether it was all a mistake, Alma adapts and makes major changes for himself. He has the courage to make these revisions because he carries God's Spirit with him. This protects him against despair.

Alma 5:1–5

Alma's ministry fundamentally differed from his friends who went to the Lamanites. He works within his own people, Nephites who have had some experience with the church and wandered from it, or who overtly fight against it. It is a challenging call because he tends to address people who are familiar with the gospel and have rejected it.

Alma starts as close to home as possible, first speaking to the people of Zarahemla, and then goes further out. As he reintroduces himself to the people in Zarahemla, he names his history and social location. So often in the Book of Mormon, speakers introduce themselves by describing their families and their place in society. This kind of introduction, before moving in a role of spiritual leadership, is important; so much of our testimony is linked to who we are and who we were raised to be. Helping people understand how you interpret the world is a meaningful part of pastoral work. What would a religious community that is aware of and sensitive to the effects of

---

24. Alma 8:12

social location in interpreting scripture and understanding testimony look like?

In Alma's case, much of how he understands his own identity is tied to ancestral history. He invokes his father's experiences with king Noah and founding a church by the waters of Mormon. He also reminds the people of their time as slaves of the Lamanites and their exodus to Zarahemla. Alma's testimony and sense of self is deeply tied to his father's journey and the oppression that his people suffered in the past. We all inherit family legacies and histories that affect our perception of God.

Alma 5:6

This verse contains three questions that offer guiding principles for establishing a person's relationship with God. It begins a kind of exploration or examination, giving prompts meant to lead a person through a spiritual inventory. *Do you remember your ancestors' captivity? Have you remembered God's mercy and long-suffering toward them? Have you remembered his deliverance of their souls?* Each of these questions could be used as a spiritual discipline, where people think deeply about the answers for ourselves, our community, and our church.

Mormons have an exodous story. They have a deluge of exodus stories, not all of them from nineteenth-century America. Every ward or branch has a story of how the Church established itself in a new and unfamiliar place. Every individual has a conversion story, a narrative that calls them back to remember miracles. We each have many interlocking ancestral stories. For example, Fatimah Salleh has the collective African-American story of the path toward civil rights. She has her Malaysian grandfather's story of coming to America. She has adopted the Mormon pioneer story. We are not one communal memory. We each house a multitude of stories and each of them matter.

To remember our personal and collective histories of captivity and how God emerged in those spaces is a critical part of our relationship with God. This is why times like Pioneer Day and Juneteenth are important—recognizing the pivotal point of liberation from a state of oppression, and then recommitting to not replicate those same systems. Remembering our own exodus stories helps us care for the marginalized.

Do we remember where we came from? What is it that remembrance is meant to do beyond parades and fireworks? How does it call us to a life of justice, to disrupt the systems that exclude and oppress? How do our stories call us to a higher humanity and deeper empathy? How do they prompt us to increase compassion toward others? Knowing the stories of your ancestors, being familiar with where your religion and people have been, is a crucial part of caring for the least of these. The questions in this verse call each of us into repentance through memory, turning us back to our origins. First do the internal work of seeing your own personal stories, then use those stories to connect to others' stories of liberation. As each of us does the work of memory, our stories should empower us to create a wider and deeper embrace of others' stories. If we don't use our ancestors' memories to connect with others, we will not internalize lessons on how to avoid perpetuating oppression. That path leads toward a mindset in which people cannot connect with others' suffering unless it is identical to their own.

Alma 5:7–12

So much of Alma's language about conversion centers around light, liberation, and expansion. The idea of souls illuminating and filling their highest potential is poetic. Alma sees sin as a real form of bondage, a state that keeps people in darkness. He makes clear how tightly the spiritual is tied to the physical, and how our capacity to experience expanded souls and to "sing the song of redeeming love" (v. 9) is dependent on the narratives we hold in our hearts. Elder Jeffrey R. Holland has spoken of how the world's suffering affects his ability to fully sing the song of redeeming love. He named economic inequality, mental and emotional illness, racism, and violence as factors that influence the state of his soul.[25] Alma speaks of a "mighty change" (v. 12) that occurs in the hearts of the converted. As the audience at king Benjamin's sermon cried out,[26] that "mighty change" prompts disciples to continually do good in the world, trying to erase the works of darkness that Elder Holland described.

Alma 5:16–20

A robust spiritual journey requires imagination, particularly in the area of faith. We talk about knowledge in regards to testimony, but it starts with simply being able to imagine a relationship with God. *Imagine it, without feeling like you have to know anything.* Throughout this sermon, through questions and invoking imagination, Alma sets up readers with a set of practices for developing a deeper spiritual life. Here, he offers the idea of an interview with God, one in which people review their lives and what they have done, what they have stood for, and who they loved. At that moment, how would you feel about those answers? Do not just imagine the answers, imagine how you might feel. This wild imagination brings along the heart.

Alma 5:26

This verse, as Mormon feminist Aimee Hickman writes, "is a genuine question about ability. *Can* you sing this song? Implicit in the question is the possibility that perhaps we cannot. Unlike so many 'questions' we can self-righteously pose to each other, Alma's question is not a chastisement, or even a call to do better than we're doing; rather, it's a genuine question about what we're capable of feeling and doing in the face of life's sometimes stark realities." She continues, "In the end, I believe the song of redeeming love will sound

---

25. Jeffrey R. Holland. "Songs Sung and Unsung." April 2017 General Conference. https://www.churchofjesuschrist.org/study/general-conference/2017/04/songs-sung-and-unsung
26. Mosiah 5:2

remarkably different than we might imagine. The song is not about perfect knowledge or perfect faith or doctrinal certainty, but a hymn of redemption, freedom, mystery, and most of all, God's mercy, compassion, and love."[27]

Alma 5:28–29

The word "stripping," more than other similar verbs, connotes intensity and vulnerability. It indicates the way pride and envy must be intentionally removed; they will not easily fall by the wayside. The way Alma describes it—being stripped of pride, not stripping yourself of pride—implies the involvement of a third party. This is an uncomfortable, possibly painful process, yet Alma emphasizes the urgency of it.

Although we often discuss pride, the Book of Mormon does not often reference envy. Envy is one of the deadliest sins because of the way it stealthily works to prompt people to endlessly acquire social power. Envy festers in structures of social hierarchy, and it leads to persecution and consumption. Pride is also rooted in a focus on social hierarchy, but it concerns an arrogance about what a person has already attained. Both pride and envy value power at the cost of dehumanizing people.

Alma 5:30–31

Those who heap on persecutions or mock others "cannot be saved" (v. 30). Persecution does not require face-to-face interactions; it can mean participating in a system that oppresses people. The strength of this assertion indicates that we should each ask ourselves: in what ways am I a part of institutions that heap persecutions on God's children? Alma speaks decisively about the importance of acting right now to see and correct these problems in ourselves. We waste time

---

27. Aimee Evans Hickman. "Dissonant Chords in the Song of Redeeming Love" *Exponent II*, Vol. 32 no. 4 (Spring 2013), 28–29.

if we are not actively moving to strip these things away and change our hearts. Appropriately internalizing the seriousness of Alma's call, again, requires using some imagination: imagine your future accountability before God now.

Alma 5:38–41

These verses contain one of the few references to "the good shepherd" (v. 38) in the Book of Mormon. It is unsurprising that this name follows the invitation to repent and come to God in verses 33–35 because the Good Shepherd calls all of us into God's fold. Alma presents the fold of God and the fold of the devil as binary, though the reality is far more complex. God's fold is vast and wide, and we may be part of it one moment but not follow the Good Shepherd the next. Perhaps that is why Alma reminds us that God will call us back into God's fold all day long.

Alma 5:45–46

This poignant moment shows Alma speaking about this work from personal experience. He knows these truths because he worked hard to gain them. Alma is one of the prophets who frankly shares how he has deeply struggled with God. His knowledge did not come from a simple epiphany; it was work. When he says "this is the spirit of revelation which is in me" (v. 46), he grounds his testimony in the efforts he has made to know God individually. It has become a part of him as he has sought truth.

Alma 5:49

The language here brings to mind other instances of inclusive scripture that defy the social divisions of the people in the Book of Mormon, mentioning "bond and free," "male and female," etc.[28] Yet

---

28. For example, 2 Nephi 10:16, 2 Nephi 26:33, Alma 1:30

this verse is distinct in its focus on age rather than sex or race. Alma nods toward generational divides multiple times only to underline their lack of importance before God. This may hint at the conflicts within Zarahemla's society; Alma's community may need a prophetic call to generational healing.

Alma 5:53–55

Just ahead in verses 59–60, Alma will return to his language of the good shepherd and describe the responsibility of a shepherd to drive out and destroy wolves that sneak into the flock. But in verses 53–55, Alma first names and describes the wolves: being "puffed up" in pride, "wearing of costly apparel" and idolizing riches (v. 53), "supposing that ye are better one than another" (v. 54), and "turning your backs upon the poor" (v. 55). Alma repeatedly uses the word "persist" to describe these actions, linking these problems to a language of work or effort he has previously employed. He calls out this behavior as a kind of commitment to disenfranchisement and devaluation of others. This is how a flock turns on itself and lets in the wolves.

Alma 6

Chapter 6 serves as a bridge chapter, describing how Alma organized the church in Zarahemla and then toured through the Nephite lands, teaching and preaching. He speaks in each place he goes to in an individualized way: highlighting and elevating the good works of Gideon, while calling the people of Ammonihah to repentance. The following chapters speak to the different ways churches may function in following the gospel. This can act as a guide for readers: do we look more like Gideon or Ammonihah? In what ways? The Book of Mosiah compares different kinds of societies, governments, and tax structures. These chapters of Alma zero in specifically on churches, examining how a church can go astray, how a good church looks, and how a community moves with the gospel.

Alma 6:1–3

When the sermon ends, what happens next? After a great orator inspires a mass conversion, the actions that immediately follow tell readers what is most important. Alma ordains priests and elders, although the church was already established in Zarahemla. So although there is already some form of organization, they needed some kind of new leadership or reconstruction.

The division between those who are officially part of the church and those who are not gets muddled here. There are those who do not belong to the church and are ready to repent, and there is a group of people who are members of the church but are *not* willing to repent. The pride that has become such a problem for this society continues to cause issues within the church. Church membership does not signal a perfect predictor of who will embrace humility and accept the gospel and who will not.

Alma 6:5

This verse reveals a gospel of deep inclusivity. Notice the repetition: "The word of God was liberal unto *all*, that *none* were deprived of the privilege of assembling themselves together to hear the word of God" (emphasis added). It does not matter who you are or where you came from; one of the very first tenets of this newly restored church is that God's word is liberal to all, and no one is deprived of the gospel. Has our own church always followed this precept? Consider the implications for a church that, at some points in its history, has not been liberal to all. A church that does not preach to or give full membership to certain people gets mired in the pride that proved so destructive to Alma's Zarahemla. Not recognizing God's word as liberal to all is deeply wicked. For a people who were drowning in pride at the moment of cleansing and reestablishment of the church, the crucial first step was to organize leadership that recognized this essential principle: the gospel is for everyone.

Alma 6:6

A community fasting and praying for others is always a beautiful scene. Yet, this is a church that very recently needed to do some serious self-reflection and repentance work to deal with the dysfunction of hierarchy and pride. That being the case, immediately moving into praying for *others* to know God may be premature. These verses make clear that we should be careful about assumptions of who knows God and who does not.

Alma 6:7

It is not a coincidence that the Book of Mormon gives names of places so intentionally. Sometimes, as it does here, the text even reminds readers of the significance of those names, giving a short history of the person and the role they played in Nephite history. Gideon was a beloved figure, as shown by the way he is memorialized in landmark names. Verse 7 takes time to name Gideon and asks readers to recall him and offer a small moment of respect for him. This is why the history of names matters in public spaces. If roads, public squares, geographical landmarks, and cities are named after people, it draws collective remembrance to their works and how they lived their lives. In scripture, names matter. The text does not just name the city of Gideon, it reinforces the importance of the name: "the city of Gideon . . . Being called after the man who was slain by the hand of Nehor with the sword." Scholar Grant Hardy notes that while the text does not make the connection explicit, the repetitive use of the name Gideon may be to remind readers that this same valley was the site of the Amlicite war just four years earlier. The death toll of those events, including the deaths of "many women and children"[29] would have been on the minds of everyone present at this sermon, including Alma.[30]

---

29. Alma 3:2
30. Grant Hardy. *Understanding the Book of Mormon.* New York: Oxford University Press, 2010.

The naming of a space yields a harvest in the public imagination. The names we use call attention to our collective values. They imbue land with meaning, giving a geographical space the power to hold our history. Our choices of names indicate what kind of history we want our land to hold.

Alma 7:1–6

Reading Alma's sermon to the people of Gideon is delightful because of how much they are doing right. As Alma says, these people are "blameless" before God (v. 3) because of their humility. This gives Alma great joy, which is wonderful to notice because his ministry holds so few moments of pure happiness. His joy must have been compounded by the peace in an area which had recently experienced dissension, fracturing, and tragedy. So much of his work is fraught with trying to get the Nephites to act right, to convince the church to recognize their own wickedness, to call his own people to repentance. In this moment, Alma gets to experience joy undiluted by "afflictions and sorrow" (v. 5). That kind of grace deserves recognition. Although Alma did experience joy in the midst of struggle in Zarahemla, his time in Gideon is special. It is important that Alma spent time in places that brought him pure joy, not just places that were a struggle. Anyone doing God's work needs to seek out restful places and rejuvenating times.

Alma 7:6

As Alma names the things that Gideon's people do right, he implicitly names the sins of the church in Zarahemla through comparison. They struggled with pride. They placed their hearts upon riches and other "things of the world." They worshiped idols. The church in Zarahemla may have borne the thin veneer of Christianity, but they became mired in pride and idolatry. Just as individuals need daily self-reflection on how they may not live up to their covenants, churches need to interrogate themselves regularly to ask who they actually worship. Is it the true and living God? Or has the membership of the church gradually shifted their hearts toward vanity?

Alma 7:7–16

Alma's testimony affirming the value of community sounds completely different from his testimony to call folk to repentance. This testimony evokes a joyful, shared hope in the future of this people. In these verses, Alma offers some of the most powerful descriptors of the Atonement in all of the Book of Mormon. They portray a God who felt it necessary to step into the flesh so that God could know and help people personally. Alma knows a God who chooses to suffer pain and horror in order to be filled with mercy and have the capacity to succor people in the best way possible. These verses radiate the love of God, and the people of Gideon receive them because of the way they have lived with humility.

Verses 11–12 are notably important in this exploration of Christ's humanity. The need for Jesus' earthly life is often explained as giving him the universal experience of mortality. Verse 11 underlines this, saying that "he shall go forth, suffering pains and afflictions and temptations of *every* kind" (emphasis added). Yet, we sometimes forget that outside of the moment of the Atonement, Jesus lived in a particular body, with particular experiences of that body, and there is a different kind of a power in that particularity. As Black theologian M. Shawn Copeland has written, "Jesus of Nazareth was born and died in subjugation to the Roman Empire. His flesh, his body, was and remains marked by race, gender, culture, and religion: he was a practicing Jew in a territory controlled by Roman political, military, and economic forces. Jesus was and remains marked by sex, gender, and sexuality: he was male, and although we cannot speak about his sexual orientation, tradition assumes his heterosexuality. In his flesh, in his body, Jesus knew refugee status, occupation and colonization, social regulation and control."[31] Understanding the ways Jesus' body was marked by his individual life circumstances gives a greater richness to comprehending how "his bowels may be filled with mercy, according to the flesh, that he may know according to the flesh how to succor his people according to their infirmities" (v. 12).

Alma 7:18–26

Here, a prophet affirms over and over again a church and a people who are getting it right. Although Alma never says so, it cannot have been easy for the church of Gideon to live into the gospel so well. Keeping covenants and building beloved community require daily work, which makes Alma's choice to offer them time and love even more beautiful. He seals his testimony with a list of divine traits: humility, gentleness, patience, submissiveness, temperance, and diligence in keeping the commandments. This list of qualities make a person easy to move with God. It is amazing to think of a society so extraordinary that they have earned this sermon.

Alma 7:27

Unfortunately, the final words of this lovely sermon veers in a problematic direction. Women and children—again—are not possessions and should not be named with houses, lands, flocks, and herds. This language should not be put into the prophetic voice. Other speakers, such as Jacob and Benjamin, do a better job of affirming the worth of individuals, including women. Alma is speaking within the cultural constraints of his time, which is understandable, but unfortunate. The women are a part of the church, part of the city. The work of men alone has not made Gideon into a reflection of Zion. By rhetorically placing women as passive objects, not the subjects of the sermon, Alma ignores their crucial contributions.

---

31. M. Shawn Copeland. *Enfleshing Freedom: Body, Race, and Being.* Minneapolis, Minnesota: Fortress Press, 2010. 58.

Alma 8:1–5

The text takes space to note that Alma returns to Zarahemla to rest at his home. Prophets need a break. They need a home. God's work is not easy, and this is not the last time Alma returns home for an unspecified length of rest. Everyone needs a Sabbath, and this verse should give readers the license to rest. Do the work, and then come home and rest from your labors.

These verses comprise Alma's time in the land of Melek. While we do not know much about this period, notice that Melek is on "the borders of the wilderness" (v. 3). This geographical description of the land gives readers a hint of his mission there, who Alma taught and how it went. The people came from the margins, from the edges of the land; the text even emphasizes that those who came to Alma came from "the wilderness side" (v. 5). Once again, the Book of Mormon offers a sermon in itself by the use of land names.

Alma 8:7

A small hint in this verse shows how the Nephites think about land, ownership, and the naming of land. Why did the author take the time to note that the cities and villages were named "after the name of him who first possessed them"? The text consistently refers to the occupation of land as possession, not as a stewardship or cultivation. In Nephite culture, the first person in a land has the naming rights. To possess land and then be named for that possession indicates an interesting cultural practice. In a book in which the names of places often hold significance, consider noting who holds the power of naming.

Alma 8:10–13

Alma's description of work in Ammonihah makes clear the struggle: he labors and he wrestles on behalf of people unwilling to repent and change. No matter how much effort Alma puts in, the people harden their hearts and reject him. The language of verse 11 is particularly cruel; they tell Alma that they know who he is, but they do not believe in his church, and he no longer has any power over them. If Alma was still the chief judge, he might wield some influence, but as he has given up that position, they will not listen to him. The people cast him out and spit on him, actions they likely would not have dared to do if he still held political power. This reveals the people of Ammonihah's state of heart. They frankly admit that they would treat Alma differently if he held traditional power. Because he left the judgment seat, they feel free to enact violence on his body and throw him out of the city. How people treat those with less power than themselves reveals much more about them than does their treatment of people with privilege and status. When the text states in verse 9 that "Satan had gotten great hold upon the hearts of the people of the city of Ammonihah," this may be what it means: the people are focused on power and are willing to brutally dismiss those without it.

Alma 8:14–18

In reaction to this wicked treatment, Alma carries on with his work, leaving behind Ammonihah and moving toward the city of Aaron. Although he is "weighed down with sorrow, wading through much tribulation and anguish of soul" (v. 14), he continues his mission. This is the deep grief of the prophetic, not just for Alma, but for all who do God's work. Part of witnessing the cruelty of humans and experiencing the harm they willingly enact on others is feeling the weight of sorrow and anguish. Heaviness comes with this role.

And yet, when the angel appears, the heavenly messenger calls Alma blessed and tells him to rejoice. In response to being weighed down with grief, the angel says to "lift up thy head" (v. 15). This is the comfort and affirmation God offers. It is also the second instance in the text of Alma interacting with this angel. In the first, the angel knocked Alma to the ground and called him to repentance.[32] In this

---

32. Mosiah 27:11–17

second experience, the angel consoles and heals Alma's sorrow. These two encounters exemplify how the gospel afflicts the comfortable and comforts the afflicted. Both are the errand of angels.

A call to return to Ammonihah comes with the angel's encouragement. The text repeats the call: "preach again unto the people of the city; yea, preach unto them" (v. 16). One of the hardest parts of following God's call is that when you are done preaching, you must preach again. This shows a Jonah moment for Alma, as he is asked to go back to cruel people and give them another chance to turn toward God. Returning to speak truth repeatedly to people who have rejected you is not easy. For those who have experienced mistreatment and trauma, returning to those places to speak up again and again may require a kind of divine urging. Yet, this may be exactly what God asks of us, to go back and preach again.

The angel gives Alma some caution, telling him the people *study at this time that they may destroy the liberty of thy people*" (v. 17, emphasis added). The people of Ammonihah work—with effort, struggle, and an intentional plan—to destroy liberation. Satan's strong influence in this city has the inhabitants focused on power and those who hold power, but also on a desire to disempower others and curtail their liberty. Alma responds "speedily" (v. 18), returning to Ammonihah quickly, even though he suffered so much there. God cares about the destruction of freedom, and Alma immediately acts to prevent it.

Alma 8:19–22

Alma displays a very human moment of hunger, a moment of vulnerability that leads to an inspired encounter. He has just received directions from an angel, yet the angel did not perform a miracle to answer this need. Instead, Alma's need leads him to the person who will become his closest companion and support in his work. This exhibits the beauty of how God works to use our vulnerabilities to bring us into relationship. Social justice work makes us realize that we need one another. Despite appearances, God did not call Alma to

do this work alone. To find the miracle, Alma had to acknowledge that
he needed another person and ask for help to meet the most basic of
human needs: he is hungry. But Jesus taught that those basic human
needs are some of the most crucial moments in which we can offer
care to Christ.[33] When we donate food or drink, visit people in prison,
or offer hospitality to a stranger, we do not know what will grow out
of those relationships, but we do know that we are doing God's will.

Amulek offering Alma food displays a beautiful, simple description of the seemingly mundane. Amulek approaches someone doing
the work of the prophetic, meets him in a vulnerable space, and offers
him resources. Before they talk about theology or strategy, Amulek
cares for Alma's basic human needs. Alma eats until he is full. This is
not a moment to pass over. This foundational experience establishes
one of the important friendships of the Book of Mormon. It will be
a partnership that changes both of their lives. And in the moment of
its creation, the text mentions twice that Alma ate until he was full
before he mentions his role as the high priest. We cannot overstate
that the work of providing food and care is a spiritual work.

Alma 8:26–27

Consider these two stunning verses. Alma was fasting and hungry as
he left Ammonihah. Amulek fed and sheltered him. Alma then stayed
many days with Amulek, resting and building a relationship before he
began preaching again. Although the angel warned Alma of impending danger and Alma hurried back to Ammonihah,[34] Alma and Amulek
take this time together. Setting aside space to build companionship
in justice work is priceless. Before we can begin to do the work, it is
worth asking whether we need to mend old relationships or form
new ones. That does not pause or stop the work; it is part of the
work. We do not want to miss how relationships are a part of what

---

33. Matthew 25:37–40
34. Alma 8:16–18

God wants for us. Taking time to build or strengthen relationships is crucial to the health of individuals and the power of the message.

Alma 8:30–32

The text emphasizes the power and dynamism of this friendship with this foreshadowing of what will happen to Alma and Amulek in the coming years. As they are filled with the Holy Ghost together, their combined spiritual strength seems greater than the sum of its parts. They cannot be kept in dungeons, cannot be killed. In the following section, the text of the Book of Alma shares space with the words of Amulek. They have become a powerful partnership, and God forged this friendship from a simple request for hospitality.

Alma 9:2–6

These verses illustrate the possibility of asking bad questions. The people focus on why God would send one man to call them to repentance. In some ways, it seems reasonable. But the question shows a fundamental misunderstanding of the miracles God can do, including the multiplicity of ways that God communicates: speaking through a donkey, a Samaritan, a younger brother, a shepherd, or a farmboy in rural New York. Because they want to hear God in a certain way, they do not see the ways that God "could do such marvelous works" (v. 5) as speaking through a single person without any fanfare. Their lack of imagination and openness limits how they can hear God. The hard-heartedness and stiff-neckedness the text references means that they do not understand that God does marvelous things by choosing the unexpected spokesperson. Their bad questions reveal that they do not know that God shows up in unlikely places and in seemingly small and powerless people. They are basically asking, "Why would God work through something so small and insignificant?" It is another version of the question, "Can any good thing come from Nazareth?"[35] God comes in ways we do not expect. To avoid missing the message, we need to let go of our expectations of how we want God to tell us truth. It may not be with a host of angels with trumpets. It may be a brown child in Syria or a queer woman in Chicago. Can we avoid asking questions like, "Who is God that God shows up like that?"

Alma 9:8–13

In response to the bad question of why God would speak through one person, Alma invokes their common ancestor, Lehi, whose individual actions changed the history of nations. Alma brilliantly responds to the crowd's criticism while also counseling them to turn their hearts to their forefather. "Remember" may be the most important word in the Book of Mormon, and much of that remembering relates to ancestral legacy. Alma seeks to tie people to their roots, reminding them of the way they descend from the bravery and faith of Lehi.

Verse 13 includes another reference to prosperity, and it is worth reviewing the logic behind Alma's use of the term. First, Alma says that following God's commandments leads to prospering in the land. Then, he says the inverse: "Inasmuch as ye will not keep my commandments ye shall be cut off from the presence of the Lord." The word "prosper" here can be examined. Imagine these two statements as a mirror image: if you follow the commandments, you prosper; if you do not follow the commandments, you are cut off from the presence of God. In this rhetorical structure, prospering is equated with being in the presence of God. Unlike some writers in the Book of Mormon, Alma does not invoke wealth or material success or battle victories. Alma's definition of prospering is to be with God. His statement is one of logical consequences, not promises of riches.

---

35. John 1:46

Alma 9:14–19

Alma claims that the Lamanites "have been cut off from the presence of the Lord." This type of claim deserves strict scrutiny: What does he mean? How does he know? Does it appear to be true?

Alma, according to the record, has little to no experience or relationship with the Lamanites. As far as the text tells us, his only knowledge of them comes second-hand from people who suffered at their hands. It is almost unimaginable that he would not harbor a negative bias against them. And while it is possible God has cut off the Lamanites at this time, Alma's claims contradict the work happening with the sons of Mosiah and raise a few warning flags.

First, we should be suspicious about claims made by anyone who has not been in a place, who has not spent time with those folk, or who lacks any relationships with a given community. Alma does not know how God has been moving in the land of the Lamanites. If he did, he would know how the sons of Mosiah are finding many people primed to receive the gospel, ready and willing to repent and be baptized. The stories of king Lamoni, Abish, and thousands of Lamanites who convert, indicate God has been working in this land, softening hearts and preparing people to listen to the Nephite missionaries. The way Alma speaks about an entire nation of people he has never met, and with whom he lacks any kind of relationship, is not just or healthy.

Second, this invocation of the Lamanites does not bring people to God. Pointing out the sins of others does not encourage people to repent. It only amplifies the hatred and prejudices that already exist between the people. Alma has a tendency to step into this kind of comparative theology that is rooted in distinguishing between two groups of people. He also uses the Lamanites as a kind of threat for the Nephites, a tool God would use to punish the Nephites for not being righteous enough. When Alma claims that "the Lamanites shall be sent upon you; and if ye repent not they shall come in a time when you know not, and ye shall be visited with utter destruction" (v. 18), he uses an entire nation as a way for God to execute punishment. It erases the agency of the Lamanites, giving the responsibility of their violence to God. When a prophet uses other people as a method of instilling fear, it adds to the distrust and suspicion that triggers anger and an increased likelihood of violence. It turns the Lamanites into a symbol of everything evil and scary while stamping God's approval on that terror.

The Book of Mormon prophets are part of a society that sees the Lamanites as separate, strange, and usually subordinate to the Nephites in some way. The antagonism between the nations has an enormous influence on Nephite culture, including their religious language and ideas. But this kind of theology does not move people toward inclusivity or love for God's children. This rhetorical device—a cultural inheritance—seems unlikely to have the outcome Alma desires. Listeners are not inspired to soften their hearts. Comparative theology is generally not useful in inspiring repentance in a people, but it will appear again and again throughout this book of scripture.

A final point to note in these verses: Alma states that God will extend mercy to the Lamanites because of the failings of their ancestors. Alma recognizes that not all people start out in the same place; the legacy of our ancestors affects the choices we can make today. Ancestral trauma gets passed down, sometimes in ways that inhibit the growth or health of later generations. God does not judge all people with identical metrics: "to whom much is given, much is required."[36] Giving the Lamanites grace for what they have inherited is the important truth nestled in this problematic comparative theology.

Alma 9:20–24.

Verse 20 continues Alma's use of comparative theology, this time telling the people of Ammonihah that they are elevated above others. Does telling people that God favors them "above every other nation, kindred, tongue or people" encourage them to repent? Does

---

36. Luke 12:48

it encourage them to be humble and love their neighbors? This does not lead people to a God who is no respecter of persons.[37] Alma's evidence of the Nephites' blessed state comes from the spiritual gifts they have received (v. 21). The list, though impressive, offers no reason to believe that other nations and people have not also received these gifts from God. The Nephites are not the only people on the earth who have seen angels or been visited by God. Alma should not claim a God who particularly belongs to them. It is one thing to say, "You have been visited by angels. There is something required of a person who has had that kind of extraordinary experience." It is another to say, "You have seen angels, which makes you favored *above* all others." The list of gifts is beautiful, but the exclusionary framing is not. In fact, not being able to see God's favor outside of a structure that elevates your people above others weaponizes God's blessings. It takes powerful spiritual gifts and says, "This is how we are better than those other people." That can do terrible harm.

If Alma removed the references to the Lamanites and the framing of being favored above all others, his message would be just as effective, if not more so. He could remind the people of Ammonihah how God has shown up in their lives and the lives of their ancestors. He could emphasize the need to recognize their blessings and show gratitude and humility without drawing a contract between them and another nation. Elevating the Nephites above the Lamanites in these verses adds nothing to Alma's sermon and instead detracts from the vital message of recognizing God's grace in their lives.

Alma 9:26

This verse names what God is full of: grace, equity, truth, patience, mercy, and long-suffering. God is quick to hear. Later, in verse 29, we learn these are the words of an angel. The description gives a glimpse into God's nature. These are the qualities that all of God's children should seek.

---

37. Acts 10:34

Alma 10:1–4

Just as many writers in the Book of Mormon introduce themselves and give their social location, Amulek shares his genealogy and describes his social standing within his community. This opening gives readers a sense of the importance of lineage in this society: Amulek uses his ancestral history to establish his authority. He also references his reputation, wealth, and social connections to set himself up as a respectable person. These are all markers people use in cultures around the world to encourage people to listen to them. Ancestral history, particularly in Mormonism, holds a certain rhetorical sway: a claim to ancestors who were pioneers or General Authorities may lend social capital to a speaker. Consider what that means for people who have been deracinated or lost knowledge of their ancestors through slavery, colonialism, or other violence. Family legacy brings significant meaning to many people in the Book of Mormon and in the LDS Church today. Those who know about their ancestors should consider the significant loss experienced by people without that privilege.

Alma 10:5–6

Amulek bears all the traditional markers of success, but he has not known the Lord. This is a living argument against the idea of prosperity gospel. Amulek—a well-respected man, with an important lineage, wealth, and many social connections—had all of this, but he did not know God. In fact, his conversion to the gospel leads Amulek to lose all that he has.[38] Amulek loses his prosperity because he comes to know God.

As Amulek lists his privileges—wealth, status, and lineage—he connects it to how he chose to not hear God, even though God was speaking. His wonderful summary of the known and the unknown describes both what God showed him and what he refused to see. He

---

38. Alma 15:16

corrects himself as he speaks, acknowledging that God moved in his life, but Amulek hardened his heart. "I knew concerning these things, yet I would not know" (v. 6) is what Black theologian James Cone described as a "willful blindness."[39] It is knowing but deliberately looking away in an effort to remain ignorant, which Cone noted as one of the hallmarks of white supremacy. What Amulek describes as a hard heart is a practice of not letting oneself know the things that are going to convict you and move you to change. This stance insists that your life is fine because you have comfort and social respect. It signals a turning away from a God who calls you to change and sacrifice your privilege.

Alma 10:7-11

There is a saying in Black church: "May God go before me." It speaks to the wish for God to soften the hearts of the people a person is going to meet or interact with that day. In Alma and Amulek's case, an angel came to prepare the way for companionship and allyship. That way of God "going before" is part of Amulek's testimony.

Scholar Kylie Nielson Turley has noted a kind of tragic symmetry in the blessing Amulek describes in verse 11 and the losses Amulek experiences later in the story.[40] According to Amulek, Alma blessed Amulek's house, his wife, children, and kin. Shortly after, Amulek leaves his home, "being rejected by those who were once his friends and also by his father and his kindred."[41] The story never explains what happened to Amulek's wife and children, but Turley argues convincingly that they may have died in the fire described in chapter 14. If that is the case, then Amulek ultimately lost everything Alma had blessed. This anti-prosperity gospel story offers a distressing

---

39. James H. Cone. *The Cross and the Lynching Tree*. Maryknoll, New York: Orbis Books, 2013.
40. Kylie Turley. "Alma's Hell: Repentance, Consequence, and the Lake of Fire and Brimstone." *Journal of Book of Mormon Studies*, Vol. 28 (2019), 1–45.
41. Alma 15:16

account of someone whose life appears cursed because he followed God.

Alma 10:12–17

The people of Ammonihah claimed to reject Alma because he acted as a single witness,[42] and yet they promptly attack the second witness Amulek offers. People wrapped up in their own malice, hatred, and pride may offer conditions in which they will change their hearts, but giving them what they desire will not necessarily move them. As Amulek described in verse 6, they will refuse to see and hear the evidence right in front of them.

Instead, the people of Ammonihah choose to use systems and laws designed to punish the righteous. We should not assume that social structures, even those built on law, are created or used for the purpose of justice. Just as the lawyers here use willful entrapment to harm Alma and Amulek, some laws and systems are not built for righteous purposes. The mere existence of a law does not mean it is moral. As Dr. Martin Luther King quoted from St. Thomas Aquinas, "an unjust law is no law at all."[43] If a law is unjust, if lawyers deliberately use it to harm truth-tellers, that law does not deserve our compliance or respect. Here, the people wield the laws as a weapon, seeking to have Ammon and Amulek "judged according to the law, and that they might be slain or cast into prison" (v. 13). Justice is not the goal in this community; killing or imprisoning people is the goal. This prompts the question: if people can find ways to imprison and murder people who speak uncomfortable truths, what kind of system does that society have? In this city, the laws seem to exist to uphold the status quo rather than to bring about justice.

---

42. Alma 9:6

43. Martin Luther King, Jr. *Letter from Birmingham Jail*. Penguin Modern. London, England: Penguin Classics, 1963.

Alma 10:17–21

The lawyers—or politicians, as they have been selected "by the people to administer the law"[44]—lay the foundation to entrap "the holy
ones of God" (v.17). But it is the people who build on that foundation
and spring the trap. While the lawmakers have built the structures
of harm that lead to death and imprisonment, they rely on people to
enact those laws on the backs of the vulnerable. It is a manipulation,
a way of twisting and turning something into evil that does not have
to be that way. Those who work for social justice need to ask what
the foundations of our own societies were designed to do. Do our
governing documents and structures work to protect people or to
disenfranchise them? In what way have our own foundations been
perverted, and how do we begin to set things right?

Notice that after this indictment of people and systems who
work to imprison and kill people, Alma warns of a God who will come
"with equity and justice" in God's hands. When a society embraces
a perverted foundation and chooses iniquity through laws that
oppress, harm, kill, and imprison the vulnerable and righteous, God
visits not with grace and mercy, but with justice and equity. This is a
serious warning.

Alma 10:22–23

The "prayers of the righteous" can prompt God to spare a society.
When Rabbi Abraham Joshua Heschel returned from marching with
Dr. Martin Luther King, someone asked him, "Did you find much time
to pray, when you were in Selma?" He responded, "I prayed with my
feet." Walking, protesting, and organizing are each a kind of prayer
against unjust laws. Prayers move in action when facing a society
that manipulates systems against the vulnerable. The prayers of the
righteous may save an entire nation. But if people cast out the righteous, God's hand will not be stayed. Notice that the promise here is

---

44. Alma 10:14

not that the righteous will always have divine protection. They may experience persecution, and suffer or even die for their work. While we may want God to act in ways that will save and rescue the faithful, instead God simply promises justice in the end.

Alma 11:1–20

At a first glance, these verses about the monetary system seem extraneous. Yet, they reveal a society extremely focused on money and a system built to protect wealth and those with wealth. Verse 2 explains that people who could not pay their debts were stripped or cast out from the community. In a world in which the community offers safety and the wilderness likely leads to solitary death, this stands out as an extreme sentence. Who benefits from this financial system? What does that say about Ammonihah? Compare this to the financial system king Limhi created to care for the widows and children,[45] or that Alma the Elder instituted to protect the poor and sick.[46] How a society judges the worth of money, and who monetary systems protect, says a great deal about what and who that society values.

The city's legal system incentivizes conflict through paying judges for each case. This exemplifies how to create laws and systems that lead to greater unrest and discord. If the people exist in a contentious state, the judges make more money. Anytime someone profits off of conflict, they have cause to create a demand for it. Be wary of any political system that receives gain through conflict.

Distinguishing between those who stir up conflict for their own gain and those who do it to cause "good trouble"[47] can prove difficult. Every social organization and movement leader should carefully examine their finances to determine whether they use conflict to further their mission or for self-promotion. The line between them can

---

45. Mosiah 21:17

46. Mosiah 27:4–5

47. United States civil rights leader John Lewis famously encouraged making "good trouble" to push for a more just society.

be thin, so members of the movement have a responsibility to insist on accountability. Trafficking in outrage is easy and highly profitable. Hypocrisy and corruption can be avoided through self-awareness and thoughtfulness on this issue.

These twenty verses give a detailed backstory of the political and financial structures of this city that will influence what happens to Alma and Amulek. While readers may find this section tiresome or unimportant, it serves as important context. Feminism informs us that the personal is political. It is not possible to separate how governmental and monetary policy works from the hearts and well-being of the people. This chapter acknowledges that fact beautifully, explaining how the judicial and financial systems work so that readers understand better why events occur as they do and how they reflect on the people. Structures deeply impact people. In this case, the way the government encourages conflict and oppresses the poor reflects a spiritual illness that will cause terrible suffering for Alma and Amulek.

This illustrates why claiming a lack of interest or investment in politics or social systems is a kind of privilege. Disinterest or disinvestment indicates an ability to insulate oneself from those issues because they do not have personal impact. Knowing who has power and how they get it, how money moves through an economy, and how peace and justice are enforced, will better prepare people to work for social change.

Alma 11:21–25

Sometimes people ask bad questions with ill intent. Rather than coming from a place of desiring greater understanding; bad questions simply exist to do harm. It is okay to follow Amulek's example and refuse to answer those questions directly. Amulek simply responds that he will answer as prompted by the Spirit and out of his own truth experience. This is a good answer.

Zeezrom's next question asks whether Amulek will deny the existence of God for the offer of money. While asked in bad faith, this is an evocative question for each of us. Can money, or the pursuit of money, cause us to deny certain things we know about God? In what ways can we each say we profit from not acknowledging parts of God that would cost us in convenience, money, or comfort? Amulek's accusation of Zeezrom's idolatry of money prompts the question for each of us: what do we love more than God?

Alma 11:26–46

The rest of this chapter gives the dialogue between Amulek and Zeezrom, a powerful conversation about important principles of the gospel. Zeezrom is a special character in the Book of Mormon, a person deeply committed to opposing the gospel but who comes to an awakening of his guilt and turns his life around. His story makes this chapter an interesting balance of the general and the particular: an explanation of the social structures that undergird this story, and then an examination of this one person who is personally affected by those institutions but changes the direction of his life anyway. Ultimately, the systems in Ammonihah do not change, but Zeezrom changes. And those decisions by an individual human can sometimes have incredible impact.

Alma 12:1

What do we know about the relationship between Alma and Amulek at this stage? An ally would provide Alma with food and housing. An accomplice would take him around the city and introduce him to people. A co-conspirator is right beside him in the work and the repercussions of that work.[48] The story of Alma and Amulek exemplifies true friendship, but also a shared commitment to the work.

---

48. Bettina Love. *We Want to Do More Than Survive: Abolitionist Teaching and the Pursuit of Educational Freedom*. Boston, MA: Beacon Press, 2020.

Amulek is with Alma to the end, even if that means facing prison, losing his family, and giving up wealth and social power. Although they walk the road together, Amulek ultimately sacrifices so much more than Alma because of the privilege he gives up. This chapter closely examines two people—Amulek and Zeezrom—with complex, rich stories around conversion, the challenge of changing one's life to embrace truth, and taking huge risks in that process.

Alma 12:3

There are two types of lies: the lies we tell one another and those we tell God. Zeezrom lies not only to his community, but also to God. Zeezrom denies a truth inside of him. Sometimes people lie to God by refusing to acknowledge or act upon the truth God has given them. These are truths we know deeply, but which we deny because they would require changes and sacrifices we do not want to face. The light of God will call us to work we do not want to do and growth we may not want to experience. When we deny those internal truths, those moments that prick us to acknowledge wrongs and injustices in the world, in a way we are lying to God by turning our backs on the light of Christ.

Alma 12:6–8

Subjection, captivity, and enslavement are all goals of the devil. The adversary holds people in chains. Although the text implies a spiritual enslavement, part of reading for the least of these means considering what literal enslavement is like here.[49] Staying on a theoretical or intellectual level indicates some privilege. Living in oppression is a physical experience, one that cannot be contained in the mind. The physical and the spiritual are inextricably tied together, prompting questions. Who are the ones in this society living in chains? Where

---

49. Miguel A. De La Torre. *Reading the Bible from the Margins.* Maryknoll, New York: Orbis Books, 2002.

are there people held in cages? If holding people captive is evil in the spiritual realm, then it is also evil in the physical world. Verse 6 clearly tells us who inspires the work of enslaving people.

Although Zeezrom enters into dialogue as a kind of intellectual interrogation, Alma and Amulek engage more expansively. While we usually think of "thoughts and intents" as a realm of the mind, Alma and Amulek place that work in the realm of the heart. This moves the conversation out of the realm of theory and into a place of lived reality. They focus on the ways in which Zeezrom has lied to God and the truths he feels inside of himself. And that focus is what shifts Zeezrom to begin to ask real, authentic questions, designed not to trick or deceive them, but to find truth.

Again, not every question or conversation is intended for better understanding. Sometimes people like Zeezrom initially engage in order to entrap, ensnare, and deny lived truths. Alma and Amulek's response is not to answer Zeezrom's disingenuous questions, but instead to respond, *"Look inside yourself for the light and knowledge God has given you."* Their discernment allows God to reveal Zeezrom's heart and prompts Zeezrom to change course.

Alma 12:9–15

This beautiful theology, woven through with language about hearts and humility, shows how people come to know about God. We receive the knowledge we are prepared to receive. We prepare ourselves through softening our hearts and embracing humility and a willingness to learn. The more confident we are in our rightness, the less likely we are to know the mysteries of God. And yet, Alma is also saying here that God is knowable to those open to listening. A theology that writes off questions about the world and about God as unfathomable to the human brain is not complete. Although it may be that some parts of the universe are unfathomable in mortality, a healthy theology welcomes the struggle of asking questions and exercising faith in the potential for answers.

Understanding God more deeply requires the willingness to open ourselves to the vastness of the answer. Sometimes the mysteries of God remain unknown because we do not truly want to confront the answers of a God who is more wild and untamed and bigger than we ever imagined. It can feel scary to let go of what we have always thought, when God breaks the confines of what we previously believed. Answers to questions about justice and love may ask more of us than we are prepared to do. They may force people to change in ways they do not want. Those moments can shake a testimony, as we pursue a God who leads us to lands that feel strange and unknown. But that is how Alma says we uncover the mysteries of God—with the questions which may not be answered in the pews.

For example: simply saying, "We do not know why there was a temple and priesthood restriction for Black people in the LDS Church" lets us off the hook far too easily. It allows people to continue the status quo because they evade the struggle of real answers. But we lie to God if we do not question and truly seek an answer when something inside prompts us to ask. Religions give good templates for asking God questions because nearly all of them started with good questions. Embracing that model of inquiry, having the humility to admit ignorance and seek for more, can lead us to moments like Zeezrom's conversion, when he "trembles"[50] with a new consciousness. We see God in new and beautiful ways as we honor the divine within ourselves. Curtailing that divinely-given curiosity, silencing questions, or refusing to seek for answers, oppresses spirits and advances ignorance. It "hardens our hearts against the word" (v. 13).

Alma describes a state in which the word of God is not found within us. When we harden our hearts against God and against one another, truth, justice, mercy, and grace cannot enter. That indicates a profound loss, a state of suffering. Alma writes, "For our words will condemn us" (v. 14) or, in the language of Dr. Maya Angelou, "Words are things. You must be careful, careful about calling people out of

---

50. Alma 12:1

their names, using racial pejoratives and sexual pejoratives and all of that ignorance. Don't do that. Someday we'll be able to measure the power of words. I think they are things. They get on the walls. They get in your wallpaper. They get in your rugs, in your upholstery, and your clothes, and finally into you."[51] The language we use to talk to and about one another gets into our hearts, into our cellular being. Our words can bring light and life or deal death. If we think about people as inferior, or find excuses and justifications for their suffering, Alma tells us that we will not even "dare to look up to our God" (v. 14) and we will try to hide rather than face who we have become.

Alma 12:21–26

The LDS creation story rests on the idea that Adam and Eve needed to transgress in order to ultimately fulfill God's plan. God's plan depends on them being tricked, and God sets up the conditions for that to happen. Could life have happened otherwise? Be wary of scripture that sets forth narrow, necessary pathways with God, because it may unintentionally bind and limit God. The LDS creation story is, in some ways, a liberating text for Eve and women, but it also contains problematic theology that limits God's potential plan. This story invites readers to wrestle with the text and doctrine.

Alma 12:32–35

The plan of redemption is a work of justice. Justice is integral to redemption's ability to save souls. We miss some of the goodness of God if a commitment to justice is not part of our testimony. The plan of redemption is also a work of mercy. Notice the words that orbit the word justice in scriptural text: grace and mercy frequently appear there. They walk together as divine characteristics of God.

---

51. Maya Angelou. Interview with Oprah Winfrey, Oprah's Master Class, podcast audio, March 7, 2019. https://oprahs-master-class-the-podcast.simplecast.com/episodes/dr-maya-angelou-FqtXFBcP

Justice and mercy are intertwined, not simply in tension. Here, verse 32 promises justice, verses 33–34 offer mercy, and verse 35 returns to justice. They are beautifully interwoven.

Alma 12:36–37

The concept of a divine rest is so important, particularly to oppressed communities. For those who have been overworked and undervalued all their mortal days, rest is godly. Offering that kind of rest acknowledges the struggles people face. God calls living with God a rest. Do we value rest with that kind of intention? Do we see it as a way of drawing closer to God? Allowing ourselves a practice of rest—a Sabbath for our bodies and spirits—can give us a taste of the goodness of an eternal life with God.

Alma 13:1–9

The ordination of priests provides organization and direction for the church, but its main function is to teach people about God. However, when we talk about men following after "the holy order of God" (v. 6), we should keep in mind that our human attempts will always fall short. If we are acting after the order of God, we need to accept that we are *way* after in the line. We are after the order of God in the way we may be following after legendary sprinter Usain Bolt in a race. We follow far after, even in our best attempts to follow. So any claim to following the order of God should come with a large injection of humility, one that recognizes the wide expanse between where we are and where God stands.

Alma describes what it means to be called to a certain work, and while he writes particularly about a religious order, readers can expand it to better understand their own callings in a variety of areas. Reading these verses with the understanding that we might feel called to anti-racism work, immigrant advocacy, or gender equality, opens the possibilities of what it means for God to call us. Following God's call to move in justice requires exercising an exceeding amount of faith. If you feel called in that way, recognize it as a holy calling. Say it out loud to yourself, recalling that anyone who professes God's will can be called a prophet.[52] Part of a life's work is to identify and follow the space to which we are each called. While these verses are deeply linked to institutional church, we can also understand them as referencing any holy order that brings people to God. To begin the process of that kind of ordination, we can ask ourselves the questions: *"How am I partnering with God in my life? When do I feel God's rest in what I'm doing? Which spaces draw me to share God's word?"* While we may crave the stamp of institutional validation, God ultimately reveals to us our holy work. The text describes a "holy calling" (v. 5) as eternal, existing "from the foundation of the world" and "being without beginning of days or end of years" (v. 7). An institutional church does not exist from eternity to eternity. A calling from God comes from before the premortal life and stays with our spirits forever. It is part of our core identity, a divine piece inside of us, bigger than we can understand in mortality. No organization or person can regulate or withhold it.

Alma 13:13–14

People committed to social justice often unintentionally enact harm by not making humility part of their work. Social justice demands learning and repentance. True repentance means willingness to give up that to which we are most attached. In ancient times, people of faith sacrificed the purest lamb and the best of their harvest. Today, we cannot simply give up the smallest part of our privilege, protecting our choicest investments. Repentance combined with humility in justice work may look like recognizing when we have hurt others, weaponized our call to injure someone, or hurt the cause of Zion and beloved community. Embracing justice without humility is a dangerous way to be in the world.

---

52. LDS Bible Dictionary entry for "prophet." See also Numbers 11:25–29

Alma 13:21–23

The glad tidings of great joy are that the Savior was born in the most unlikely of places to the most unlikely of women. God broke through into an unexpected, unwelcome place and brought salvation to the world. The God we believe in brings great joy because no matter how bad the world may be, new life and hope breaks forth. Although Alma claims that this makes the people "highly favored" (v. 23), it is in the context of a universal gospel that is "declared unto us in *all* parts of our vineyard (v. 23, emphasis added) and "unto *all* nations" (v. 22, emphasis added). How can any people be highly favored when the joy of the gospel spreads to everyone on the face of the earth? The context indicates that "highly favored" may simply mean beloved and not intended as a comparison with any other group of people.

Alma 13:25

This assertion that God will come, even if the author does not live to see it, sounds like the preaching in Black American churches. Preparing to rejoice at a distant time—having the faith to rejoice—resonates with the kind of hope Dr. Martin Luther King described when he told his people, "I've been to the mountaintop . . . I've seen the Promised Land. I may not get there with you. But I want you to know tonight that we, as a people, will get to the Promised Land."[53] Alma's call to rejoice, whenever the time comes, is built on a similar platform of faith and patient resolve.

Alma 14:1

This chapter examines the many responses people have to truth-telling and what can happen to people who speak hard truths. Do truths convict us? Do they infuriate us or make us defensive? Do they make us want to change? Alma and Amulek pay a heavy price for speaking

---

53. Martin Luther King, Jr. Speech given in Memphis, TN, April 3, 1968. https://kinginstitute.stanford.edu/encyclopedia/ive-been-mountaintop

truths to an unjust, unrighteous people. Their experience evidences what Dr. J. Kameron Carter calls "a fugitive gospel."[54] Just as Lehi went hungry in the wilderness and Abinadi was burned alive, Alma and Amulek suffer the cost of confronting systems, institutions, and a wicked population's failings. Compare this chapter to Mosiah 5, in which king Benjamin's people react to his calls for repentance. In that case, the community willingly confronts their need to be better, serve one another, and care for the poor. In this way, Benjamin experiences a certain amount of privilege: the benefit of speaking to an audience that accepts your authority and reacts with generosity of spirit. Alma and Amulek, lacking that privilege, suffer terrible violence in response to their calls for justice.

Alma 14:2–5

The people of Ammonihah, unsatisfied with merely stopping Alma and Amulek from speaking or with expelling them from the city, want to "destroy" (v. 2) them, a term more violent even than killing them. The word destroy implies wiping away any record of a person, eliminating their bodies. Intense rage underlies this response, an anger caused by the way Alma spoke to Zeezrom and their perception that Amulek lied about and reviled their law. The crowd seeks to "put them away privily" (v. 3), a phrase evoking Joseph's desire to privately separate from Mary when she reveals her pregnancy.[55] This case seems more violent, as if the mob wanted to hurt them outside of the eye of the justice system. These people are hungry for destruction.

However, instead of private violence, the people tie up Alma and Amulek and bring them before the chief judge. Witnesses claim that the men disparaged the laws, the judges, and the people. The accusation? *Alma and Amulek said negative things about us and our justice system. Alma and Amulek broke the law by speaking about injustice and*

---

54. J. Kameron Carter. *Dietrich Bonhoeffer course*, Lecture at Duke Divinity School, Spring 2015.
55. Matthew 1:19.

unrighteousness. The laws of Ammonihah intend to keep people silent, and Alma and Amulek defied those laws. Dr. Martin Luther King said "an unjust law is no law at all."[56] This story indicates that, sometimes, laws and judges are wrong. Alma and Amulek had to violate the law in order to follow God's commandments.

Mormons believe in "being subject to kings, presidents, rulers, and magistrates, in obeying, honoring, and sustaining the law,"[57] but our own sacred text offers a more nuanced perspective. Sometimes governments and laws of the land are immoral and unjust. Sometimes the oppressed experience brutality by enforcers of the law who wield their power. Alma and Amulek, as well as many others in the Book of Mormon and LDS Church history, were persecuted, jailed, and tortured under the law. Insisting on obeying the law without exception ignores our own history and scripture, disregarding the ways in which laws and judges have enacted violence on our people. Telling stories similar to Alma and Amulek reminds us of ways governments and people in power can use laws to persecute the marginalized and those fighting for liberation.

Alma 14:6–7

Some forms of guilt immobilize people, keeping them paralyzed with shame and unable to progress or undo the harm they have enacted. The guilt Zeezrom experiences is more productive: it propels him forward and serves as a catalyst to spur him to change the situation. Knowing that he has done something terribly wrong, he immediately confesses the role he played in what is happening. Author Brené Brown describes this as the difference between guilt and shame: shame is a focus on the self—"I am bad"—while guilt is a focus on behavior—"I've done something bad and I need to do bet-

---

56. Martin Luther King, Jr. *Letter from Birmingham Jail.*
57. Article of Faith 12. Church of Jesus Christ of Latter-day Saints.

ter."⁵⁸ Shame is a form of relinquishing your power to change yourself while guilt pushes people toward repentance and trying again. Vitally, shame does not help heal people or fix problems. Zeezrom's choice to take action reflects not only his understanding of his complicity, but also a willingness to make himself more vulnerable in confessing his mistakes.

In response, the mob attacks him and the other men who believe Alma and Amulek. The mob's violent response to those who say, *"We believe the truth-tellers"* reveals the power of witnesses. Although Zeezrom and the other believers are not able to stop the horrific fire which follows, the crowd's immediate and devastating reaction of brutality and expulsion underlines the ways in which allies have the potential to be powerful forces for good.

Alma 14:8–13

These six verses depict some of the most harrowing of the Book of Mormon. Women and children suffer horrifying deaths while Alma and Amulek stand by watching helplessly. This exemplifies what theologian Phyllis Trible describes as a "text of terror": a scriptural story in which women are the victims of violence for a narrative or instructional purpose.⁵⁹ The violence that occurs is an unintended consequence of their choice to preach and call the people to repentance, and yet they do nothing. Alma's explanation for inaction—that God allows the most vulnerable of a society to die in order to exercise justice on their tormentors—is a theological failure. Readers are left with a story of unimaginable pain, overly simple answers, and the question of what to glean from this difficult text.

Amulek raises questions shared by many people who fight for liberation for the oppressed: *Can we help these vulnerable people? How could we possibly witness destruction and suffering and do nothing? Could*

---

58. Brené Brown. "Listening to Shame." TED Talk given March 2012. https://www.ted.com/talks/brene_brown_listening_to_shame
59. Phyllis Trible. *Texts of Terror*. Philadelphia, PA: Fortress Press, 1984.

the strength of God give us the power to change this terrible situation? In response, Alma says that the Spirit constrains him from interfering. This implies that they *could* change the situation but that God stops them. This answer seems so heartless, a refusal to seek a way that God might mete out justice and intervene. Alma's response does not stand up to the scrutiny of the people's pain in front of him. His explanation—that the victims will be welcomed by God "in glory" and that God allows it in order to exercise judgment on the perpetrators—is far from sufficient. As Rabbi Irving Greenberg has written about the Holocaust, but which may also apply here, "No statement, theological or otherwise, should be made that would not be credible in the presence of burning children."[60] We should not create theology that cannot withstand the most horrific events in human history. Along with Alma and Amulek, we are left with the difficult question of why a loving and omniscient God permits evil acts to occur, particularly against innocent people.

Alma believes that he could have done something to stop the agonizing inferno before him. In some ways, believing he was helpless would have been easier because then at least he bears less responsibility. As it is, his mission to Ammonihah triggered the scene before him—it may even have been Alma's own words about "a lake of fire and brimstone, whose flame ascendeth up forever and ever"[61] that prompted the people of Ammonihah to choose a massive pit of fire as the means of torturing the faithful.[62] Alma has faith in a God who

---

60. Irving Greenburg. "Cloud of Smoke, Pillar of Fire: Judaism, Christianity, and Modernity After the Holocaust," in Eva Fleischer, ed. *Auschwitz: Beginning of a New Era?* New York: Ktow Publishing, 1977, 23.

61. Alma 12:17

62. Kylie Nielson Turley. *Alma 1–29: A Brief Theological Introduction.* Provo, UT: Neal A. Maxwell Institute, 2020. Turley also brilliantly notes that while the phrase *lake of fire and brimstone* appears many times previously to these events of Ammonihah, afterwards the phrase is never again used in the Book of Mormon. This may be because of the pain Alma felt at seeing his words weaponized against innocent people and how the horrifying incident was remembered in broader Nephite culture (p. 92).

called him to this place, who could have stopped these events. Alma believes that the God he loves and trusts not only allows this to happen, but asks him to witness it and not intervene. That is a severe kind of trauma. And when people experience that level of trauma, they sometimes need to construct a reason for its existence in order to relieve the nearly unbearable spiritual dissonance they experience. People build their own imperfect answers that serve them for that moment when they lack answers in the face of terrifying atrocities. These are long-standing, pervasive issues for everyone who seeks for God and works for justice. What do we say to a God who does not seem to use God's overwhelming power to protect the most vulnerable and innocent? What theology erupts from the sites of our inability to change horror? We all live with spiritual trauma every day, simply by looking at current events and wondering why God does not intervene.

If you have a commitment to justice in the world, seeing the news every day can wreak havoc on your spirit and your relationship with the divine. This part of the Book of Mormon deserves a lot of attention because it challenges the narratives we construct around God. Alma and Amulek's experience teaches us this: God may not always show up in the way we need. If we do not talk about the harm to testimony and spirits in times of deep wounding, then we are not really speaking to the complexity of people's faith and their relationship with God. Like Alma, we may not have any satisfying, complete answers to these incredibly difficult questions. But the discussion can be deep and rich and invite people to think about how they wrestle with God and make meaning from the struggles of mortality.

Alma and Amulek rested after this time, and some speculate that Alma did not preach for a period.[63] While we do not know what the immediate aftermath looked like, there is good reason to believe that Alma was deeply affected by this experience for many years, possibly for the rest of his life. Although the moment of his conversion phys-

---

63. Kylie Nielson Turley. *Alma 1–29.*

ically shook him, it is this event that left him spiritually devastated. Some evidence shows that it changed Alma permanently. He never again used the phrase "lake of fire and brimstone" in his preaching. Also, before his experience at Ammonihah, he left women out of his sermons or included them as part of a list of property.[64] After Ammonihah, he includes women in his rhetoric and describes them as individuals with agency, such as when he says that God speaks "not only [to] men but women also [and also to] little children."[65] Perhaps watching the suffering of women and children in the fire changed Alma's perspective on the condition of women and children in Nephite society.[66]

Alma 14:14–22

These verses document many days of abuse, torture, and cruelty. The chief judge—a man tasked with upholding the justice system— repeatedly beats and taunts Alma and Amulek. In addition to the physical violence, he perpetrates spiritual abuse, reminding them that God did not save the women and children who burned in the fire. Imagine the heartbreak Alma and Amulek experience in this period, likely one of the worst of their lives. The chief judge exploits that, encouraging their doubts at a time when they are wondering why God did not perform a miracle to protect innocent people. For those working in any social justice cause, the question of where God is, and why God has not intervened, will sometimes weigh us down. Maintaining hope and faith in times of the "dark night of the soul" can feel impossible at times.

In the midst of their suffering, Alma and Amulek refuse to answer the chief judge's questions. As noted in our discussion of Alma 12, not every question is worth engaging. There needs to be space for silence. Discerning whether the questioner asks with good or malicious intent

---

64. For example, Alma 5:49 and 7:27.
65. Alma 32:23
66. Kylie Nielson Turley. *Alma's Hell*, 33–34.

is an important skill to hone. Declining to answer bad questions is a form of nonviolent resistance, a refusal to acknowledge someone else's claim to power over you and showing they do not have power over your body. They cannot force you to answer. The chief judge recognizes that Alma and Amulek's silence undermines the legitimacy of his power, which is why he reacts with rage. Their choice to employ nonviolent resistance ultimately increases the violence enacted against them, which is a common effect of nonviolence. The implication that one's adversary cannot ultimately control a person, no matter how they bind them, hurt them, or threaten them, infuriates people who want to exert power over others.

The officials of Ammonihah withhold food, water, and clothes. They repeatedly batter Alma and Amulek and leave them tied up. After witnessing such terrible violence against innocent women and children, Alma and Amulek survive days of torture themselves. God allows it. The question that hangs over this section is why God allows these terrible things to happen to people of faith. The text does not necessarily answer the question; it simply invites us to sit with it.

Alma 14:26–29

After being unable to stop the burning of innocents and then suffering days of torture in silence, Alma finally cries out to God for help. His lament in verse 26 radiates their pain and grief: "How long shall we suffer these great afflictions, O Lord?" His words are similar to the psalmist who cries out, "How long wilt thou forget me, O Lord? Forever? How long wilt thou hide thy face from me?"[67] A scriptural lament is a cry to God in the darkest of times. As scholar Jacob Baker has written, "No hope for a better world can silence the lament; indeed, the lament might be seen as the soul cry for hope in the face

---

67. Psalm 13:1

of hope's final abandonment."[68] Alma's lament in this moment can be read as his admission of absolute heartbreak and despair.

Then, Alma and Amulek are able to break the ropes that bind them. They escape the prison as it collapses and kills all the cruel people who have hurt them. Alma and Amulek walk away naked, starving, and probably covered in dirt, blood, and bruises. In some ways, this dramatic end to their imprisonment feels satisfyingly heroic. But even though the miracle happens, an undertone of sadness remains. If God was going to perform a miracle, why did God not act earlier? If God could have ended it at any time, why did God allow these men to suffer for so long? Theologically, the climax is unsatisfying. It does not tie up neatly or leave the reader feeling like all is well. Those deaths cannot be undone. Their trauma does not go away.

Those who work for justice must face that, often, the price of truth-telling is deeply unsatisfying. The consequences may not make sense and things will not go right. Justice will feel too late and God will not move when we want God to move. Even when we are doing the work of God, it will sometimes feel as if God is not there with us. We do not always want to face this part of the story of social justice: it requires watching the needless suffering of innocent people. It takes a massive spiritual and physical toll. Miracles sometimes come too late, if they come at all.

---

68. Jacob Baker. "Theologizing in the Presence of Burning Children: From Theodicy to Lament." *Sunstone*, Sept. 21, 2012. https://sunstone.org/theologizing-in-the-presence-of-burning-children-from-theodicy-to-lament/.

Baker convincingly argues that Alma's period of silence in prison following the fire and his cry of lament can be seen as a kind of abandonment of his earlier attempt to explain the burning of the women and children. Rather than attempting a doctrinal explanation to respond to the judge's questions, Alma chooses silence and then finally, a lament for the injustices of the world.

Alma 15:1–2

As Alma and Amulek leave the city, they find the men who were cast out and stoned and tell them what happened to the women and children. They have to be the bearers of an account of unspeakable violence as they also tell the story of their deliverance. The juxtaposition of those things, telling people about the suffering and deaths of their families while also explaining how they survived, is emotionally overwhelming. Alma and Amulek have just barely escaped with their lives, but they must also carry the burden of the violence they witnessed. The text does not describe the men's responses, nor does it pause to reflect on the grief and anger that must have followed this moment. Because the text moves past it so quickly, readers must make an additional effort to slow down and sit with the pain of this story. Spending time in the lament, imagining the mourning of these men and the guilt Alma and Amulek must have felt, gives a richer, fuller experience to the scriptural account.

Alma 15:3–11

This moment with Zeezrom is complex. Although he is suffering and repentant, he stays very centered on himself and his experiences and feelings, which is extraordinary given the context around him. Alma and Amulek have just been through hell. The other men have just learned their families died after horrible suffering. Zeezrom suffers from a burning heat, an echo of the fire that killed the women and children, but which does not kill him. He experiences pain that pales in comparison to the pain he caused other people. Yet, he immediately calls Alma and Amulek to him and begs them to heal him.

On the one hand, this beautiful story demonstrates care and compassion. Alma and Amulek go immediately to this man, who has deeply harmed them, and offer him relief. In a time when they still suffer from their own torture, they extend forgiveness. On the other hand, Zeezrom's actions reflect the entitlement and self-centeredness he previously showed. While he has repented, he has not fully interrogated his privilege and ego. He is surrounded by pain and suffering he helped cause, yet his entire focus remains on himself. He cannot stand the weight of his own guilt and so he "immediately" (v. 4) sends for Alma and Amulek, asking for help from those whom he has harmed.

Upon facing a reckoning for their actions, perpetrators of violence sometimes ask their victims to save them. Zeezrom's failure to examine his own entitlement does not make his pain any less real. He is suffering. But he is also in a place of privilege, one in which he can send for people and have them come to him directly. Those two things exist simultaneously, and the text allows readers to wrestle with it. In times when we feel guilty with the realization of ways in which we have harmed people, we can choose to not ask marginalized people to relieve that burden. We do not have to expect people who suffer from our actions to come to our aid and heal us. We can sit with the pain we feel and interrogate it, asking ourselves, *What caused this suffering? Who is responsible for it? What can I learn from it?*

Alma 15:13–14

The church Alma and Amulek build at this time starts with men who were cast out and stoned and who then lost their families for their faith, a population of widowers. This church begins with people who have been tortured and marginalized, who are in deep grief. The church of Sidom is a church of the wounded.

Every time a church gets established, it is worth pausing to examine the surrounding context, because a church becomes a site of gathering, a place that anchors a community. In a time of deep grief and distress, people flock from all over the region to Sidom because of the church. Here, grief-stricken folk—who have been cast out by their own city—start a church, and in turn that church draws people from all over the land. Do not miss how often the most vulnerable, the survivors of deep trauma and grief, create a deeply inviting church space, one that people will "flock" (v. 14) to join.

Alma 15:15

The people who stay in Ammonihah ascribe Alma and Amulek's power to a different source. Their corruption and pride re-narrates God's saving miracle into an act of the devil. Be careful of the ways in which stories of God and God's people get reimagined and retold in the hands of the oppressors. This surprisingly important verse illustrates the power of stories. The people of Ammonihah convince themselves that they are right and that the people they have wounded are of the devil. They strip God from a site of miraculous liberation and place the devil there instead. That is spiritual violence. By claiming that God was not in that space where people suffered and died, they tell a story in which God was not present for the worst moments of these people's lives. The right of people, particularly oppressed people, to claim their own story—narrating God into that story in ways true to their experience—is vitally important. The power to move God into our stories of trauma and suffering is part of the healing process.

Alma 15:16

This verse contains an entire sermon. Amulek gave up his gold, his family, and his friends to follow God. When Amulek introduced himself to the people of Ammonihah,[69] he cited these markers of identity. He had family, wealth, connections, and influence. He lost it all. Amulek's experience, of all the individual stories in the Book of Mormon, reflects one of the greatest personal losses because of his decision to follow God. Even Lehi kept his family when he wandered into the wilderness. The closest comparison in the text is that of Moroni at the end of the book: no family, no community, no possessions. Amulek's experience underscores one of the most important messages of the Book of Mormon: following God does not lead to an easy life. Instead, God's disciples often suffer abuse, lose their wealth, and become estranged from their communities. The joy that comes with the gospel is often inextricably intertwined with hardships and loss.

---

69. Alma 10:2–4

Alma 15:18

This verse offers a hope for consolation after Amulek's suffering in verse 16. Remember, Amulek took Alma into his own house and fed him and cared for him at the beginning of their relationship.[70] Here, Alma takes Amulek to his house and "administer[s] unto him in his tribulations." Amulek suffers from the loss of his community and the abuse he endured in prison. As he faces the great griefs in his life, Alma succors him. Imagine a church community in which we each fully followed the guidance of this verse and administered to one another in our tribulations. If Amulek needed to be strengthened, then he must have felt weak at this moment. Possibly it was hard for him to feel God in all of the heartache he experienced. When people offer love and care, it helps others to see God a little more clearly. Recommitting ourselves to administering to others in their tribulations is radical faith.

Alma 16:1–8

Although the text claims the Nephites have enjoyed "much peace in the land" (v. 1), only six years have passed since the last war with the Lamanites, which makes it closer to a ceasefire than a period of peace. Something seems broken in a society that views such short periods of time without overt violence as "much peace." The Lamanites then soon destroy the city of Ammonihah. However, the Nephites' focus now is on recovering the captives taken away into the wilderness. Notice the total lack of interest in retaliation or punishment; chief captain Zoram's sole objective is to retrieve the prisoners. Zoram even invokes prophetic help in this effort, which fulfills the description of the role of the prophetic in Isaiah 61:1 and Luke 4:18: "The Spirit of the Lord God is upon me; because the Lord hath anointed me to preach good tidings unto the meek; he hath sent me to bind up the brokenhearted, to proclaim liberty to the captives, and the

---

70. Alma 8:21–22

opening of the prison to them that are bound."[71] Freeing prisoners literally, not just spiritually or metaphorically, is one of the works of God. God is invested in the liberty of all people. Those who seek justice should not only engage in the work of freeing captives—such as immigrants jailed at the border, victims of trafficking, and enslaved people—but should also ask the prophets, seers, and revelators for direction on how to liberate those in captivity.

Zoram fulfills his mission without any deaths among the captives. Although the text says the Lamanites "were scattered and driven into the wilderness" (v. 8), it does not specifically state any deaths on their side either. This offers one of the great success stories amid violent conflict in the Book of Mormon. Rather than escalating the conflict, the Nephites choose to merely recover their people from captivity. When the former captives get brought home, the Nephite society ensures the continued possession of the lands they had before. The military, the prophetic, and the general population work together to restore victims' lives in a beautiful way. It exemplifies a whole community enacting social justice.

Alma 16:9–11

These verses detailing the total destruction of Ammonihah are unsettling, even for readers who are fine with unleashing punishment on people who burned women and children alive. It is worth noting the way the Nephites name places of deep destruction and sever them from the rest of the land. By naming the land Desolation, they remember the violence that land holds. Both the name and the way it remains empty help the stories survive.

---

71. Isaiah 61:1. Luke 4:18 is slightly different: "The Spirit of the Lord is upon me, because he hath anointed me to preach the gospel to the poor; he hath sent me to heal the brokenhearted, to preach deliverance to the captives, and recovering of sight to the blind, to set at liberty them that are bruised."

The Book of Mormon previously attributed the destruction of Ammonihah to an act of God.[72] It will later ascribe responsibility to the Lamanites' anger because of the Anti-Nephi-Lehies.[73] Did God put anger in the hearts of the Lamanites in order to cause the annihilation of the city? The inhabitants of the city were vile, past feeling and willing to commit atrocities against the most vulnerable in society. If God cares about the oppressed, it is difficult to comprehend why God would not respond to such evil. But to claim God worked through war gives a kind of divine approval to the Lamanites' rage and violence. This interpretation also removes the Lamanites' agency, supposing a God who moves people as pawns in a game of war. While the people of Ammonihah deserved justice, the narration of God inspiring or supporting the Lamanites in their campaign of complete desolation is problematic.

Alma 16:13–17

In *Lectures on Faith*, it reads, "But it is also necessary that men should have an idea that [God] is no respecter of persons; for with the idea of all the other excellencies in his character, and this one wanting, men could not exercise faith in him."[74] This strong language emphasizes this crucial aspect of deity. Here, the text urges imparting the word of God without regard for social distinctions or hierarchies. The gospel is for everyone, and the ways in which we spread the gospel ought to reflect a commitment to that principle. In the case of Alma and Amulek, their lack of constraint in teaching the gospel appears to build a church that lacks inequality entirely (v. 16). The feeling of abundance is moving: "the Lord did pour out his Spirit on *all* the face of the land" (v. 16, emphasis added). Building a church that does not

---

72. Alma 8:16

73. Alma 25:1–2

74. "Lecture 3," *The Lectures on Faith in Historical Perspective*, ed. Larry E. Dahl and Charles D. Tate Jr. Provo, UT: Religious Studies Center, Brigham Young University, 65–73.

recognize social divisions leads to a community with no inequality, which in turn allows God to pour out God's spirit on all the people. This, in turn, sparks joy and prompts people to "enter into the rest of the Lord" (v. 17). Only a few years earlier, Alma witnessed a Nephite church in which people turned away from faith because of the terrible inequality within the community.[75] Here, the opposite occurs: a revolutionary social equality helps spread the gospel. With no restriction in how the gospel is taught and to whom, God's spirit pours out on all the land. This is a joyful moment.

Alma 16:19–21

A beautiful hope gets invoked in these verses—a hope not for themselves, but for their descendants several generations away. They believe God cares about them and God will show up. Not for them, but for their kin someday in the future. They hear this with "great joy and gladness" (v. 20), almost as if Christ's appearance will be for themselves. This is the kind of mutuality that exists in an equal society. They can feel joy for something they will not see in mortality, simply because other folk will experience it and others' joy is like their own. Verse 21 reiterates God pouring out blessings on the people, not in the language of wealth or prosperity, but in community. This is a relationship-bound blessing for a beloved community that has managed to teach with equity and rejoice as they receive God's word together.

Alma 17:1–2

Like the Book of Mosiah, the Book of Alma takes the stories of different groups of people, occurring simultaneously but in different lands, and binds them together into a single volume. This kind of bundling of disparate experiences symbolizes how different perspectives and backgrounds become stronger in their union. This first

---

75. Alma 4:11–13

verse of chapter 17, describing the joy these men felt as they regroup after fourteen years of separation, encapsulates this principle of the power of coming together. They went down different paths and had distinct experiences and challenges, but they have in common their past repentance and a commitment to a life with God. They can celebrate the ways their lives are the same and different.

Alma 17:4–5

"Now these are the circumstances which attended them in their journeyings" (v. 5) is a phrase we should use more often. How would our conversations change if we asked people what circumstances attend them in their journeys? The sons of Mosiah and Alma suffered a great deal in their work, and the text explicitly acknowledges those physical, mental, and spiritual hardships. So while they are happy for their success, they do not separate that joy from a recognition of how challenging this time has been. The circumstances that attended these men in their journeys were simultaneously tragic and joyful, and the details of those journeys are part of sacred text.

Alma 17:9–12

This group with the sons of Mosiah had a work to do during their time in the wilderness. As they began their call, they first had a period of transition. People often ignore the points in between Zarahemla and the exciting stories of the land of Nephi, but the sons of Mosiah spent time preparing themselves for their years as wanderers in a strange land. They fasted and prayed for a "portion of [God's] spirit," so they could become "an instrument in the hands of God" (v. 9). The text gives greater insight into this interval several chapters later, when Ammon reminds his brothers that the Nephites mocked them for attempting to convert the Lamanites and even suggested that instead, they should raise an army and "destroy" the entire nation.[76]

---

76. Alma 26:23–24

These men grew in crucial ways over the course of their travels as they let go of the prejudice and hatred of their native culture and prepared to serve their enemies and act out of love. Once again, time in the wilderness in the Book of Mormon is when some of the most important and transformative events occur.

God tells them to be comforted, and they are, yet the words God gives hardly seem comforting. God does not tell them that things will be okay or that they will be safe and successful; they are exhorted to have patience and long-suffering in their afflictions. God's words indicate a hard path ahead, which could inspire apprehension instead of comfort and courage. Yet, these men take heart and continue on a journey that required a great deal of courage merely to begin. Their concerns and response indicate God's patience with us as we undertake hard things. It is okay to have doubts and worries after we have started a new effort. As we go on, God will help build our courage.

Alma 17:14–16

This language about the Lamanites is problematic in so many ways. The text just finished describing the Nephite city of Ammonihah, which burned women and children alive and stoned believers.[77] Yet it names only the Lamanites as a "wild and a hardened and a ferocious people; a people who delighted in murdering the Nephites" (v. 14). According to the stories in this book, both nations struggle with the exact same sins and weaknesses. For all the sons of Mosiah suffer in the land of Nephi, the Lamanites never do anything to them that is comparable to what the people of Ammonihah did. Yet only one group consistently gets described as wicked, vain, indolent, and murderous. The language here is intense and unrelenting. Only one group is called "cursed" and faulted for "the traditions of their fathers" (v. 15). One great failing of the way the Nephites narrate their own story is their blindness to how similar they are to their enemies.

---

77. Alma 14

They do not see how their own people do the same terrible things the Lamanites do. This gets particularly problematic when it accompanies missionary work and traveling to other lands to teach people. A narrative built on prejudice does not serve the cause of evangelism. When we can name all the problems and failings of others but do not see the ways our own people engage in the same behavior, we do not recognize our common humanity. The relationship becomes inherently hierarchical, which is not how God sees God's children.

This reductive description of the Lamanites comes from a physical and emotional distance, a time before the sons of Mosiah have actually met any Lamanites. When the sons of Mosiah actually engage in a personal, up-close way with the Lamanites, they do so with humility and love. These verses do not represent how they actually behave in relationship with the Lamanites they come to know. The language does not align with the stories that follow, but it is possible that it represents the attitudes they had as they entered the wilderness and asked for God's help. Noticing this language in the text helps readers to see the enormous growth the sons of Mosiah experience during their time with the Lamanites. The Lamanites are not the only ones to undergo a conversion; the missionaries' hearts are also changed.

Alma 17:22–23

The way Ammon enters into this relationship with Lamoni is extraordinary. At some point, possibly during his time in the wilderness, he decided that his commitment to the Lamanites will be long-term, possibly permanent. He feels prepared to accept a life in a strange land with folk who have been taught to hate him. His language demonstrates a strong commitment, and he speaks with humility and servitude. This posture differs from verse 17, which describes their efforts as one of correcting and saving the Lamanites. To enter a hostile space and simply say, *"I'm here to be in relationship with you and serve you in any way I can,"* is a radical act of love. It is these actions of service and love, not the later impressive display of weaponry, that lays the foundation for a healthy and peaceful exchange between the two men.[78]

Alma 17:24–39

This section depicts one of the strangest and most well-known stories in the Book of Mormon. It includes bizarre moments, such as the servants carrying a bundle of arms to the king while Ammon returns to the pastures (v. 39). Lamoni and Ammon are complex characters. Lamoni shows the intense hospitality of offering a stranger his daughter as a wife (v. 24) but then also has the bloodthirsty history of killing his own servants for their inability to protect his flocks (v. 28). Ammon displays bravery in his service to the king, but also vanity with his heart "swollen within him with joy" because of his chance to "show forth [his] power" to men trembling with fear (v. 29). The story reads like a kind of fairytale, a legend of a prince who single-handedly defeats a terrible enemy in order to save the neighboring king. Ammon's skills with a sword—a weapon likely unfamiliar to shepherd-servants—points to his privileged life as a son of the Nephite king. There is also the important question of whether God sanctioned the extreme violence Ammon uses to prevent the theft of animals.

While this story at times seems so extreme as to venture into the absurd, it raises important questions about violence. Ammon has entered a culture in which violence is normative: the king kills his servants for mistakes, robbers regularly attack, and people live in fear. If we live in a violent world, what actions are we justified in taking? Are we limited to self-defense, or does God approve of seeking justice through bloodshed? If we expect and assume that people will respond to the work of social justice with aggression, should we plan

---

78. For further reading on this, see Patrick Q.Mason and J. David Pulsipher. *Proclaim Peace: The Restoration's Answer to an Age of Conflict*. Provo, UT: Neal A. Maxwell Institute, 2021. 86.

to respond in the same fashion? These are all questions this story raises without necessarily giving a definitive answer. It offers the opportunity to wrestle with the problem of how to live in a violent world. If we evade those questions and tell Ammon's story superficially, we miss the chance to examine how God wants righteous people to act in a complex, fallen society.

Alma 18:1–6

When the servants testify to Lamoni about what happened in the pasture, the king asks, "Behold, is not this the Great Spirit?" and wonders whether the Great Spirit is punishing the people for their sins (v. 2). This connection Lamoni makes immediately indicates an existing understanding of God. When Lamoni's wife first speaks with Ammon, she also uses the language of religion and displays an understanding of God.[79] The Lamanites have some kind of religion, at least enough for Lamoni to have a name for God and connect that God with a morality that punishes people for bad behavior. When he sees something that goes beyond his understanding—in this case, a man cutting off the arms of a group of attackers—he puts it in the language of the miraculous and divine. Although the Book of Mormon sometimes describes the Lamanites as inheriting wrong or corrupt traditions from their ancestors and having no concept of God,[80] Lamoni's words indicate a more complex faith culture. Verse 5 states that Lamoni's father taught Lamoni about God, even if he gave God a different name than Ammon and the Nephites use. Readers do the Lamanites a disservice if we assume the text is always correct in its assumptions about the Lamanites' culture, religious understanding, and ancestral legacy.

Although the Lamanites believe in some kind of God, they simultaneously believe "that whatsoever they did was right" (v. 5). Lamoni

79. Alma 19:4
80. For example, Alma 9:16 and Alma 17:9.

has caused his servants to be killed for a relatively minor failure beyond their control and now begins to fear the Great Spirit is angry about those actions. Believing in God while also consistently believing oneself to be in the right is a path to justifying terrible sins. This moment with Ammon is a reckoning in which Lamoni has to examine his assumption that the Great Spirit approved of everything he has done, including murdering people. In some part of himself, Lamoni knew killing his servants was wrong, which is why he immediately perceives his own guilt and begins to worry God is angry with him. His previous belief that "whatsoever they did was right" only allowed him to lie to himself for a time. Eventually, he had to acknowledge the truth he already knew.

Alma 18:8–21

After this dramatic and violent moment in the pasture, Ammon apparently returns to the stables and goes back to work (v. 12). When Lamoni calls Ammon in, the king struggles to know what to say (v. 14), and Ammon acts as if detecting the reason for the conversation is a moment of great discernment and prophecy (v. 16). Readers might chuckle at these verses, wondering why Ammon acts so bizarrely and why the text insists that Ammon needed God's help to know the king might want to discuss Ammon killing and cutting off the arms of a large number of men.

Again, reading these chapters as a certain kind of storytelling helps us understand the strangeness. Recognizing the fantastical packaging digs into the text in a deeper way. This particular story has characteristics of literary heroes and villains, as well as the hyperbole of other scriptural texts like the Book of Job. The narrative gets told not first-hand, like a memoir, but by an unnamed author who has the goal of spreading the gospel. In this layered missionary story, one about more than missionary work, the author tries to move the reader into believing certain things about God. There is nothing wrong with that—the scriptures are meant to help bring people on a journey with God. But when stories get told in a way that leaves out complexity and flattens characters to stereotypes and tropes, readers may miss important messages. Taking this story and considering which parts need unpacking helps us realize far more nuance and subtlety to the narrative. Asking the question of why a story and characters are being told in a certain way assists in this effort.

Ammon's character arc is extraordinary. He was born a prince, chose to become a missionary/servant, and eventually is forced to develop into an impassioned advocate for the converted Lamanites. He walked away from kingship,[81] only to have Lamoni's servants call him "great king" (v. 13) and to have Lamoni briefly believe that he is God (v. 18). Ammon grew up privileged, then forsook it to act as a servant and do the grueling work of teaching the gospel among his enemies. All the sons of Mosiah followed a call that took them away from the seat of power and traditional forms of influence. God asked them to leave the comfort of their homes and communities and go to a people who hate them and treat them terribly. They then come to love the Lamanites and work hard to protect the faithful from harm. Ammon, in particular, spends much of the rest of his life teaching and protecting the converted Lamanites. The author of this section writes about Ammon as a superhuman with impossible skills in battle and an unflappable demeanor. That is the problem with scripture packaged into a story: it sometimes overlooks the complexity and humanity of its subjects. Slowing down and asking questions reveals an intense narrative of personal growth, a true change of heart, and activism on behalf of vulnerable people.

Alma 18:41–42.

One of the first concepts that Lamoni references after listening to Ammon is the idea of "abundant mercy" (v. 41). Mercy is not a word he used before in recorded conversation, and it is certainly not a

---

81. Mosiah 28:10

principle he exercised in regards to his servants. He understands mercy as a gift God has offered the Nephites, and one of the first prayers Lamoni offers asks God for a similar blessing. Immediately following that prayer, he faints. It seems to be this moment of asking for mercy that prompts Lamoni's collapse. The moment seems similar to Alma's moment of falling to the ground and his description of the mercy he experienced during that time.[82] Abundant mercy is an overpowering feeling, and the realization that God offers it to each of us has the power to knock people to the ground. Whenever we share the gospel, the truth of God's abundant mercy should be one of the first principles taught.

Alma 19:1–5

Lamoni's wife and the power of her advocacy cannot be overstated here. By calling in Ammon after challenging some people's claims that Lamoni is dead, this deeply dedicated woman defies cultural norms and the pressure of the opinions of her community. Although she identifies the conflicting ideas about what has happened to Lamoni, she clearly states what she believes, sharing her own truth in an extremely confusing and upsetting time. Although the text never offers her the respect of recording her name, these few verses give a too-brief insight into an extraordinary woman.

The focal point of this story shifts deliberately as it develops. It begins with Ammon, who from a Lamanite perspective, carries three markers of privilege: he is Nephite, male, and from a royal household. The spotlight then turns to the king, who is missing one of these markers: he is royal and male, but not a Nephite. When the king falls to the ground, the story shifts to the queen, who is a female Lamanite, but still royal. Finally, with the queen's collapse, Abish becomes the focal point. Abish is Lamanite, a woman, and a servant, making her one of the lowest-ranked people in the Book of Mormon. Yet she

---

82. Mosiah 27:28–29

is the turning point of the story, the one who ultimately raises the queen from the ground and calms the raging crowd.[83]

Alma 19:6

This beautiful verse describes Ammon's understanding of the state of Lamoni's mind. "A marvelous light of [God's] goodness—yea, this light had infused such joy into his soul," is a lovely way to describe the effect of the gospel. God and joy are inseparably intertwined. In a moment when a man looks dead, he is actually being infused with joyous light. As people grieve around him, "the cloud of darkness" inside of him gets "dispelled." The gospel is so often counterintuitive and surprising.

Alma 19:7–10

Ammon and the queen share a virtuous quality of a willingness to listen to others, including people from other social standings than themselves. Ammon's "only desire" in this moment is what the queen desires (v. 7). He is so entirely focused on her that any other interest in missionary work or his own personal safety fades to the background. He follows her desire for him to visit the king. The queen, for her part, listens to him not because of her own witness, but because of the witnesses of Ammon (a Nephite and a stranger) and her servants (v. 9). Her curiosity and willingness to listen to people on the margins gives her powerful faith.

Her faith is so remarkable that Ammon tells her, "there has not been such great faith among all the people of the Nephites" (v. 10). What an extraordinary moment. The text has repeatedly claimed that the Lamanites are depraved, ferocious, and godless. And yet, the queen of the Lamanites has greater faith than any of the Nephites, including Ammon. She will not be the only Lamanite who exhibits exceptional faith: the entire household of Lamoni is so open to the spirit that the

---

83. Joseph Spencer. Email message to authors, Mar. 3, 2022.

simple act of Ammon preaching to them for a short while overpowers them with joy, and they fall to the ground.[84] Lamoni, Abish, and the Anti-Nephi-Lehites will be part of a narrative which displays some of the greatest faith and courage in the Book of Mormon. They make risky decisions out of a deep commitment to God. Their stories of faith contradict a reading of the Book of Mormon in which the Nephites are the righteous heroes. While many Lamanites did terrible things, there were many who showed greater faith than any of the Nephites.

Alma 19:11–13

Women watch. Women in the scriptures stay at the cross and sit at the bedside. They attend and keep vigil, even when the text refuses to name them. When it seems all hope is gone, women continue to watch and witness. Their faith holds them there, whether it is the three Marys standing at Golgotha[85] or Sariah waiting for her sons to return from Jerusalem.[86]

Lamoni's first words as he returns to consciousness are to bless God and to bless the queen. He recognizes the power of a woman whose incredible faith, greater than any Ammon has witnessed, is built on the words of her servants and a stranger. It seems not coincidental that much of Lamoni's vision appears to have been about Mary. He speaks about a Redeemer who will "be born of a woman" (v. 13). Possibly Lamoni is more aware of and thoughtful about women, making him more likely to recognize the spiritual power of women in his visions and in his waking life. Or maybe his vision of Mary prompted him to better appreciate his wife as he awoke.[87] Either

---

84. Alma 19:13–15

85. John 19:25

86. 1 Nephi 5:2

87. Joe Spencer, "(Something Like) A Feminist Interpretation of a Book of Mormon Text, 3.1: Conversion of the King, Or, Lamoni's Feminist Moment," posted April 29, 2011 at Feminist Mormon Housewives (https://www.feministmormonhousewives. org/2011/04/something-like-a-feminist-interpretation-of-a-book-of-mormon-text-3-1-conversion-of-the-king-or-lamoni%e2%80%99s-feminist-moment/).

way, Lamoni apparently connected the two women in his mind. The queen is an amazing woman and the text ought to give her name.

Alma 19:16–28

A second woman of incredible faith enters at this moment. Abish is a "Lamanitish" servant who has been following God for "many years, on account of a remarkable vision of her father" (v. 16). While many assume that Abish's father had a vision, the text could also be read as Abish having had a vision of her father (earthly or heavenly).[88] Given the miracles Abish performs later in the story, this interpretation of the text of Abish as a visionary is quite likely.

As Abish sees the wild moves of the Holy Spirit, the uncontainable joy spreads to her and she immediately runs out to tell as many people as she can. The fact that she has never shared her conversion with anyone before this time tells readers that she previously feared how her community would react to her beliefs, but she is now sure that the moment for their conversion has arrived. Yet, events do not transpire as she wishes or anticipates. Instead, the crowd splinters into arguing factions, some accusing the king of bringing evil on their society by harboring a Nephite (v. 19), some believing the king is being punished for killing his servants (v. 20), and some feeling angry at Ammon for killing the robbers (v. 21).

All of these stories are incorrect, but that does not stop the people from using them to justify a course of action. One of the messages of this story is that our actions have repercussions we do not anticipate. As Ammon defended the king's flocks, he killed many people. One of them has a brother who is grieving and enraged. The violence Ammon used circles back to him as the brother tries to use Ammon's own sword to kill Ammon (v. 22). This is a complex moment: God may have inspired Ammon, but there is a violent consequence to

---

88. Jerrie W. Hurd. *Our Sisters in Latter-day Scriptures.* Salt Lake City, UT: Deseret Book, 1987, 23. Kevin Christensen and Shauna Christensen. "Nephite Feminism Revisited: Thoughts on Carol Lynn Pearson's View of Women in the Book of Mormon." *Review of Books on the Book of Mormon*, Vol. 10, No. 2 (1998), 16.

what Ammon did. Whatever Ammon's intentions, he caused deep violence that harmed people in the Lamanite community. That does not mean the action was wrong, but it does show how violence tends to perpetuate itself. As Dr. Martin Luther King said, "The ultimate weakness of violence is that it is a descending spiral, begetting the very thing it seeks to destroy. Instead of diminishing evil, it multiplies it."[89]

The people do not interpret the events in the joyful way that Abish does. She sees the moment as an opportunity for conversion; they see it as divine retribution. Although Abish invited them to come witness God, the immediate consequence is fierce arguing and a threat to Ammon's life. As the contention escalates, Abish despairs (v. 28). The servant woman who hid her faith, then had a moment of intense hope for change, believes she failed.

Those who seek for God and work for justice will sometimes anticipate something good and be deeply disappointed in others' refusal to accept the invitation for change. People do not interpret events in the same way, and their reactions may seem frustrating or confusing. Look at moments of great opportunity to see God at work and witness what people's reactions are to those times. Moving in social justice will mean hearing incorrect narratives and experiencing unintended consequences. We cannot know how people will perceive our actions. Testifying of God is particularly difficult because our testimonies are subject to others' narration. While we may see our social justice work as the work of God, other people may not. They may even react with violence, causing us to feel "exceedingly sorrowful, even unto tears" (v. 28).

Alma 19:29–36

While Abish's story is one of despair at this moment, the narrative does not end at verse 28. In the following eight verses, the story

---

89. Martin Luther King, Jr. *Where Do We Go from Here: Chaos or Community?* Boston, MA: Beacon Press, 2010, 181.

changes dramatically. Abish's actions prove vital to the community. At those times when we have acted in faith and hope, and yet believe we failed, God is still at work. Abish's willingness to continue on changes everything between verses 28 and 29. She takes the queen by the hand and raises her from the ground (v. 29). The power of this woman! Abish restored the queen, who in turn takes the king by the hand and brings him back to consciousness. This is a miracle akin to Paul raising Eutychus from the dead.[90] Abish uses her faith and the prophetic power rolling through her to raise the queen.

After testifying to the group, the queen then raises the king from the ground, using the same faith and power Abish and Ammon employed (v. 30). As he awakens, the king also teaches the people surrounding him (v. 31). The servants who had collapsed also begin to preach, "declar[ing] unto the people the self-same thing—that their hearts had been changed" (v. 33). All of these extraordinary events began with two women who had patiently acted as witnesses before acting in faith.

Verses 31–32 explain that while many people heard Lamoni's words and believed, many others "would not hear his words; therefore they went on their way" (v. 32). Anyone working to share God's message of social justice will find people ready to hear and others who simply want to continue with the narrative they already have. In those cases, it is best to follow Lamoni's example of letting people walk away. Those who have ears to hear, let them hear.[91]

Ammon has experienced two miraculous moments in which God moved in mass conversion—the first when he saw an angel with his brothers and Alma,[92] and the second in this chapter. In both, a group of people shared a communal spiritual experience that ultimately ties them tightly to one another. We see the first hint of how close Ammon will become with Lamoni and the Lamanites in verse 33.

---

90. Acts 20:7–12
91. Matthew 11:15
92. Mosiah 27

The text states that Ammon, the servants of Lamoni, and some of the crowd of people administer to one another and then "*they did all declare unto the people the self-same thing*—that their hearts had been changed; that they had no more desire to do evil" (emphasis added). Ammon appears to be part of this testimony, one witness in a group of people stating their hearts were changed. So even if Ammon went into the land thinking he would teach them, a reciprocal relationship developed in which God converts and reconverts all of them together, and they testify to one another. Starting in this verse, the text begins to present Ammon as part of a faith community, not as simply a missionary for others.

The text indicates that Ammon's presence in the Lamanites' land starts God's work there and even claims that this marks the beginning of the Spirit being "pour[ed] out" on the people. Yet, the story's narrative contradicts these assertions. Abish converted to the gospel long before Ammon's arrival. The king and queen knew about the Great Spirit before meeting Ammon. The widespread, deep conversion of these people indicates hearts and minds that were already touched by God. One man is never the lynchpin for God's presence among an entire nation. So what the narrator believes is the start of God's work may not be the true beginning, and God's arm truly is "extended to *all* people" (v. 36, emphasis added).

Alma 20:2-7

This beautiful chapter illustrates how God cares about people in prison and how people can use power and relationships to bring about liberation. In this verse, God moves Ammon to change his plan for further missionary work and instead go to relieve the suffering of Ammon's brothers. Like Jesus counseled in his sermon about "the least of these," Ammon goes to those in prison.[93] But this is not limited to a visit or temporary relief and comfort. Ammon follows God's commandments by bringing freedom to those wrongfully incarcerated.

---

93. Matthew 25:36-40

This story of the sons of Mosiah has important ramifications in a world in which the prison-industrial complex has wrongfully imprisoned innocent people. Exoneration and liberation is God's work. In a beautiful example of allyship, king Lamoni chooses to use his political and personal power to assist Ammon in his call. By offering to ask for help from his friend king Antiomno (v. 4), Lamoni rejects any potential shame, embarrassment, or fear he might have of publicly taking up common cause with a Nephite. Instead, he immediately offers his full and complete support (v. 6) upon hearing Ammon's statement that God has called Ammon to this work (v. 5). Ammon's acceptance of Lamoni's offer is also a lovely example, one of recognizing and accepting the ways others may have spiritual, relational, or structural power that we may lack. As someone with a call from God and his own history working miracles, Ammon could have rejected Lamoni's offer of support. Instead, each man comes to the work with their own skills and access to power while also affirming the other. This is a critical component of community work.

Alma 20:10–14

The conversation between Lamoni and his father exemplifies the way prejudice and discrimination evolve from dehumanization into overt physical violence. Lamoni's father first reveals his bias when he talks about Ammon without acknowledging him: "Whither art thou going with this Nephite, who is one of the children of a liar?" (v. 10). To the king, Ammon is not a person worthy of notice. He is a faceless member of a group, not someone with a name and individual history. The king places Ammon in the category of Other, which allows him to call Ammon names to his face without recognizing his personhood.

The king's anger erupts into violence when Lamoni explains he is going to help free the sons of Mosiah from prison. To Lamoni's father, the Nephites are all liars and thieves, descended from a man who stole the brass plates and Urim and Thummim from the Lamanite ancestors.[94] This offers a small glimpse into the Lamanites' narrative of their dueling nations' origin story and what happened between Nephi and his brothers. Told from another point of view, the conflict might appear quite different from the one the text presents initially.

Although Ammon has yet to speak a word to Lamoni's father, Lamoni's father wants Ammon dead (v. 14). The king's anger suddenly escalates into physical threat, apparently in response to Lamoni's desire to help the sons of Mosiah escape prison. As far as the text reveals, none of the contemporaneous Nephites have hurt Lamoni's father, and Ammon certainly has never interacted with him. But his hate for an entire people is so great that he wishes for the death of a stranger. That is the logical end result of prejudice.

Alma 20:15–21

Lamoni's choice to stand up to his father shows an impressive moment of bravery. A person's rejection of prejudice and refusal to participate in violence and oppression may lead to internal family strife, as it does in this story. Lamoni transformed his personal views about the Nephites because of his association with Ammon. He sees injustice in the situation of the imprisoned sons of Mosiah and is ready to take action to help them. The way he has changed prompts him to see the world differently, and he reaches across systemic lines to help his former enemies. In response, his father becomes violent, ready to see his son—in addition to Ammon—dead rather than forming relationships and coming to the aid of those he hates. The father's overpowering prejudice primes him to want to kill his son for understanding the world in a different way than he does. Rejecting social divisions and loving our enemies is such a powerful threat to violence and hatred that those who hate will lash out, even at those they love most deeply.

---

94. 2 Nephi 5:12

In the section on Alma 3:8–10, we discussed how the Nephites' narrative around the curse of the Lamanites worked to keep the two people separate, effectively preventing them from loving one another. This exemplifies the same force of division, this time from the perspective of the Lamanites. The king's narrative of the Nephites as liars and thieves drives a fear that propels him toward violence. The entire purpose of that violence is to keep the two groups of people separated because love is too powerful a threat. To prevent individuals breaking that social constraint and loving one another, both sides enforce the division of the nations through violence and fear.

The idea of "blood [that] would cry from the ground to the Lord" for justice (v. 18) is not unique within the Book of Mormon. Other verses reference this concept of innocent blood calling out from death for the punishment of oppressors.[95] Yet this is the only one singling out an individual, both for the person who would die and the potential killer. Putting a face and name on this idea of a victim calling from the grave for justice changes the feeling of the verse. Rather than an anonymous group of saints who suffered at the hands of unnamed persecutors, this verse is about Lamoni's (potential) spilled blood and his father's soul. It tells readers God cares about each individual who dies at a site of oppression. To read this verse from a social justice perspective means replacing Lamoni's name with others who have been killed in innocence.[96] Ammon's warning to the king about the potential consequences of his actions is alarming but important to consider in these cases.

---

95. Such as 2 Nephi 26:3, 2 Nephi 28:10, 3 Nephi 9:11, Ether 8:22, and Mormon 8:40
96. At the time of this writing, that could mean replacing Lamoni's name with Breonna Taylor's name or with Eric Garner's. Or it may mean the names of immigrants who perish on their journey to reach safety, their names unknown to us but known to God. It is important to consider who, at the current moment, continues to die in innocence. Does their blood, like Lamoni's, cry out from the ground for justice?

Alma 20:22–27

Ammon asks for his brothers to be released from prison and for Lamoni's father to no longer be "displeased" with Lamoni (v. 24). This request is stirring. In a moment of intense emotion and danger, Ammon worries about the relationship between father and son. He does not want Lamoni's newfound love for him and God to disrupt the family relationship, no matter how prejudiced and reactionary Lamoni's father acts. Ammon's choice to privilege that family relationship and the wellbeing of Lamoni changes the king's heart as he sees how much Ammon loves his son. The testimony of "the great love" Ammon has for Lamoni smooths away the fear he has of the Nephites (v. 26). This is the power of love, moving almost immediately to conquer fear, anger, and prejudice. Once the king is no longer afraid for his son, his anger changes to generosity and gentleness.

Alma 20:29–30

The last two verses of this chapter describe the grief Ammon experiences as he sees the suffering of his brothers in prison. Between this story and Alma and Amulek's time in prison,[97] this section of the Book of Mormon gives a lot of detailed description of people in prison. The conditions of incarcerated people may be different, but these verses should prompt readers to consider those whom society puts in prison today and what sufferings we deem acceptable there. The words of Joseph Smith, written during his own time in prison, sound similar to the miseries of Ammon, Amulek, Aaron, Muloki, and Ammah: "O God, where art thou? And where is the pavilion that covereth thy hiding place? How long shall thy hand be stayed, and thine eye, yea thy pure eye, behold from the eternal heavens the wrongs of thy people and thy servants, and thine ear be penetrated with their cries? Yea, O Lord, how long shall they suffer these wrongs and unlawful oppressions, before thine heart shall be softened toward

---

97. Alma 14:18–26

them, and thy bowels be moved with compassion toward them?"[98]
With a modern history of wrongful incarceration and a sacred text
that testifies of God's concern for the sufferings of those imprisoned,
Mormons should have particular concerns about this issue today.

Alma 21:1–3

Names of people and land appear in interesting ways in these verses.
The Lamanites call their land Jerusalem, despite not having their
ancestral records and having "dwindled in unbelief."[99] The Lamanites have held on to at least part of their legacy through naming the
land. Jerusalem retains meaning for them, even when so much else
has been lost.

These verses also describe the nuance of the different groups living in the land of Nephi: the Amalekites and Amulonites, as Nephite
dissenters, remain distinct enough to have their own communities,
although the text will later reduce them to the label of "Lamanites."
Compare this use of a single name to king Benjamin's sermon in
which he gives the Mulekites and Nephites the unifying name of
Christ.[100] This purposely brought people to God through covenant.
In contrast, the text's tendency to erase different nationalities, and
to refer to diverse groups under the single identity of Nephite or
Lamanite, heightens conflict and oversimplifies the narrative.

Alma 21:4–6

Perhaps in the hopes of finding believers, Aaron first goes to the synagogues to preach. But while the Amalekites have built edifices and
gather to worship God, their belief is entirely superficial. Their religion does not reorient them toward justice or community. Instead,
it insulates them from having to change themselves or work for good

---

98. Doctrine and Covenants 121:1–3
99. Mosiah 1:5
100. Mosiah 1:11–12

because their religion tells them they are good. One of the great misconceptions of religion is that checking off a list of behaviors—in this case, building churches and gathering there to worship—makes people good, even when they continue to harm others and uphold systems of oppression. The Amalekites' focus is entirely on what their money and their hands can build, not on transforming their hearts.

Alma 21:15–17

Following their release from prison, Aaron and his companions return to the Amalekites. God frequently asks prophets and teachers to return to places where they have been rejected and mistreated. Moses returned to Egypt, Alma to Ammonihah, Abinadi to Lehi-Nephi. Harriet Tubman returned to slave states repeatedly. These people are not necessarily able to convince everyone or change the entire system, but they offer hope and freedom to some people. Their bravery in returning to places that hold great pain for them offers relief for the listeners who need their message and assistance. While Aaron and the other men did not reform the Amalekites as a whole, they brought liberation to a few.

Alma 21:20–23

These verses serve as an interesting comparison to verses 4–10 about worshiping in synagogues. King Lamoni also builds synagogues, but the faith community he creates is completely different. While the Amalekites' religion was superficial, Lamoni understands that faith requires structural change. While keeping the monarchical system, he tells the Lamanites "that they were a free people, that they were free from the oppressions of the king" (v. 21). A community truly transformed by God requires a political shift that emphasizes liberation.

Alma 22:1

Like Lamoni's wife—the inspiring queen of the Lamanites—Lamoni's father remains unnamed, creating some confusion about who is referenced under the title of king. Ammon's work could not have moved forward without Lamoni's wife or his father, and Ammon appears to have deep regard for them. Yet they do not have names. Telling someone's conversion story without naming them is problematic because it strips personhood from the story. Mere titles such as "father" and "king" are faceless and disempowering. It would be better for the text to leave out the name Korihor and refer to him as "an antichrist" than to exclude the names of these good Lamanite people. Repeatedly, who receives a name in the Book of Mormon indicates who the author regards as important. These people who made radical moves to love and follow God deserve recorded names.

Alma 22:2–3

Aaron uses the same language Ammon used when he approached king Lamoni.[101] The way these princes engage with people, demonstrating humility and willingness to serve, is extraordinary. Yet the king refuses Aaron's offer of servitude, instead asking for ministry and clarification for his confusion. He is troubled because Ammon's actions of goodness toward Lamoni disrupt the narrative he has of the Nephites. How incredible to be such a force for good in the world that a person troubles people's minds. Although it was not his intent, Ammon has overthrown the king's prejudices about the Nephites, causing disorientation and changed behavior. Ultimately, Ammon's love for Lamoni has caused Lamoni's father to question who he believes is good and what relationships ought to exist.

---

101. Alma 17:25

Alma 22:7–12

When Aaron asks the king whether he believes in God, the king responds by citing the Amalekites and their faith, indicating his knowledge of and acquaintance with people of faith. In this interesting moment, the king references his own willingness to allow religious freedom among the Amalekites, and his experience with them seems to have given him some kind of foundation to speak about faith. By letting God flourish in others' lives, the king has a spiritual connection that helps him in his own journey. Yet, the Amalekites were some of the most violent people in the Book of Mormon,[102] and they end up leading the effort to destroy the people of Anti-Nephi-Lehi.[103] Ultimately, the Amalekites are not good examples of people of faith. However, that does not stop them from inadvertently acting as a catalyst for the king's conversion.

Aaron begins the dialogue with two questions about what the king believes, and both times the king responds with trust in Aaron's witness (v. 7 and 11). When talking about issues of social justice and oppression, the questions of what people believe are foundational: Do you believe? Do you believe the stories of undocumented immigrants? Do you believe in the experiences of queer members of the church? The king's willingness to believe in Aaron's words, without his own witness, is powerful. Believing someone else's words, trusting in their stories without needing to experience them oneself, is a spiritual gift. Lacking omniscience, our willingness to be in relationship with people who provide a diversity of witnesses can help us understand injustice in the world with greater clarity. This is why the king's response is so beautiful: he repeatedly hears Aaron's witness, restates it back, and has faith in its truth.

---

102. Alma 43:6
103. Alma 27:2–3

Alma 22:15–18

As Lamoni's father cries out with longing for atonement and eternal life, he falls to the ground as if dead. This is incredibly similar to Lamoni's experience, as well as the experiences of Lamoni's wife and household,[104] yet conversion does not appear again in this specific way anywhere else in the Book of Mormon. Possibly, spiritual collapse is a cultural practice within this group of Lamanites, or maybe there is another cause. The way God moves with these Lamanites looks distinct from the way God moves with other nations. How can we better note the freedom in which the Spirit shows up in its varying particularity for different people? Not everyone experiences a burning in the bosom or a still small voice or a desire to weep. Sometimes God speaks in a shout; sometimes people fall to the floor. Religions should avoid confining spiritual movement to a small number of acceptable experiences. The Book of Mormon itself offers a multitude of disparate examples of people experiencing God in strikingly diverse ways. The breadth and depth of worship in the Book of Mormon would not necessarily be welcome in the pews today. That is a loss. When a church insists on worshiping only through quiet, calm, and sedate environments, it cannot hear the rich and varied languages of a wild and untamed God. Worship, praise, and song do not have to look a certain way for God to speak to people. By acknowledging and celebrating the great diversity of ways in which people feel the Spirit, a greater number of people feel they belong in the faith community.

Alma 22:19–22

Aaron's fear in the face of "the determination of the queen" is unsurprising given his personal experiences with "the hardness of the hearts" (v. 22) of the Lamanites.[105] His time of suffering in prison gave

104. Alma 18–19
105. Alma 20:29–30

him a very different perspective than Ammon about the cruelty of the Lamanites. What do prisons reveal about our hearts and the hearts of others in our community?

Alma 22:25–26

The king uses his power to calm the people, putting his body between the angry crowd and Aaron and his brethren. Immediately afterward, he gives the platform to Aaron, letting him speak directly to the people while simultaneously ensuring Aaron's safety. This is a great use of his own privilege. The king intervenes to stop violence, prepares the people to overcome their prejudice and listen to a Nephite, and then steps back to allow someone else to speak. Anyone with authority seeking to give voice to a marginalized population should follow this example.

Alma 22:27–33

This long section about the details of land boundaries, where it divides between nations, and who lives where, seems a strange interjection in the narrative. At first, the particular details of geography and location appear unnecessarily specific. The importance of these verses lies in the context of what is about to happen with the people: all of these land borders and delineations of nations will radically shift with the conversion of the Lamanites and the creation of the Anti-Nephi-Lehies. That reformation of identity will breach boundaries between peoples and territories. While humans carefully drew these specific lines to divide the land, God will enter in and entirely disrupt it all. The gospel brings Nephites—the sons of Mosiah—into Lamanite land, and then Lamanites—the Anti-Nephi-Lehies—into Nephite land, prompting the Nephites to voluntarily give up territory to their former enemies. This passage emphasizing the rigidity of borders underscores how both nations knew exactly which people belonged where and which land belonged to each group. But the gospel breaks down borders, upends expectations, and destroys divisions.

Alma 23:1–2

The king establishes policies that protect Ammon, Aaron, Omner, and Himni's safety, hinting at their experiences in the past. The list of what is no longer allowed in the Lamanite kingdom tells the history of what has happened in the past. A society's laws give insight into what that society has been doing. The particular list describes what the sons of Mosiah have suffered. These verses give a greater sense of the animus between the nations and the bravery of these men to go into such a violent place. The change in the law is also one of the most important outcomes of their work. Even if they did not gain any converts to the church, the sons of Mosiah could celebrate the institutional change of a policy that moves a society away from violence and toward acceptance. The work of the gospel can include the establishment of laws that respect others' humanity. Any effort which increases inclusion and dialogue, breaking down divisions between groups of people, is of God.

Alma 23:4–7

How is "success" defined and used for missionaries and those sharing the gospel? Be careful of definitions which count numbers of converts as success. While quantitative numbers may matter, the focus should always be on the qualitative changes of the people. If success is rooted in large numbers, then having few or no baptisms is failure. Transformations of hearts and minds may occur over a long period of time, and we do not want to ignore how God moves us into places and outcomes which may not be what we wanted or anticipated. Setting goals and defining success narrowly may cause people to not see how God performed miracles through their work. In this case, the miracle is less about how many thousands of people converted and more about how God changed their hearts to such a degree that they laid down their weapons and came to love their former enemies. These extraordinary people undergo an experience so transformative that they create bridges across chasms of hate between people. That is the measure of what the gospel can do.

In verse 5, the text pairs a "knowledge of the Lord" with believing "in the traditions of the Nephites." Those two things are different and ought to be kept separate. Not all of the traditions of the Nephites are rooted in righteousness, as can be seen in the lives of king Noah,[106] the people of Ammonihah,[107] the cleansing of the church in Zarahemla,[108] and many other stories in the Book of Mormon. The Nephites are frequently misaligned with God, and some of their traditions—such as bloodlust and hatred toward the Lamanites[109]—are wicked and destructive. Linking one nation's traditions so closely to a knowledge of God labels an entire complex culture as righteous while also stamping another culture as evil. That teaches people that part of conversion means despising their own history and disavowing their heritage rather than carefully sifting through what is good and true and what they want to leave behind. Every nation has historical failures and cultural malpractices. But if groups get reductively labeled as good and evil, then converts may feel a pressure to leave behind healthy, beautiful traditions that may strengthen their new faith community. A relationship with God should not be linked in any way to an acceptance of the superiority of Nephite culture. It eradicates an important process of carrying on ancestral truth and replaces it with self-loathing.

Alma 23:14–15

Superficially, the Amalekites and Amulonites may seem the likeliest of converts: the Amalekites already had churches and religion; the Amulonites were former priests. Yet these two groups not only do not convert, they actively stir up violence against those who do.[110] Their dangerous pride leads them to believe that they know everything they need to about God. They appear to have the structures of religion,

---

106. Mosiah 11
107. Alma 8
108. Alma 4
109. Alma 26:23–25
110. Alma 24:1

and yet their anger is so destructive that they engage in some of the most terrible violence of the Book of Mormon. Their membership, or even leadership, in a religious institution does not prevent them from dehumanizing others. Witnessing the soul-changing conversion of their brethren enrages them to the point of engaging in genocide.

The heart-hardening language used to describe the Amalekites and the Amulonites echoes of contagion spreading into villages and cities. Violence is a contagious disease that can move through communities as an epidemic.[111] Importantly, this hardening of hearts occurs simultaneously to the gospel moving through the land. The two run parallel as one reacts to the other. When social justice spreads and grows, violence finds a way to evolve and reappear in newly malicious ways. The protests of the suffrage movement moved in tandem with imprisonment and forced feedings of women in the United States. Gandhi's noncooperation movement and the protests of Tiananmen Square met a surge in violence and oppression. Efforts to increase justice and righteousness often prompt greater persecution and abuse.

Alma 23:16–17

The ability to rename oneself after a personal or communal transformation is a powerful and liberating ritual in human identity. It distinguishes oneself from a previous life or a past way of being in the world, particularly if the previous name had associations of oppression. This is why many descendants of enslaved people decide to rename themselves, removing the enslaver's name from their family identity. It is why respect for a transgender person's chosen name is so important. Throughout sacred text, renaming gives people a way of showing their internal change. Abram and Sarai's shift to Abraham and Sarah represented their new relationship with God.[112] The chil-

---

111. For more on violence as an epidemic and how public health strategies can stop it, see the organization Cure Violence at www.cvg.org.

112. Genesis 17:5–17

dren of Amulon and the other priests of Noah adopted the name of Nephi.[113] This powerful gesture displays how a person is no longer a part of a former community and how their previous life no longer represents who they are. Respecting and celebrating a name change shows regard for the other person's humanity.

Alma 23:18

The final verse of this chapter is one of the most violent in the Book of Mormon because of the place it occupies in this story and the way it has been interpreted and contextualized. Claiming that the Anti-Nephi-Lehies "began to be a very industrious people" and "the curse of God did no more follow them" strips the power of this incredible conversion story, rooting it again in deep racism. It denies the power of a people willing to upend their lives in their desire for a consecrated life. While "the curse of God" could be interpreted in a multiplicity of ways, including as simply an absence of a relationship with the divine, the official footnote to the phrase directs readers to 3 Nephi 2:15, which specifically describes the Lamanites' skin turning "white like unto the Nephites." This recasting of the Anti-Nephi-Lehies' story as a transformation to whiteness is violence. Their narrative marks an extraordinary transformation of a community in the Book of Mormon, and these words reduce that change to the color of their skin. God runs through all people, and no change of skin tone can affect that eternal truth. Claiming otherwise manipulates the gospel, a terrible tragedy in a moment of miraculous conversion.

This verse could be interpreted completely differently than in terms of skin color. However, that is not what has historically happened in Mormonism. This has caused generations of harm as children and families suffered the burden of colorist theology.[114] The damage

---

113. Mosiah 25:12

114. For an excellent personal essay on this topic, see April Carlson's "Whiter My God to Thee," *The Exponent Blog*, January 30, 2020. https://www.the-exponent.com/whiter-my-god-to-thee/.

this verse and its history causes cannot be undone through simply removing it from the text. Therefore, it should remain in place with added commentary making explicit that the idea of skin lightening due to righteousness is racist and wrong. The prophets and scholars who wrote and interpreted these words in that way made a mistake. Like so many others in the Book of Mormon attempting to follow God, they are human, fallible, and worthy of love and compassion.

Alma 24:1-4

The Lamanites may have resented and hated the Anti-Nephi-Lehies, but it is the Amalekites and Amulonites—people who had some relationship and history with religion—who are so enraged that they promote violence and rebellion. Although the text will later simply refer to them as "Lamanites," in verse 5, these verses give a better view of this complex society and who within it has a propensity for aggression. The increase in hatred from the Lamanites, Amulonites, and Amalekites is a direct reaction to the Anti-Nephi-Lehies' increased love for God and goodwill toward the Nephites. Love will frequently prompt hatred, and scripture depicts how hatred will rise in parallel with a rise in love and tolerance.

The text indicates that the Lamanite king confers the kingdom on his son, and renames him Anti-Nephi-Lehi, then dies soon afterward. Still we never learn the king's name, this important character who played a critical role in a beautiful mass conversion story. The king dies at a difficult time for the people as they mobilize for war within their society, one of the most challenging times for him to die as the community struggles with the divisions resulting from conversion and resentment. Death is always hard to understand, but this season of compounded trials prompts difficult theological questions. This must have been an extraordinarily troubling time for the Anti-Nephi-Lehies.

Alma 24:5–6

This council of the sons of Mosiah, Lamoni, and Anti-Nephi-Lehi signals an incredible meeting in which they definitively articulate their decision to follow through with their promise to never participate in violence again. These statements of commitment from the people are lived testimony, alive and vibrant with how they act and what they do, not just what they believe. They add a breadth and depth to their faith beyond what even most disciples experience. This group seriously and substantively changed their societal structures as a reflection of their beliefs. They share their testimony through their lives, not simply their words. This is what a "mighty change" of heart, or radical conversion, looks like.[115] It prompts readers to question what conversion looks like in their own lives. How have we changed and lived differently because of what we know? The Anti-Nephi-Lehies model individual and structural change due to faith in God and love for others.

Alma 24:7

"Beloved brethren" is a beautiful phrase employed by Book of Mormon prophets, particularly Jacob[116] and Alma.[117] But the more inclusive phrase, "beloved people" gets used in dialogue by Anti-Nephi-Lehi and, in all the Book of Mormon, only describes the Anti-Nephi-Lehies.[118] Perhaps it is not coincidental that disciples from the Lamanite nation use language inclusive of women, given the Book of Mormon's hints that the Lamanite men treated women with greater respect than did the Nephite men.[119] Jacob preached of a

---

115. Mosiah 5:2

116. For example, 2 Nephi 9–10

117. For example, Alma 5 and 7

118. The text refers to them as "beloved people" in Alma 27:30.

119. Jacob 2:35 and 3:5–7. For more on this, read Joseph Spencer's *1 Nephi: A Brief Theological Introduction* Provo, Utah: Neal A. Maxwell Institute, 2020 and Deidre

radical and necessary change in the Nephites' treatment of women.[120] Here, another prophet counsels his people on a revolutionary and structural change needed in their society. The choice to call them beloved emphasizes the close relationship between prophet and people, a tie that helps a leader usher in difficult transformations.

Alma 24:8–9

For the second time,[121] correspondence with the Nephites is identified as part of the evolution of this community. Never underestimate the power of speaking across enemy lines, developing relationships with people who have been historically and systematically kept distant from your own people. Established religious restrictions and cultural divisions successfully prevented dialogue and friendship between the nations for almost their entire existence. Friendships which cross boundaries and expectations are one of the most powerful tools in the work of God, including the work of social justice. For the Anti-Nephi-Lehies, opening a correspondence with the Nephites pivoted their conversion narrative because it disrupted the demarcations of identity and provided an impetus for changing their hearts and abandoning their hatred.

Alma 24:9–11

One of Atonement's greatest gifts is the ability to change and not carry guilt for our past life and former versions of ourselves. Bearing unproductive guilt only prevents us from the growth which prompts us to do better and be better.[122] Part of Jesus' work is to assist us

---

Nicole Green's *Jacob: A Brief Theological Introduction* Provo, Utah: Neal A. Maxwell Institute, 2020.

120. For more explanation, see Fatimah Salleh and Margaret Olsen Hemming. *The Book of Mormon for the Least of These, Vol. 1*, Salt Lake City, UT: BCC Press, 111–115.

121. The first was Alma 23:18.

122. The way Alma uses "guilt" here is closer to how we defined "shame" in the section on Alma 14:6–7.

in moving into the next season of our lives once we have filled the requirements of true repentance.

Anti-Nephi-Lehi speaks of his own people as "the most lost of all mankind" (v. 11), an unhelpful comparative theology. While he may be speaking hyperbolically, he just testified of the gift of setting down guilt. Clearly, their violent society did terrible things, but trying to assess which society is the wickedest in human history seems beyond the human mind. People can be lost without being the most lost, and clearly seeing one's own failure and sins without self-loathing is more productive and healthy than claiming to be the worst in human history. Whether claiming blessings from God or personal sin, it never serves people well to compare themselves to other individuals and groups. Everyone travels their own journey with God, and none can compare with any other. The phrase "most lost" also sits in tension with Anti-Nephi-Lehi's description of them as his "best beloved" people (v. 12), a unique phrase in all the standard works of scripture. The love for God and one another in this group inspires awe.

Alma 24:12–16

God told the Anti-Nephi-Lehies to lay down their weapons and never fight again because God loves their souls and God loves their children. The references to future generations speak to how this covenant to renounce violence is a work of the present being seen from the future. The Anti-Nephi-Lehies perceive how their decisions affect not only themselves, but also their posterity. The change starts with them, but it will ripple with consequences into the future. They become good ancestors through thinking about how their choices will impact their descendants. Our testimonies, ideas about the nature of God, cultural practices we change, and sacrifices we make all influence those who follow us. By taking notice of that at the site of lived testimony and structural change, the Anti-Nephi-Lehies transform the trajectory of their people.

The Anti-Nephi-Lehies hide their weapons in the ground so they are not even tempted to use them. To avoid lives of violence, they renounce their tools of violence. Their self-awareness acknowledges a propensity to slip back into their old ways, so they make a provision to prevent it. They take actionable and clear steps to walk away from hatred and violence. They are extraordinary examples of setting up boundaries for themselves to prevent a return to harming others. These actions are intrinsic to their testimonies. By naming the ways they have hurt people, and laying a plan for substantive change, the Anti-Nephi-Lehies testify of God with their lives.

Social justice from a spiritual perspective relies on action as testimony. That requires recognizing our social location and privileges, educating ourselves, and then becoming engaged. Voting, protesting, abandoning violence, working to build an equitable society, and standing in and speaking up about sites of oppression become a form of vibrant, lived testimony. Given that each of us carries some kind of blood on our metaphorical swords, a life of social justice prompts us to explore how we can begin a life in which we wipe those swords clean and then take concrete actions to never stain them again. The Anti-Nephi-Lehies bury their swords in the dirt "that they may be kept bright," a paradox that nicely parallels others in the gospel, like the Savior of the world being born in a lowly manger. The steps God asks us to take in order to keep our own personal swords clean and bright may surprise or even scare us, but this is the call the Anti-Nephi-Lehies followed.

Alma 24:17–19

Their testimony is to God but also to all people, making their covenant not just with God but with humanity. Their testimonies resulted in real change, at great cost. They name the harm of the past and replace it with something else: "rather than shed the blood of their brethren they would give up their own lives; and rather than take away from a brother they would give unto him" (v. 18). They did not just give up their weapons of war, but "buried the weapons of war, for peace" (v. 19). What we give up needs replacement by something good and true: *Rather than acting with prejudice, I will speak into a new love. Rather than grinding the faces of the poor, I will share what I have. Rather than simply not being racist, I will be anti-racist.* There is a part of testimony that is "rather than"—that acknowledges where we have been, who we were, and accepts a new life with new ways of being in the world.

Alma 24:21-27

The narrator of this story—almost certainly Mormon—gives his own summary and interpretation of this horrible moment of genocide. It is a shame that in a story as heartbreaking as this one, readers do not have a firsthand account from those who experienced it or watched as their loved ones died. Instead, a Nephite—far removed geographically and historically—describes and comments on the meaning of events. In this case, the narrator is far too eager to make this story clean and acceptable. By writing, "we know that they are blessed, for they have gone to dwell with their God," (v. 22) the narrator glosses over the grief and suffering of a thousand innocent people dying in terrible violence. There is no description of the lamentation and mourning that the text sometimes shares in the wake of war.[123] Here, the text does not hold space for the deep violence that occurs, nor the grieving afterward. Instead, it tries to assure readers that what happened was acceptable, as in verses 26-27, which attempts to justify the deaths by numbering new conversions. More than a thousand righteous people died horrible deaths for their faith. Their families and communities mourned their loss. Sitting with that anguish can be more important than making meaning from it.

The complex conversions occur in a period of bloodshed and death. The fact that it took watching so many innocent people die for the Lamanites to recognize the wrong in their actions is disturb-

---

123. For example, Alma 28:4–6

ing. Conversion should not have to happen at the sites of harrowing violence. If nothing moves us but death and destruction, our hearts are far too cold.[124] When death is the moment of our awakening, we need to carefully interrogate our conversions. Questioning why we had to witness that level of violence will help point us to the further progress we need to make.

The narrator problematically asserts that those deaths were part of God's plan to bring people to salvation. A theology that professes people die and suffer for God's purposes—"thus we see that the Lord worketh in many ways to the salvation of his people" (v. 27)—does not withstand close investigation. Those people who loved God and died following the covenant they made deserved protection. It is wrong for people to show up to bear testimony and do good and lose their lives. While some good came of it, claiming that it happened for the purpose of that good is not right.

At the same time, this story exemplifies a society transformed by the power of nonviolence. The relationship between victim and aggressor is so utterly transformed that they are able to lay down weapons of genocide and become a peaceful, integrated, welcoming community. This critical moment of choosing nonviolence has more lasting influence than all the coming bloodshed between and within the nations. It is a beautiful illustration of Dr. Martin Luther King's statement: "The aftermath of nonviolence is the creation of the beloved community, so that when the battle is over, a new relationship comes into being between the oppressed and the oppressor."[125] This violent event differs from many others in the Book of Mormon because of the nonviolent component. The action of nonviolent pro-

---

124. For instance, while the death of George Floyd acted as an awakening for many white Americans in 2020, we should not need to watch nine minutes of a person struggling to breathe and ultimately dying on the sidewalk to believe that Black lives matter.

125. Martin Luther King, Jr. *The Birth of a New Nation*. Sermon delivered at Dexter Avenue Baptist Church, Montgomery, AL, April 7, 1957.

test by those who died reconstructed the society in an incomparable way to any other brutal period in the text.[126]

Alma 24:28–30

In the description of who converted, the label of "Lamanites" becomes more complex again. The Amalekites and Amulonites— people who once had or currently have religion and who were descended from Nephites—were the most vicious attackers and also declined to repent and convert. Not a single one regretted their actions enough to open their hearts to the gospel. While the Lamanites sometimes get described as bloodthirsty,[127] at this site of one of the most disturbing battles in the Book of Mormon, the people who were descended from Nephi remained hardened while some of those who descended from Laman and Lemuel repented. Once again, the differences between the nations are far more complex than the text superficially indicates.

Alma 25:1–3

After committing genocide against their own people, the Lamanites blame the Nephites rather than engaging in introspection. They take out their guilt on the people of Ammonihah, the city that burned women and children alive in front of Alma and Amulek. Their response to having done something for which they seem to feel shame or regret is one of self-loathing. Instead of confronting their own actions, they enact violence on other folk. This happens when people cannot live with what they have done, so they continue with the same behavior and simply change their victims. Responding to guilt by blaming someone else and repeating the same kind of harmful actions again is not an uncommon reaction. This is how violence and oppression shift and reincarnate in new forms but with

---

126. For further reading see Mason and Pulsipher. *Proclaim Peace.*
127. Such as in Mosiah 10:11–12

similar results, something those who fight for social justice too often witness.

Although the text previously claimed God called on the Lamanites to destroy Ammonihah because of the inhabitants' wickedness, here the text explains the Lamanites' rage and how they redirected their aggression toward the Nephites. Is the text claiming the Lamanites' anger and aggression stemming from their own violent actions were sanctioned by God? Or that God used the Lamanites' murderous hatred for God's own ends in an effort to punish Ammonihah? It seems more likely that this violent society—one in which one nation burns women and children alive and their adversary cuts down a thousand of their unarmed kinfolk—is so far from God that none of their actions have divine approval. Too much evil exists on both sides.

Alma 25:4–5

The distinction between the Lamanites and Nephites gets blurred throughout this story, but this verse underlines how strange the distinction has become. The text states the Nephites killed almost all of the Amulonites, who were descendants of the priests of Noah. It places that group of Amulonites within the umbrella term of Lamanites. Yet the priests of Noah were descendants of Nephites who intermarried with Lamanite girls. When the Nephites kill the Amulonites, they kill people who genetically belong to both the Nephites and the Lamanites, yet the text labels the conflict as simply between Nephites and Lamanites. Clearly Nephite and Lamanite have no biological meaning. These are social groups, where belonging depends on social networks, not on blood. This makes any claim of a hereditary physical curse which distinguishes one group from the other even more absurd and harmful.

The Amulonites' use of fire to torture and kill the converted Lamanites emphasizes the blurring of nationality and cultural legacy. Three other instances of death through fire have occurred in the Book of Mormon: the deaths of Abinadi, king Noah, and the execution of women and children in Ammonihah. It is the Nephites who use fire as a weapon in all three cases. When the Amulonites attack the Lamanites with fire, they echo the actions of their ancestors and kin. The differentiating labels become almost meaningless as righteous Lamanites suffer and die at the hands of descendants of Nephi, through a practice unique to the Nephites within the text. Who belongs to which group depends on the choice of individuals regarding beliefs and traditions, not on genetic inheritance.

Alma 25:6–9

Once again, a mass conversion of Lamanites occurs at the site of war. The loss of life prompts the Lamanites to remember the words of the sons of Mosiah, although they refused to listen in a time of peace. Although abundant evidence points to the enormous problems of this society, the fact that so much conversion occurs in moments of horror signals something terribly wrong. The cycle of mass conversion prompting anger and violence, which then encourages more conversion, seems never-ending in these chapters, a theme underscored by the narrator's claim that the Lamanites continue "at this day" (v. 9) to hunt the Amulonites. It perpetuates just as powerfully as the pride cycle throughout the Book of Mormon.

In the Bible, conversion and faith typically lead to God's protection and victory, just as exile and suffering frequently follow disobedience. In the Book of Mormon, the opposite often appears true: faith and obedience lead to persecution, fleeing to the wilderness, or even death. In the conversion stories of the people who followed Alma, the women and children of Ammonihah, the Anti-Nephi-Lehies, the Lamanites in these verses, and so many others in the Book of Mormon, collective trauma accompanies people's choice to follow God. In this text, living into faith comes with serious and often violent consequences. People suffer terribly for the decision to repent and believe. While individuals, particularly prophets, sometimes struggle in the Bible, no Biblical examples of conversion lead to genocide or slavery. More than any other book of scripture, the Book of Mormon tells us that following God is a dangerous road to take. Faith does not guarantee safety and security; it simply takes us on a journey with God.

Alma 25:17

The "success" the sons of Mosiah "rejoice" in appears complex and difficult to define. Large numbers of baptisms among the Lamanites get interwoven with genocide, war, and torture. God may have answered their prayers, but that came in the midst of horror. Readers can hold those two facts simultaneously and feel gratitude for the mass conversions and also recognize the sufferings of martyrs. Do not let one overpower or usurp the other. Notice how God came through for these people in the darkest of times, but do not ignore the vile things that happened in parallel with the beautiful transformation of this society.

Alma 26:1–10

As Ammon rejoices, he drifts toward a narrative of centering himself instead of the converted Lamanites. Notice how many times he uses the words "I," "us," and "we," in these verses: "how great reason have we to rejoice" (v. 1), "we have been made instruments in the hands of God" (v. 3), and "if we had not come up out of the land of Zarahemla" (v. 9). Although thousands of innocent Lamanites have recently perished, Ammon seems to see only success. He talks about the Lamanites as living in darkness, entirely separated from God, saved through the actions of himself and his brothers. By so clearly separating himself from the Lamanites, he tells a story in which he is the critical ingredient of conversion rather than a facilitator in a relationship between the Lamanites and God. Ammon claims the Lamanites would be "strangers to God" without the sons of Mosiah, yet there is no way for him to know this. He does not know, or fails to acknowledge, the different ways (possibly through Abish, who was already converted)

God would have worked without Ammon's work. Thinking about the events that transpired as his own success has led him to speak as if he is the irreplaceable part of the story. This causes Aaron to rebuke him in verse 10. Aaron's words are perfectly framed: "thy joy doth carry thee away unto boasting" (v. 10). Ammon's reductionist view of the events, ignoring the struggles and grief the Anti-Nephi-Lehies experienced, has led him to center himself. Aaron's gentle reproof prompts Ammon to refocus on the work of God.

Alma 26:11–16

Although at first Ammon seems to double down on his message, his framing significantly changes beginning in verse 11. Instead of speaking of himself and his good work, he shifts toward praising God and singing redeeming love. Although he still veers toward celebrating himself, particularly in verses 13 and 15, overall the monolog turns toward admitting his own weakness and celebrating the power and grace of God.

In his sermon, "Drum Major Instinct," Dr. Martin Luther King Jr. warned of the human instinct to "be out front, a desire to lead the parade."[128] He told of the biblical story of James and John asking Jesus to promise them the right to sit on his right and left hand. Like Aaron in this chapter, Jesus gently rebuked James and John, telling them that glory will be given to those who are prepared and reminding them that in the gospel, leaders act as humble servants and do not ask for authority over others.[129] Dr. King warned listeners of a desire for importance which leads to "snobbish exclusivism" and about "a need that some people have to feel superior." Instead of seeking glory in our work, we ought to be, as Ammon says, "instruments in his hands" (v. 15), or, as Dr. King said, a drum major for justice, peace, and righteousness.

---

128. Martin Luther King, Jr. *Drum Major Instinct*. Sermon delivered at Ebenezer Baptist Church, Atlanta, GA, Feb. 4, 1968.
129. Mark 10:36–45

Alma 26:17–22

Ammon moves further towards a humble, egalitarian framing of the narrative. Instead of speaking solely of the Lamanites' and their failings, he includes himself and his brothers in the need for repentance and forgiveness: "Who could have supposed that our God would have been so merciful as to have snatched *us* from our awful, sinful, and polluted state" (v. 17, emphasis added). As Ammon tells the story of their conversion, he recognizes the miracle of his own salvation and the undeserved grace he received at the "everlasting gulf of death and misery" (v. 20). By openly speaking of his own story, Ammon connects himself to the Lamanites instead of setting them apart as different. God saved the Anti-Nephi-Lehies *and* the sons of Mosiah from a polluted state. While one group acted as missionaries in these events, in a broader, more fundamental way, they are the same.

This shift in perspective changes the connotation of some of his previous statements. "Yea, they were encircled about with everlasting darkness and destruction" (v. 15) is a damning description when Ammon speaks of the Lamanites as different from himself. But when he connects his own conversion to theirs, his words instead express a personal memory of how it felt to be cut off from God and a gratitude that people he cares about no longer have to experience that feeling. Tying their conversions together links their common humanity. Aaron's interruption of Ammon moved Ammon from a hierarchical framing of being the salvation of the Lamanites to one in which he sees how deeply bound up his story is with the Lamanites' and how their faith journeys are actually the same. This new mindset reflects the words of Gangulu activist Lilla Watson and Australian Aboriginal Rights groups, who have said, "If you have come here to help me, you are wasting your time. But if you have come because your liberation is bound up with mine, then let us work together."[130]

---

130. Attributed to Watson at the World Conference to Review and Appraise the Achievements of the United Nations Decade for Women, July 15–26, 1985, Nairobi, Kenya.

Alma 26:23–25

Certain moments in the Book of Mormon undermine the authors' broad claim of the righteousness of the Nephites relative to the Lamanites. These verses give important missing insight into the Nephite society, particularly their feelings about violence and their antagonism toward the Lamanites. Not only did the brethren of the sons of Mosiah laugh at the sons of Mosiah for having the idea of preaching to the Lamanites, they mocked and dismissed them. They suggested that instead of engaging in missionary work, the Nephites should raise an army and kill all the Lamanites. They believed the world would be better without the entire Lamanite society, a society which included Abish, Lamoni, and thousands of the most faithful people in all of the Book of Mormon. Hatred, prejudice, and blood-thirstiness echo in these verses.

The sons of Mosiah were called into a space in which generations of enmity and centuries of hostility had hardened into a fixed point of view. Perhaps this is why they needed their extended time in the wilderness to prepare before entering the land of Nephi.[131] It takes time and effort to divest ourselves of the prejudiced narratives our own people teach us. Coming to an enemy with a spirit of real love and service would require the kind of fasting and prayer they employed in the wilderness. To overcome racism, homophobia, sexism, or any other learned intolerance, we must be willing to reject our culture's messaging and spend time in our own metaphorical wildernesses until we are ready to come into community in a spirit of love and service.

Alma 26:27–37

Ammon returns to the language of success, but his tone has changed. For the first time, Ammon describes how he and his brothers almost gave up on their mission in a period of depression. He shares more

---

131. Alma 17:9

details of their struggles in the Lamanites' land. His account of what happened to them gives more insight into their hardships during this period than the previous several chapters. God's mercy supported them but did not remove their sufferings. First, God reminded them that the Lamanites are their brethren, not their adversaries, by telling them to "Go amongst thy brethren, the Lamanites, and bear with patience thine afflictions, and I will give unto you success" (v. 27). God asks them to bear their afflictions with patience. Then, God's comfort takes the form of a promise of success, yet the success Ammon describes in the following verses is different than readers might expect. It is the creation of a beloved community.

Ammon recognizes the depth of the Anti-Nephi-Lehies' conversion, not just the number of people converted. When Ammon states he and his brothers "can witness of their sincerity, because of their love towards their brethren and also towards us" (v. 31), he gives a much better definition of success. The witness of real success is love. And although they went on their missions thinking about the numbers of people they might convert (v. 30), Ammon upends that idea by emphasizing that what matters is the love these people now show for one another and for them. That powerful love exceeds any love Ammon has ever seen, including among the Nephites. He speaks about what love does, how it is a force for deliberate and significant action among the Lamanites. Conversion is not about a tally but about a transformation.

Do not miss that one of the greatest stories of conversion in the Book of Mormon is rooted in a love which lays down weapons, opens communication with an enemy, and builds community. The faith of the Anti-Nephi-Lehies is not without works. As Ammon recognizes that, he also acknowledges for the first time that many people died in this process. Ammon's celebration has become more nuanced since Aaron's gentle admonition, and he now speaks of his own sufferings and the death inextricably interwoven into this beautiful story. Ammon's joy also becomes deeper and richer, and he connects himself more closely with the Anti-Nephi-Lehies as he references not only his joy, but also his salvation and "redemption from everlasting wo" (v. 36). He brings in a familial tie to the Lamanites by recognizing their common descent from Israel. In a particularly poetic moment, he expresses gratitude to God for caring for them as "wanderers in a strange land" (v. 36), and praises a God who "is mindful of *every* people, *whatsoever land they may be in*: yea, he numbereth his people, and his bowels of mercy are over *all* the earth" (v. 37, emphasis added). These last few verses display some of the most powerfully inclusive and connective in all the Book of Mormon.

Alma 27:1–3

The story of the Amalekites in the conversion of the Anti-Nephi-Lehies is one of violent people seeking any justification for more violence. After slaughtering the Anti-Nephi-Lehies, the Lamanites felt so angry that they attacked the Nephites.[132] Here, after losing their battle with the Nephites, the Amalekites foment rage against the Anti-Nephi-Lehies and return to killing them. They are determined to stir up people to anger and destruction, no matter how weak their excuse. The Amalekites appear to excel in manipulating others in their appetite for bloodshed. These chapters offer a cautionary story for societies considering war. They prompt questions, such as: Who is controlling the narrative in a mobilization toward war? What is that narrative? What is the motive for violence? This account of the Amalekites and Lamanites shows that the choice of which stories to tell, and the way those stories get interpreted, affects whether people choose war.

Alma 27:4–7

Two phrases in verse 4 frame this episode of Ammon conversing with the king to save the Anti-Nephi-Lehies. The first is "dearly beloved," a phrase reminiscent of Jacob's use of "beloved brethren"[133] and almost

---

132. Alma 25:1
133. For example, 2 Nephi 10:1 or Jacob 4:2.

a direct reference to the description of the Anti-Nephi-Lehies as "beloved people" in verse 7. The sons of Mosiah dearly love these people. The second phrase is when Ammon and his brothers are "moved with compassion." Powerful compassion provokes action. Ammon does not simply pray for the Anti-Nephi-Lehies and hope things improve for them. He cares enough to do something. The phrase "moved with compassion" is unusual in scripture. The only people associated with it are Jesus in the midst of performing miracles, and the works done for and by the Anti-Nephi-Lehies.[134] Moving in compassion gets interwoven with performing miracles. It spurs people to take great risks and change lives.

Ammon's idea of asking the Nephites for sanctuary seems incredibly bold, given the Nephites' mockery and threats of violence toward the Lamanites when the sons of Mosiah proposed teaching in the land of Nephi.[135] But Ammon is so deeply "moved with compassion" that he thinks perhaps a miracle will intervene to prompt his people to act better and lay down their prejudice in this horrible moment. Ammon is the son of Mosiah and likely saw his father joyfully welcome Alma, Limhi, and their people as refugees into the land of Zarahemla.[136] Perhaps Ammon hoped the Nephites could embrace that legacy of welcoming the stranger into their lands. In the case of Mosiah, the descendants of Zeniff were ethnically Nephites. Here, the proposal is even greater: a radical hospitality of welcoming people who you once hated. Ammon's intense love for the Anti-Nephi-Lehies and their love for him give him the bravery to craft such a bold plan.

Terrified of what might happen to his beloved friends, Ammon creates an idea for action and goes to Anti-Nephi-Lehi for approval, then asks God for divine confirmation. Ammon did not wait for God

---

134. In the New Testament, Matt. 9:36, 14:14; Mark 1:41, 6:34. The other reference in the Book of Mormon is Alma 53:13, when the Anti-Nephi-Lehies consider breaking their covenant of nonviolence in order to protect the Nephites.

135. Alma 26:23–25

136. Mosiah 22:14 and 24:25

to hand him a plan; he actively created an answer and then sought confirmation.

Alma 27:8–13

Anti-Nephi-Lehi offers to submit his people to the Nephites as slaves, but Ammon declares that slavery is outlawed in Nephite land, a legacy of Benjamin's efforts to build Zion.[137] Once again, Ammon walks in this important tradition of his father and grandfather in his efforts to create a highly inclusive and liberating society. Benjamin established laws of equality within Zarahemla by forbidding slavery and other forms of wickedness. Mosiah expanded that by welcoming and rejoicing over their estranged extended kin when Alma and Limhi's people came to Zarahemla. Ammon extends the tent poles even farther by asking the Nephites to welcome and make space for Lamanites, not as slaves or an underclass, but as equals.

Anti-Nephi-Lehi's response to Ammon resembles Nephi's famous promise to "go and do." The simplicity of his commitment is beautiful: *if God tells us to go, we will go. If not, we will die here.* Because he trusts Ammon and has faith in God, he is willing to walk unarmed into a dangerous place. God's response in verse 12 is also striking: "Get this people out of this land." Although it is Ammon who approached God on this issue, not the other way around, God's response appears clear and unwavering. Get the people out. This is something God sometimes tells people to do: save themselves and their community by leaving dangerous situations in their own countries and seeking refuge in the land of their enemies. God repeats that sentiment in this verse, emphasizing the importance of getting out of the land. Moreover, the second repetition comes with an addition after the semicolon: "and blessed are this people in this generation, for I will preserve them." God pronounces a blessing on the Anti-Nephi-Lehies as they leave their land and seek shelter with former enemies.

---

137. Mosiah 2:13

That blessing indicates that the Nephites' response to the Anti-Nephi-Lehies is the effect of a miracle. It seems unlikely that entirely on their own, the people who mocked the sons of Mosiah for their missionary work and threatened violence toward the Lamanites would so quickly change their hearts. This is God moving through the people. This is God protecting the Anti-Nephi-Lehies with a blessing as they flee for safety. Do not miss the miracle of this story: that the Nephites found enough compassion to abandon hatred and violence and adopt radical hospitality.

Understanding these verses in this way gives readers direction on how we should approach and advocate for immigrants and refugees today. What does it mean for immigration policy if we believe God sends people out of their own land? What does it mean for refugee policy if our sacred text tells a story of people welcoming their enemies into their land? If God blesses the exodus, then we must not only tolerate but embrace those seeking refuge. If we want to be the people who welcome our former enemies with mercy, we need God to change our hearts and give us ideas that seem too big and wild to undertake. The sons of Mosiah walking into the land of Nephi was not a rational idea. The Lamanites laying down their weapons and following God by refusing to protect themselves was not reasonable. In this case, the Nephites welcoming their enemies and giving them the land of Jershon and providing protection is not a naturally human act. Most people do not come up with ideas like these, particularly when interacting with their enemies. This shows God performing miracles. This is community willing to follow God into new, difficult, and uncharted land.

The Anti-Nephi-Lehies set out on a wild journey. They leave their land, the land where they have lived for generations, where their babies were born and where their ancestors died. They walk away from land they tilled and harvested. They walk into the wilderness and wait at the borders of the land to find out whether they will live or die. This is the fourth time in the Book of Mormon that a large group of people has fled into the wilderness because of their obedience to God.[138] This is another example of the important recurring theme in the Book of Mormon of God calling people to leave their lands and seek safety elsewhere.

Alma 27:15–20

Ammon leaves the Anti-Nephi-Lehies at the border of the land of Zarahelma because he does not know how his own people will respond to a group of Lamanites in their land. Again, the Nephites' response of welcoming and protecting was not an obvious or foregone conclusion. Even Ammon feared what they would do, which is why he went on alone. This is a social experiment, which Ammon describes as "try[ing] the hearts" (v. 15) of the Nephites. Trying their hearts means asking them to seek deeper humanity within their souls, accept the promptings of God toward more compassion, and to make sacrifices for their former enemies. This is a stress test of their capacity for charity.

As the sons of Mosiah cross into the land of Zarahemla, they meet Alma at the borders. After so many years apart, they happen to meet in exactly the right spot at the right time. This is God fulfilling God's promise to protect the Anti-Nephi-Lehies. This historic moment is crucial for both nations, but particularly for the Nephites. It ushers in an enormous transformation for their people. Their community grows exponentially more righteous and compassionate in their efforts to protect the Anti-Nephi-Lehies. God was in the details of these events, which is why joy is expressed throughout these verses.

Just as Alma brought Amulek to his own house after a traumatic experience,[139] Alma conducts the sons of Mosiah to his own house. This is one way Alma shows care for his friends. By offering his home as the first destination during and after challenging times, Alma takes responsibility for others. He has been through his own hard journeys

138. The others were Lehi's family, Alma and his followers, and Limhi and his people.
139. Alma 15:18

and periods in the wilderness, which is perhaps why his own house is the first place he brings the weary travelers.

Alma 27:22–24

The Nephites give the Anti-Nephi-Lehies Jershon, which appears to be high-quality, desirable land. It sits next to Bountiful, whose name connotes abundance and references the land of "much fruit and also wild honey"[140] from Lehi's family's sojourn through the wilderness. The land is not a loan; it is given "for an inheritance" (v. 22), meaning the Nephites understand the importance of land legacy in building wealth and intend the Anti-Nephi-Lehies to have the land forever. The Nephites then set up armies around Jershon in order to protect the Anti-Nephi-Lehies (who they now refer to as "our brethren") from any threats. Pause to consider this extraordinary moment in the Book of Mormon. The Nephites do not take in the Anti-Nephi-Lehies and give them the worst, most barren land. They do not accept them as an underclass to assume and perform the hardest labor in society. They create structures to help these people thrive. They put their own lives at risk to keep them safe. They give up resources in order to protect the Anti-Nephi-Lehies' covenants with God, even though those covenants look different from the ones the Nephites have made. The Anti-Nephi-Lehies' journey with the divine diverges from that of the Nephites', yet the Nephites honor and respect those different choices.

The Nephites display more than mere tolerance here, offering a profound example of promoting others' faith. Following that example today may look like protecting the diet or dress restrictions of other religions. It may mean offering resources to help others worship in peace. The Nephites did not need to make the same choices as the Anti-Nephi-Lehies in order to see the necessity of aiding them so they could live their lives with the divine in a way that was right for them.

---

140. 1 Nephi 17:5

Alma 27:25-26

Notice the points of connection created in the text between the Nephites and the Anti-Nephi-Lehies. The author describes the Anti-Nephi-Lehies as having "pitched their tents" (v. 25) in the wilderness, a possible rhetorical reference to Lehi's family pitching their tents in Bountiful, then again in the promised land.[141] Alma introduces himself to the Anti-Nephi-Lehies and relates his own conversion story, narratively uniting his experiences with those of the new believers. Like them, he needed to repent and change. Like them, the Nephites' origin story began with tents in the wilderness. In this beloved connection, the Nephites choose to emphasize their commonalities with their former enemies in order to give them joy and hope.

However, amid the joy of the people as they go to live in the land of Jershon, we see a problem of honoring identity. Verse 26 explains that the Nephites called the Anti-Nephi-Lehies "the people of Ammon," or Ammonites, rather than the name they chose for themselves. The text goes on to refer to the people as Ammonites for the rest of the Book of Mormon. Despite the Nephites' interpretation, Ammon does not lead this group. They have a king, Anti-Nephi-Lehi, and they have an identity for their people. Stripping them of their name and tying them solely to Ammon, a Nephite, limits the uniting symbolism of the identity they chose for themselves. It defines them by how the Nephites saw them, not how they saw themselves. This new nation suffered so much in their conversion and went through a process of separating themselves from their Lamanite brethren and forming a new coherent group. While the text does not explain why the Nephites failed to honor their true name, it appears to stem from their perspective of centering Ammon in this story. And while Ammon may have been a catalyst for their conversion, he is not the center of the Anti-Nephi-Lehies' story. They get to tell their story on their own terms and name themselves. Therefore, this text will continue to use the name Anti-Nephi-Lehi in any reference to that group.

---

141. 1 Nephi 17:6 and 18:23

Alma 27:27–30

The Anti-Nephi-Lehies "never did look upon death with any degree of terror," at least in part because they relinquished violence and the shedding of blood (v. 2). Nonviolence theory attributes its power to this principle: an oppressor only wields power when others fear the weapons they employ. By not fearing death, one's enemy loses the power they believe they have over you. Nonviolent liberation movements around the world have dismantled systems of oppression by refusing to cave to physical force. Humans find it hard to recognize or comprehend that power. It echoes the words of Paul: "O death, where is thy sting? O grave, where is thy victory?"[142]

This lack of a fear of death and commitment to never hurt anyone sets the people apart from any others in the Book of Mormon. The Anti-Nephi-Lehies are a "beloved people, a highly favored people of the Lord" (v. 30), because they adhere so closely to their covenant to relinquish violence. Yet these people were the same ones who recently identified as Lamanites and still carry Lamanite blood in their veins. If there were a curse on the Lamanites, particularly one associated with any kind of physical attribute, the Anti-Nephi-Lehies would carry it with them. Their status as "highly favored" therefore indicates that perhaps the curse always existed only in the Nephite imagination. No curse follows the people; rather, the Jershon nation becomes a Zion-like bastion of inclusivity, acceptance, care, righteousness, and a refuge for others.

Alma 28:1–14

A terrible battle follows in the wake of the Anti-Nephi-Lehies fleeing to Jershon and accepting the protection of the Nephites. It should not be surprising that one of the greatest conversions in the Book of Mormon, in which thousands of people renounce violence and the entire Nephite society embraces radical hospitality, is followed by

---

142. 1 Corinthians 15:55

an awful battle, "such an one as never had been known among all the people in the land from the time Lehi left Jerusalem" (v. 2). Social evolution toward justice seems always to be met with an oppositional force which attempts to equal the power of good. In this case, society accepted and protected vulnerable people, gave up precious land to former enemies, and put their own bodies at risk to aid them in an unprecedented move toward beloved community. In response, the worst battle in the history of these nations erupts. The way love and justice are met with rage and violence can be sad and disheartening, but notice throughout the Book of Alma, particularly in this chapter, the way the text intertwines joy and sorrow. Alma connects those emotions because they so often occur together in the human experience.

Consider this moving description of grief: "[G]reat mourning and lamentation [was] heard throughout all the land" (v. 4) as family members cry out for their dead. These verses frankly address grief, with no pretense—as sometimes appears in the Book of Mormon—that the righteous escape suffering.[143] This public, shared bereavement, is not contained to quiet, private spaces. With so much lost, the people give themselves a season of communal lament. They set aside a specific time for grief and do not isolate people in their sorrows. The text adds that part of this solemn period was for "much fasting and prayer" (v. 6), companions which indicate that grief is a holy work. Mourning is a spiritual practice, just like fasting and prayer. It is not something to be rushed or shamed. Grieving places us in conversation with the divine. A description of "sorrows, and their afflictions, and their incomprehensible joy" (v. 8) seems like it ought not to be part of a single list, yet here they go together. This chapter moves in the complexity of what seems to be the polarization of emotions. It challenges readers to name joy and sorrow together in their own lives. Those who follow a Savior "acquainted

---

143. Joseph Spencer. Email to authors, March 3, 2022.

with grief"[144] must know grief themselves, yet doing so also comes with "joy because of the light of Christ unto life" (v. 14).

Alma 29:1–5

This chapter contains the psalm of Alma, a chance for him to interrogate his own journey with God. He explores his own desires in regards to his call and how that may sometimes conflict with God's plan. It is rooted in memory work, with beautiful references to the Old Testament. It also powerfully links to what happens in the remainder of the Book of Alma.

The first two verses express Alma's desire to shake the world with the call to repent and do better. Anyone working for social causes and trying to bend the arc of history toward justice feels this sentiment at times. When we see the suffering caused by sin and oppression, the ignorance and disinterest in the plight of the marginalized, we want to "speak with the trump of God . . . that there might not be more sorrow upon all the face of the earth" (v. 1–2). The grief surrounding Alma in this moment prompts his desire to prevent evil. After watching the terrible battles of the previous chapters, Alma knows how much human pain can be prevented, and he acts out of a wish to protect his community.

Yet in verse 3, Alma explains that he oversteps in wanting more than the mission God has given him. He acts not solely out of a desire to share the gospel, but with a wish to control others. He wants a "voice of thunder" (v. 2) because he struggles with the principle of letting people choose "according to their wills" (v. 4). Alma realizes he ought to be content with the parameters of his call and his sphere of influence. The remainder of the chapter describes the importance of humbly embracing his own limitations, respecting others' agency, and trusting the grace and power of God.

---

144. Isaiah 53:3

Alma 29:6–8

Alma interrogates his desire to do *"more* than to perform the work" to which God has called him (v. 6, emphasis added) or to be the one who teaches everyone on the earth (v. 7). He chides himself because God gives wisdom to *all* nations in their own tongue, and that practice is "just and true" (v. 8). Although Alma wants to teach the entire world the truths he knows, he realizes God moves with each nation in their language and in their time. He pushes back on his own wish for everyone else's journey with God to look like his own. Alma's failing here is his audacity in thinking he knows what the entire world needs. And as he reflects on what he has stated, he acknowledges that God moves in particular and intentional ways for each individual and community. Alma does not need to proclaim the gospel to all the world because God already has that role covered. Alma's realization that his responsibility as a prophet is for his time, language, and people reminds us that a relationship with God cannot be mass produced or forced on anyone. A just and true God speaks to everyone, in their language and in their season with the wisdom they need.

Alma 29:9–17

After describing how each individual and community experiences their own journey with God, Alma then beautifully ties all those journeys together in a common thread. He places himself into the web of humanity through the memory work of his stories, those of his ancestors, and those of his friends.

In verse 10, he recalls his own need for repentance and his gratitude for the mercy God extended toward him. Notice his repeated use of the word remember and how memory works in him: he remembers what God did for him. He remembers that God heard his prayers. He remembers that God was merciful to him. In this way, he steps down from the pulpit and recognizes the similarities between himself and others. Their progression is like his own. They are all in need of grace.

Alma then invokes one of the most potent liberation stories in scripture, the account of the Israelites being brought out of bondage in Egypt and into their promised land. He remembers that God delivered his ancestors with great miracles. He sees himself in the stories from the ancient records. He is another part of that story, and the same God who delivered the Israelites saved him as well. Although God moves in particular, intentional ways, the same God performs all these miracles for different people at different times. In remembering this history, Alma realizes the joy of being called by this same God "to preach the word unto *this* people" (v. 13, emphasis added). Alma does not need to preach to the entire world when he remembers what an honor it is to play any role in the great narrative of God's liberation of the world.

Finally, Alma connects himself to the sons of Mosiah and feels the joy of their work in the land of Nephi. He did not need to be the one to preach to the Lamanites. He can celebrate any goodness which has come into the world without him needing to be at the center. He is living into shared joy.

Alma starts his psalm with a wish for more and ends it with great joy and anticipation for the moment in which all good people may sit down and rest together in the kingdom of God. This illustrates an inclusive, open-hearted, joyful vision. It is no longer about him or his desires. His psalm now focuses on a community of believers which extends vertically into history and laterally throughout all nations. This is, indeed, cause for great joy.

Alma 30:1–2

The text juxtaposes the establishment of the Anti-Nephi-Lehies in the land of Jershon with the burial of so many bodies that the people could not number them. At the beginning of this new life in a new place, death is part of the narrative. The Book of Mormon frequently ties joyful new beginnings with death, once again implying that a work of grief will go alongside a work of righteousness and justice.

The text also links fasting, mourning, and prayer again,[145] treating the three together as spiritual practices. Unlike some other periods of relative peace following war in the Book of Mormon, the people have a small amount of time to reflect and grieve before the next conflict begins. Unceasing violence that does not give people a moment to grieve looks different (and yields different results) than a community who experienced violence but had time afterward to heal. When studying periods of war in the Book of Mormon, notice how long the ceasefires last and what happens during those times.

Alma 30:6-10

Alma defines an antichrist as someone who preaches that Christ is not coming. One of the reasons Korihor does so much damage to the Nephite society is that they legally protect the right to self-determined belief. Not only do they not have a law against belief, but they view such laws as "strictly contrary to the commands of God" (v. 7). Fascinatingly, this understanding of law came from the way the Nephites understood the scripture, "Choose ye this day, whom ye will serve."[146] While there are many different ways to interpret that scripture, the Nephites understood it to mean that agency and choice of faith are so crucial that governments should not have any laws which allow religious discrimination. They did not allow laws placing believers and non-believers into separate legal categories, even if that meant the rise of an anti-Christ who seriously damages their society. While acceptable boundaries of behavior exist, those lines are based on actions, not on personal beliefs. The Nephites interpreted and implemented the scripture in a way that ties equity to belief. The text does not apologize for this law; it seems to hold it up, despite the inconvenience and threat. This exemplifies people applying a particular understanding of scripture to political policy,

---

145. See section on Alma 28:1-14.
146. Joshua 24:15

and it offers a glimpse into how they used religious text to honor different beliefs and reflect equity.

Alma 30:13–17

Korihor attacks and mocks people for their faith, calling them foolish. This is the counternarrative of Paul's proud claim of being a "fool for Christ's sake."[147] Theologian Willie James Jennings insists that one of the worst things we can do is to destroy others' faith.[148] Faith may be interrogated or re-navigated, but it is a serious sin to harm someone else's faith. Any movement—including those meant to improve the human condition—which calls people fools for their faith needs to change its methods and behavior. Korihor's use of phrases such as "a frenzied mind" (v. 16) is meant to malign and degrade people, treating them as less than human because of their faith. That is unacceptable.

Korihor also introduces a form of atheist prosperity gospel in claiming every person fares according to their own abilities and people deserve what they can take according to their strength (v. 17). This ruthless, individualistic worldview resembles the kind of prosperity gospel many Christians embrace. Instead of God blessing people for their righteousness, Korihor teaches that people deserve any privilege they can take for themselves. Both ethical systems defend inequality and embrace individualism at the expense of community.

Alma 30:19–21

Korihor goes to Jershon and Gideon to preach to the people there. Yet, the Anti-Nephi-Lehies reject him completely and send him out of their land. They have suffered and experienced too much, and fought too hard for their testimonies, to be led away by Korihor's message. These people survived genocide and became refugees. They

---

147. 1 Corinthians 4:10
148. Willie James Jennings. *Christian Theology course*, Lecture at Duke Divinity School, Fall 2014.

recognize a theology which is not rooted in their liberation. Everything in their life experiences would revolt against Korihor's message that "every man prospered according to his genius, and that every man conquered according to his strength."[149] That is not the God they know. Their utter repudiation of Korihor's message is based on their knowledge of a God who was with them in the darkest times of their lives.

Alma 30:23–28

Korihor claims a righteous work in setting people free from the shackles of faith. These verses offer an interesting opportunity to explore the definition of freedom. Korihor's definition advocates for individuals separating themselves from families, traditions, and social structures. While that can certainly be a part of freedom, it is not a complete or robust enough definition. Korihor misses the possibility of freedom within a community and the idea of making some sacrifices for a common cause bigger than oneself.

Korihor also tries to name the bondage of other people, something that can be extremely problematic. Though his society theoretically might suffer under an oppressive religious elite class like Korihor describes, the people always have the right to name their injustice for themselves. People work out their own definition of freedom and what sacrifices they are willing to make for their own communities. Korihor is a false ally in the way he tries to take that from the people. This seems similar to the experiences of queer folk, BIPOC, and women in the LDS Church who regularly receive the message that they are "stupid" or "blind" for staying in the Church. This unhelpful approach undermines people's ability to use their own agency. It is not the work of social justice.

---

149. Alma 30:17

Alma 30:32–35

In response to Korihor, Alma first rejects the narrative of oppression. Alma knows the falseness of these claims because of the legacy of king Benjamin and his own experiences as unpaid clergy. In this community, leaders do not financially benefit from their positions—an understandably important stance for a people who have experienced oppression from king Noah and his priests' religious structures. They appear to have stayed as far away from a religious elite class as possible. This society highly values equity within their religious organization.

Alma 30:42–52

This moment shows Alma moving as a prophet in discerning that Korihor actually believes in God. He describes Korirhor as having "put off the Spirit of God" (v. 42), an active verb which connotes a forcible removal. It is possible to fully embrace a narrative which runs counter to our own deep beliefs. This proves equally true in social justice, where facing the consequences of truth may demand change. Sometimes it is easier to act on a lie than follow the truths we know.

Alma experiences grief when he realizes that Korihor continues to deny the truth he already knows. At some point, Korihor became wrapped up in a big lie. The tragedy is that he knew truth and had potential to be so much better. He lied to God and to himself, which is worse than simply not believing. Not believing is a universal experience, but betraying your own belief and living an inauthentic life not rooted in what you know is a terrible existence. This is what makes Korihor's story so sad: he deceived himself and preached something he did not believe.

Alma 30:55–60

At first glance, Alma's choice to keep Korihor muted seems brutal and punitive. Korihor's fate of being cast out of Nephite society and becoming a beggar and then being trampled to death by the Zoramites is particularly distressing. Although they seem tied together, Korihor's curse of muteness and his death require separate examination.

At this point in their history, the Nephites have built a diverse and peaceful society. It includes various branches of Nephites as well as the Anti-Nephi-Lehies. They have sacrificed and died for one another, forming a community of former enemies who now love and respect one another. However, diverse societies, particularly those formed of groups with a history of violence between them, are fragile. They are hard-earned and easily destroyed. The Nephites understand this because of the schisms and violence they have experienced. They recognize the fragility of what they have built and they see the risk of splitting apart. Unsurprisingly, the Anti-Nephi-Lehies, Alma, and the Nephites have zero tolerance for words and people who threaten the friendship and social norms they have created. They will not allow anyone to interrupt the joy they have formed through humility, sacrifice, and open hearts. Muting Korihor is their way of protecting their beloved community. Korihor has lied, incited violence, and attempted to turn them against one another. They refused to let him continue to have a platform because of the risk to their society.

However, Korihor's death from a mob is unjustifiable. Although the narrator interposes his own interpretation of the justice of Korihor's death in verse 60, the death occurs at the hands of the Zoramites. Chapter 61 will make clear that the Zoramites are not a righteous or healthy society and ought not to be used to prove a moral point. This action of trampling a man to death because of what he said is the text's first warning sign that something is poisonous in the Zoramite society.

Alma 31:1–2

The prophetic lament runs through this chapter and the story of the Zoramites. Alma witnesses the betrayal of God within the Zoramites' church, and his resulting deep grief depicts one of the lowest points of his narrative. He describes the impact of people going astray and corrupting the gospel for their own pride and privilege. Through their perversion of theology, the Zoramites build a church that harms people. They separated themselves from others through a destructive theology.

Carefully studying any scripture means putting oneself in the roles of every character of the story, not just the heroes. We must see the ways we act like Laman and Lemuel, not just Nephi. We are, at times, Jonah, Sariah, the prodigal son, Deborah, or Peter. Seeing ourselves in the successes and failures gives a new depth to scripture reading. Therefore, we should study the stories of Korihor and the Zoramites with this question: What part of my theology and beliefs look like that? What part of my discipleship and life choices look like theirs? We do not have to totalize; we do not need to stand on a Rameumptom to believe in prosperity gospel and an exclusive God. But part of our worldviews or daily choices may look like theirs.

Alma 31:4–5

The Zoramites have ideologically separated themselves so much from the Nephites that the Nephites fear the Zoramites will align themselves with the Lamanites. The text claims "a correspondence with the Lamanites" would be "the means of great loss on the part of the Nephites" (v. 4), although it does not explain that loss. Would it be a political and military threat for the two groups to align together? Or would it be an emotional loss, a separation from their brethren? The fact that the text uses the word "fear" to describe the Nephites implies the former, which underscores how closely religion and politics get tied together in this society.

Alma decides to preach the word of God to the Zoramites rather than respond with force. The text explains that preaching the gospel is more powerful than any other method to lead people to justice. Even in a society that just emerged from a series of wars, Alma recognizes the ability of God's word to speak light into dark spaces. People sometimes feel uncomfortable with the concept of justice because they link it to the use of force and violence. This verse says God's word is the most powerful tool of justice.[150]

Alma 31:8–11

The Zoramites are familiar with the word of God, yet they separated themselves from the Nephites and created their own church. While easy to read this as an example of people leaving the church, the Zoramite story seems more complex than that. It illustrates what happens when people decide to move away from a God rooted in love and create a theology built on privilege instead of liberation. Their idea of chosenness becomes their guiding ethic rather than humility, compassion, mercy, and justice. Although they continue to attend their church, they have lost the daily practices of staying connected to God. Failing to live out the gospel in day-to-day life helped them pervert the gospel for their own ends. They have not integrated God into their lives, even as they continue to attend their church services.

Alma 31:12–25

Alma and his brethren have good reason to be astonished when they see and hear the Zoramites' method of worship. Everything about this scene reinforces their idolization of exclusivity, from a tower which holds only one person to a prayer of gratitude for being supe-

---

150. Michael F. Perry provides a lovely article about the power of God's word in comparison to violence and the delayed but long-lasting impact of Alma's mission in his article, "The Supremacy of the Word: Alma's Mission to the Zoramites and the Conversion of the Lamanites," *Journal of Book of Mormon Studies*: Vol. 24 : No. 1 (2015), Article 6.

rior to others. They have made an idol of inequality through setting their hearts upon wealth (v. 24) and by excluding people they consider to be part of an underclass.

Yet the Zoramites use language not far removed from what the Nephites have historically claimed. "We believe that thou hast separated us from our brethren" (v. 16) seems similar to asserting that the Lamanites were cursed so that "their seed might be distinguished from the seed of their brethren."[151] And, "We do not believe the tradition of our brethren, which was handed down to them by the childishness of their fathers" (v. 16) sounds similar to criticism of the Lamanites for following "the incorrectness of the traditions of their fathers."[152] Furthermore, "We believe that thou has elected us to be thy holy children" (v. 16) echoes the Nephites' claim of "having been favored above every other nation, kindred, tongue or people."[153] The Zoramites have not built their theology *ex nihilo*. They took the most poisonous parts of Nephite culture and theology and amplified them. The Zoramites are a distorted reflection of the same problems the Nephites face. Their insistence on their own blessedness and the comparative inferiority of others stems from a worldview they inherited.

The theologies of the Zoramites and Nephites differ in two significant ways: 1) the Zoramites have abandoned a belief in the coming of Christ, and 2) they have an extremely poor understanding of the nature of God. They describe God as an unchanging spirit (v. 15), a static figure which is "the same yesterday, today, and forever" (v. 17).[154] Their idea of God is insubstantial and stationary. This God is unable to accept Christ or a new law. The reason for their lack of knowledge of God is clear: their only spiritual engagement is in the short period at the synagogue in which they boast of their own specialness (v. 23).

---

151. Alma 3:8
152. Alma 9:16
153. Alma 9:20
154. This language also appears in Hebrews 13:8 as a way that God describes Godself. This is a good example of people misinterpreting scripture to limit God.

They do not listen to God, they only speak. They do not have a relationship with God, only a public face of false righteousness.

The Zoramites inherited a theology mixed with toxic elements of pride, exclusivity, and perceived superiority. They lost the true parts and amplified the worst parts, tragically becoming a violent and sick society. Not even their gratitude holds goodness, as the counterfeit feeling stems from condemning others and lifting themselves up. Though their actions and beliefs point to the rot within the Nephite society, their choice to abandon the good parts of the Nephites' faith takes them down a brutal path.

Alma 31:26–38

Alma condemns the Zoramites' pride and their interest in "costly apparel" and "precious things" (v. 28) in explicit terms in these verses. According to Alma, is it wrong for anyone to wear expensive clothing and jewelry? John the Baptist taught that anyone "that hath two coats, let him impart to him that hath none,"[155] and Jesus told the wealthy young man to give all his possessions to the poor.[156] Many scriptures condemn greed, selfishness, covetousness, and immodest displays of wealth. But knowing how to apply these scriptures practically in our lives can be difficult. Rather than presuming to draw universal lines for what is appropriate, each seeker should be in honest dialogue with God about whether their own heart is "set upon" (v. 28) wealth. This merits serious contemplation in light of Alma's counsel and Jesus' observation that, though not impossible, it is more difficult "for a camel to go through the eye of a needle, than for a rich man to enter into the kingdom of God."[157]

---

155. Luke 3:11
156. Mark 10:17–22
157. Matthew 19:24

Alma 31:30–38

Alma's lament seems to stem not only from his experience with the Zoramites, but from all his troubling missions among the Nephites before this moment. His palpable exhaustion likely feels familiar to those who work in justice. A deep grief accompanies seeing people make destructive choices over and over again. All of Alma's efforts to turn the people toward righteousness may feel fruitless to him in this period as he watches the Zoramites corrupt ideas of prayer, worship, and gratitude. Readers can sense the power of Alma's sorrow described as a soul sickness: "O Lord, wilt thou give me strength, that I may bear with mine infirmities. For I am infirm, and such wickedness among this people doth pain my soul" (v. 30). Even Alma does not feel strong enough to face the wickedness of the Zoramites. As a man who has witnessed people burning alive and who has been tortured in prison, Alma knows the real consequences of a corrupt society. He understands the danger of speaking truth to these people, and he is prepared to face it because he moves in the love of God.

Alma's love for other people also becomes clear in his prayer for his "fellow laborers" (v. 32) in this work. He clearly worries for them, possibly because of his past experiences in Ammonihah and other corrupt communities. Alma also prays for the Zoramites, acknowledging that their souls are precious to God, although he says *many* of them are their brethren, instead of realizing that *all* of them are kin.

Alma then puts his hands on the men who have come with him, blessing them in a sacred moment intertwined with his lament. It is a move of the Holy Spirit during a period of fear, anxiety, and grief. Alma intertwines the spiritual and the physical, pain and comfort, so beautifully. He touches his companions as he prays for them. They experience afflictions that are "swallowed up in the joy of Christ" (v. 38). God is revealed in the paradox.

Alma 32:1–5

Two important themes run through this story, and both of them appear in these first four verses. The first explores what it means for a faith community to be exclusionary or inclusionary. In verse 1, Alma and his friends preach in the synagogues, houses, and streets. Synagogues are the most exclusive of these places and represent the gathering of a select group of people. Homes are private, intimate places for families to gather. The streets represent the broadest, most inclusive space, since everyone uses them equally. This story seems to mostly take place on the streets, given that the poor in this society are not allowed into the synagogues. Preaching in the streets is a different kind of outreach than preaching in a house of worship or in a home. It is an opportunity to be in relationship with the entire society, not just kin or people who believe as you do. This story invites readers to consider who is excluded from our houses of worship and why, and what inclusive spaces we go to in order to preach God's word.

Verse 5 digs deeper into the theme of exclusive spaces, noting that the poor people who are not allowed into the synagogues are the same people who "labored abundantly to build with [their] own hands." This phenomenon—in which an oppressed population builds the spaces from which they are then excluded—commonly appears throughout history. Sometimes we see it literally in government buildings, universities, churches, and other institutions which used enslaved or underpaid labor to construct a building and then refused entry to the workers. This pattern can also be seen metaphorically in systems such as agriculture, religion, and political spheres when the ideas and resources of marginalized people build and sustain a space but then those same people are not allowed to participate. The Zoramites' dilemma can be seen in the United States Black soldiers who fought in World War II who could not access the GI bill. It can be seen today in migrant farmers who work the land but do not profit from it. Stripping the benefits of a space from the labor force which built it repeats a historical narrative.

The second theme in this chapter interrogates ideas of humility, being poor in heart or lowly in spirit. This chapter describes humility and poverty in many different ways. Sometimes the text separates those two things as different categories, such as in verse 3: "they were poor as to things of the world; and also they were poor in heart." At other times, the text gives no distinction at all, such as in verse 4: "those of whom we have been speaking, of whom were poor in heart, because of their poverty as to the things of the world." When the latter occurs, the definition of humility gets muddied, because the two categories are not actually identical. There may be a correlation, but they are still distinct, and failing to preserve the difference creates problems of stereotyping large groups of people. It collapses the nuance of the many factors that influence people's behavior by simply saying that poor people are humble. (Although Alma sometimes fails to distinguish the two in the first half of the chapter, later in verse 25 he appears to correct himself and proceeds more thoughtfully.)

Alma 32:6–16

Alma mixes some radical, exciting theology in these verses with some very problematic claims. The precarious line he takes of rhetorically linking virtue with poverty deserves scrutiny. He expresses "great joy" (v. 6) at the opportunity to speak to a receptive audience, but his reaction deserves some caution. His chance to share the gospel comes at great cost to the people in poverty among the Zoramites. Although his message eventually brings them liberation, their current circumstances are sorrowful. Celebrating the hardships of others because they have made people humble is problematic.

Alma again weaves poverty and humility too tightly together in verse 12: "for it is because that ye are cast out, that ye are despised of your brethren because of your exceeding poverty, that ye are brought to a lowliness of heart; for ye are necessarily brought to be humble." He tries to see divine purpose in their oppression, which can be a violent way of preaching to people. He continues with this message through verses 13–16, repeating the idea that their sufferings are divinely given and the source of their morality. The problem is not that he is saying they are blessed because they are humble. The problem is when he implies they are blessed for *being compelled* to be humble; that the compulsion is a blessing in itself. Although Jesus taught that the meek and mourning are blessed,[158] the Sermon on the Mount does not imply that the cause of meekness and mourning is a blessing in itself—a crucial difference.

We may believe that folk who have struggled with great injustice will receive exceptional blessings. People who have suffered may see God in their trials. They may recognize the ways in which they have grown because of their experiences. But in those cases, people have a right to name the blessings stemming from their oppression for themselves. They deserve to describe for themselves a God who has blessed them in the sites of harrowing injustices. Drawing that line for them by saying "because ye were compelled to be humble ye were blessed" (v. 14) can compound harm. Alma takes this even further when he distinguishes between those who are "compelled to be humble" and those who "humble themselves" (v.16). Does this mean that while it may be a blessing to be poor, it would be an even greater blessing to be rich and humble? The poor are blessed in their oppression but the wealthy are blessed more, provided they are humble? Because Alma conflates poverty and humility, a poor person cannot prove that the source of their humility is voluntary and not circumstance-driven. Observers may therefore assume it was not chosen, but that the poor may somehow have the "advantage" of humility through their poverty. This is an unjust way of navigating wealth, oppression, and humility.

At the same time, Alma employs some of the most radically inclusive theology in the Book of Mormon. In answer to the ques-

---

158. Matthew 5:4–5

tion of, "What shall we do?" from one of the men excluded from the synagogue (v. 9), Alma gives an unexpected response: walk away from that church community. You do not need it to have a relationship with God, and worship ought not to be confined to one time or place. The building is not the church. This revolutionary statement breaks the mold of who has authority or responsibility for a person's relationship with God. Alma insists that the wealthy Zoramites may control a building, but their power ends there. If that building does not enthusiastically welcome people, it no longer serves its purpose. People can find God elsewhere.

Alma's words can also be read as a metaphor about privilege and inclusivity. The poor Zoramites want an invitation to an exclusive space, a place that would not actually uplift them or serve them, because it has grown into something corrupt and unhealthy. They want to be on the inside and enjoy the same level of privilege as the wealthy Zoramites. They are not deconstructing the exclusionary principles that have become pervasive in this church. In fact, if they took part in constructing the church, it is safe to assume they helped build the Rameumptom. Possibly their fight is for the opportunity to be part of something exclusive, not to welcome everyone into the synagogue. Alma's encouragement to walk away from the space entirely nudges them toward abandoning an institution that will continue to perpetuate hierarchies and segregation. He moves them toward a God who breaks down every wall and barrier, not just the ones meant for them.

Alma 32:17–23

These verses seem to belong outside of this particular time and place. Alma's musings on faith, knowledge, and signs seem to reference his experiences with Korihor in chapter 30. The Zoramites have not asked for a divine sign, nor have they questioned the value of faith. These words do not seem appropriate for the audience, but prophets are not separated from their own past experiences. Alma is working through the remnants of that problem while also processing what he saw at the Rameumptom. In fact, Alma's many encounters with gospel corruption mean he may need time to answer the Zoramites' questions with a theology which takes in and responds to his harrowing preaching experiences. These verses allow readers to see the prophetic as a process, as Alma's human experiences and his prophetic calling inseparably tied together.

Yet, as he circles back around to the Zoramites and the situation in front of him, Alma articulates a nuanced, thoughtful, inclusive lesson. First, he states that "faith is *not* to have a perfect knowledge" (v. 21, emphasis added), a teaching which would seem to be influenced by his experience with Korihor. Then, he emphasizes God's mercy "unto all who believe" (v. 22). Finally, he teaches that God speaks to all people, and particularly emphasizes women and children instead of just assuming their inclusion in the category of "men." For a book of scripture almost silent on the lived experiences of women and children, this is one of the most inclusive verses in the Book of Mormon. Angels impart the word of God to everyone. Every person can avoid being confused by allowing themselves to hear how angels speak to and guide them.

Alma 32:24–27

In this astounding moment, Alma seems to retract his earlier statements about humility and poverty. He clarifies that humility and poverty are not identical and inseparable by acknowledging that some of the people would have been humble regardless of their circumstances. This also seems to undermine his claim that being compelled to be humble is a blessing, since some of them were not compelled to humility and yet still suffered poverty. He precedes this reworking of theology with the invocation of "my beloved brethren," an expansive, loving term (v. 24). During this sermon, Alma has navigated himself from a dualistic worldview into a more complex doctrine, correcting himself as he preaches.

In the following verses, he further explores the idea that faith is not a perfect knowledge. While this thought may have been inspired by Korihor, Alma transfers it into a beautiful sermon for the Zoramites about seeking God. He even connects it to himself and his words in verse 26, explaining that understanding the prophetic is a process, not a moment. He wants people to "experiment upon [his] words" (v. 27), language which implies making mistakes, trying repeatedly, and investigating different hypotheses. Alma does crucial theological work in these verses as he corrects himself, adds complexity, and describes his own lack of perfect knowledge. All we need is a particle of faith, one of the minutest portions of measurement humans can understand. And we do not need to believe in the totality of his sermon, but simply "give place for a portion of his words" (v. 27). Perhaps the limited scope of his claim intentionally allows for judicious selection: seekers do not need to build their testimonies on the totality of what a prophet says; they can simply give place and experiment on some of them.

Alma 32:28–43

This extended metaphor of God's word as a seed which takes root, grows into a plant, and bears fruit, contains many powerful messages. It contains vivid language, such as when Alma illustrates how a good seed growing within someone will "enlarge [their] soul" and "enlighten [their] understanding" (v. 28), or when he links the physical and spiritual by describing truth as "delicious" (v. 28). Alma shares the importance of continually interrogating the values and statements of truth we develop in our lives, asking repeatedly whether what we grow is a good seed and casting it away if it is bad. Again, this is faith as an experimental process, not a destination.

Alma describes the good seed as "light" while staying within the metaphor of seeds and plants. Light is one of the five things necessary for a plant to survive, yet Alma links the good seed to making light, not requiring it. Something circular happens in this metaphor:

the good seed requires that which it is. The seed is light but it also needs light. This makes sense in a divine ecology: what truth needs is also what it produces.

Growing plants from seed requires nurturing and caregiving. It also demands adaptability and curiosity. Alma repeatedly reminds readers to not neglect the work of growing, asking questions, and reassessing. He also points out that while sometimes the seed is bad (v. 31), in other cases a lack of growth points to environmental factors (v. 38). If we do not take care of good ideas and truths in our midst, they wither and fade away. Knowing there can be multiple causes of failure to thrive—bad seeds and bad soils—means we must spend time interrogating ourselves and our faith communities. Have some God-given principles failed to take root in our spaces because we did not offer a safe and healthy home for them? Are we cultivating theological ground in our lives which allows new and good seeds to thrive? Have we ceded space to bad seeds which need to be removed? Sorting through this requires diligence and thoughtfulness.

The last three verses of Alma's sermon invoke the tree of life from Nephi's vision.[159] This is the ultimate goal for our garden of faith—to enjoy the fruit of eternal faith. Placing the tree at the center of our garden can help us determine with wisdom which good seeds to grow.

Alma 33:1–11

Alma tells the excluded Zoramites they have focused on the wrong problem—that of not being allowed access to the synagogues. His revolutionary answer, again, is that the people do not need the synagogues to worship God, who can be found anywhere. To illustrate this, Alma offers a wide spectrum of physical locations, increasingly smaller and more domesticated, and names God in each place. God is in the wilderness, in the field, in the house, in the closet. God is too big to be contained by a narrow number of acceptable places to wor-

---

159. 1 Nephi 8

ship. God hears us when we are alone and in crowds. God hears the "cast out" and "despised" (v. 10). Nobody can erect barriers between a person and God. And because of that, joy erupts into this moment, even as Alma speaks of anger with his enemies and struggle with his afflictions. God has been with Alma throughout all his hardships and grief, and so Alma recognizes that "in [God] is my joy" (v. 11).

Alma 33:16–23

God feels anger toward people who "will not understand [God's] mercies" (v. 16). Alma, through Zenock, offers examples besides the Atonement of Christ: a prophet who gets stoned and Moses raising a serpent in the wilderness. Throughout history, God has consistently offered people awesome gifts and received a blind eye or even violence in return. Pride, complacency, and plain contrariness get in the way of us looking at God's mercies and receiving healing. It may take the form of an unwillingness to acknowledge our illness of fat-phobia, homophobia, or sexism and avail ourselves of the resources to learn and do better. Which prophets in our midst do we choose to stone because of our unwillingness to work on the ways in which we are sick? Alma criticizes people for being "slothful" (v. 21), indicating that our response is indeed a work—a labor to uncover our own unhealthiness and then make use of the mercies of God as a hospital to heal us.

The final verse of this chapter emphasizes once again that this work is a process. Alma returns to the metaphor of a plant which has the potential to grow into a tree of "everlasting life" (v. 23). God promises the easing of burdens, not the entire removal of them. This ongoing work is a step toward liberation, which is cause for joy.

Alma 34:1–7

Alma concludes his sermon and Amulek stands to speak. If the books of Mosiah and Alma are a gathering of different stories from different nations and communities, they are also a gathering of many concurrent prophets speaking together. The sons of Mosiah work cooperatively.

Alma and Amulek partner in their call and sometimes bring along their sons and friends. They preach in a faith community, and the narrative alternates between scenes and speakers. The result is a beautiful, chaotic multiplicity of stories instead of the series of singular speakers that prevails in the first third of the Book of Mormon.

Amulek begins his address with a reference to this abundance of prophetic leaders and chides the Zoramites for ignoring the "things [which] were taught unto you bountifully before your dissension from among us" (v. 2). He invokes Alma, Zenos, Zenock, and Moses as a community of prophets before adding his own voice. And while Amulek's tone and message differ from Alma's, both men fulfill their prophetic call. Their different approaches are meant to be taken together, with their distinct experiences and social locations adding to the collective understanding of God.

Alma 34:15–17

Alma and Amulek, while companions and associates, approach the tension between justice and mercy differently. Here, Amulek preaches that mercy "overpowereth justice" (v. 15) and "mercy can satisfy the demands of justice" (v. 16). Compare this to Alma's teachings a few chapters later, in which he says, "What, do you suppose that mercy can rob justice? I say unto you, Nay; not one whit. If so, God would cease to be God."[160] Amulek sees the Atonement—"the great and last sacrifice" (v. 14)—as an opportunity for people to be enveloped in mercy. In comparison, Alma focuses on the need for repentance. Alma leans more toward mercy and justice working in tandem, with justice as an unalterable feature of the divine, while Amulek seems to trust more in the power of grace. Yet both men ultimately conclude that the purpose of mercy is to move people toward repentance and greater mercy toward our fellow human beings. It is interesting that two men who were close associates had differing

---

160. Alma 42:25

explanations for such an important doctrinal issue, but these various teachings—and what they share in common—can offer readers wisdom about the divine role of justice and mercy in the world.

Alma 34:18–29

Amulek continually emphasizes prayer. He renames all the places for prayer and worship Alma described: the closet, house, field, and wilderness. He adds praying in "secret places" (v. 26), implying even greater intimacy and solitude. He also describes some of the things we may pray for, including praying for our crops and fields (v. 24–25), and praying for ourselves and for the welfare of those around us (v. 27).

But we need to be careful to continue reading past verse 27 because verses 28–29 put all the previous verses in a different context. Amulek strongly urges the Zoramites to not stop at prayer, because "if ye turn away the needy, and the naked, and visit not the sick and afflicted, and impart of your substance . . . behold, your prayer is vain and availeth you nothing, and ye are as hypocrites" (v. 28). Even after this long description of all the places and ways in which we should pray, Amulek makes clear that God will not know us if all we do is cry unto God. Nothing can stop people from praying to God in any place, but prayer is in vain if we do not take care of the least of these. Amulek goes even farther, describing those who pray without taking action for the needy as "dross, which the refiners do cast out, (it being of no worth) and is trodden under foot of men" (v. 29). Charity, the pure love of Christ, prevents God from saying to us, "I never knew you."[161]

Taken together, Alma and Amulek give a revolutionary answer to the questioning desire of the poor Zoramites to use the synagogue. They tell the people that place and social hierarchy do not matter and that they need to leave it behind. Where they pray has no importance; they can pray to God in the wilderness, field, house, or closet. But they must do more than pray or attend church once a week.

---

161. Matthew 7:23

They have to reorient themselves away from the privilege they desire and toward those who have less than themselves. They have to take action for the most marginalized in their community.

Alma 34:30–41

Amulek stated in verses 15–16 that we receive mercy through faith and repentance and that mercy has the power to overcome justice. In verses 30–31, he asks the Zoramites to "harden not [their] hearts any longer," but instead "bring fruit unto repentance." Yet the previous two verses made clear that one of the important fruits of repentance means caring for the marginalized. Although his earlier statements seemed to separate mercy and justice, these verses bring them back together. Repentance leads to receiving mercy, but one of the fruits of repentance is engaging in justice work. God's mercy ultimately leads us to enact justice. Awareness of the gift of mercy acting in their own lives moves people to care for the needy.

Amulek's words contain an urgency that goes beyond Alma's. He reminds the people again and again to take up this labor now. He urges them to "not procrastinate the day of your repentance," underscoring the idea that now is the time to work. We can hope for rest one day, but not in this life (v. 41).

Amulek ends his sermon with the counsel to continue with a "firm hope" (v. 41) and "not revile against those who do cast you out," a pertinent warning for people experiencing oppression. Black theologian Willie Jennings describes hope as "a discipline . . . not a sentiment," but he also ties hope to a certain need for anger. In the wake of George Floyd's death, he said, "If you have hope, if you wish to be disciplined by hope right now, you need anger. Anger is the engine that drives hope because this anger, this God-bound anger, turns us toward the urgency of the moment, as Martin Luther King, Jr. said so eloquently, and the deep desire for a changed world." Yet Jennings strongly counseled against pairing anger with hatred, because those two emotions touching one another creates disastrous results:

God invites us into a shared fury, but only the kind that we crea-
tures can handle. You all know that anger is frightening because
it is not easily controllable. Anger can easily touch hatred, and if
anger enters into hatred, then we will be drawn into violence, and
way too many people in this world have been drawn deeply into
violence. What Christian faith knows is that the way to keep anger
from hatred is not to deny anger, to pretend that it is not real. No,
we can't do that. What keeps anger from touching hatred is not the
cunning of reason or the power of will. It is simply Jesus.[162]

Jennings and Amulek agree that hatred is a dangerous possibility
for those suffering oppression. Faith in Christ offers the antidote to
get us through. Anger may spark our hope, igniting our energy and
visions of what may be, but the work of change lies in harnessing our
will to God's with compassion for those we engage and seek to teach.

Alma 35:1–2

The land of Jershon again becomes a place of safety, this time providing refuge or rest for people other than the Anti-Nephi-Lehies. Alma,
Amulek, Ammon, and the other men of their group appear to travel
there in order to rest after a difficult time with the Zoramites. They
withdraw themselves from a challenging space and move into a land
of peace, full of people they love. Consider the symbolism: they need
to depart from a group of people who used to be Nephites and go to
find rest with people who used to be Lamanites. This emphasizes the
limitations of the labels of these groups but also points to how some
of the most beloved and godly communities will grow from oppressed
populations. It also exemplifies how new communities can be a safe
harbor when your own people are no longer safe. These relationships

---

162. Willie Jennings. *For the Life of the World*, podcast audio, produced by the Yale
Center for Faith and Culture, June 2, 2020.
https://for-the-life-of-the-world-yale-center-for-faith-culture.simplecast.com/
episodes/my-anger-gods-righteous-indignation-willie-jennings-response-to-the-
death-of-george-floyd-FXkkWh9b/transcript

between the Nephite religious leaders and the Anti-Nephi-Lehies are radical because they defy notions of who can offer love and kinship to one another. These nurtured spaces offer rest in ways we could never anticipate because they come from unexpected sources.

Alma 35:3-6

When anger shows up in scripture, pay particular attention to the cause. The Zoramites are angry "because of the word" (v. 3), meaning because of the gospel truths Alma and Amulek taught. Sometimes truth incites anger. Speaking, as Alma and Amulek did, about a God who is at the margins, who welcomes everyone, who requires everyone to care for the least of these, will always threaten certain people. The powerful and wealthy Zoramites react with offense because the word "did destroy their craft" (v. 3). It disrupted their hierarchical systems of power. If they listened and internalized what Alma and Amulek said, it would force them to make changes to their society that they are unwilling to make. Their kind of privilege requires an underclass, an oppressed population who can be excluded and exploited. The word of God can dismantle the parasitic nature of their society, which is why they react so violently.

The rulers, priests, and teachers orchestrate the investigation and expulsion of anyone who approved of Alma and his brethren. These groups in this society have the most power to lose if the oppressed class is no longer under their control. In an echo of king Noah and his priests, the Zoramite church and political leaders united to form an elite class that enacts violence on those below them. In order to find out who disagrees with them, they find out "privily the minds of all the people" (v. 5). These ecclesiastical and governmental leaders act in the darkness and background in order to judge people and execute punishment. Their questions and concerns about beliefs are not rooted in community, care, or even curiosity. They are self-preservational and focused on their own power.

For the second time in a few verses, Jershon becomes a place of safety as the Zoramites now seek refuge there. The converted Zoramites have been expelled from their own land after experiencing long-term exclusion from their own synagogue. And the Anti-Nephi-Lehies, carrying the woundedness of experiencing all the horrors they faced at the hands of their own people, offer a site of acceptance and safety. The Zoramites knew where they could go for asylum. They go to Jershon because the Anti-Nephi-Lehies will give them empathy and compassion.

This moment must be particularly poignant for Amulek, who experienced rejection from his family for his religious beliefs[163] and also watched many of his people die by fire for their faith.[164] Alma's father also faced violence from the government after his conversion and had to lead his people into the wilderness to find safety. Uprooted communities traveling to a new land is an important and prevalent theme of the books of Mosiah and Alma. These men know the dangers of choosing faith. Readers can only imagine the heartfelt way in which "Alma and his brethren did minister unto" the beleaguered refugees as they came into Jershon (v. 7).

The LDS church has its own narrative of religious persecution, eviction, and immigration to a new land. Imagine if we let that story work on our hearts in the way the Anti-Nephi-Lehies did. We could make LDS spaces well known around the world as destinations for people seeking refuge. What if immigrants, refugees, exiles, and people persecuted for their beliefs around the world knew they would find safety and care with our folk? What if Mormon pioneer legacy was a driving force for us to create our own land of Jershon?

---

163. Alma 15:16
164. Alma 14:8–9

Alma 35:8–11

The Zoramites' anger increases and focuses on the Anti-Ne-phi-Lehies for their willingness to take in the converted Zoramites. Unsatisfied with expelling the believers of their society, now they feel rage toward anyone who helps them. This is power determined to punish and destroy. They *want* the oppressed to suffer. They crave the demise of a people. They created an underclass, cast them out, and still feel threatened because this group may have found happiness, peace, and safety somewhere else. There is something diabolical and pathological about someone else's liberation sparking an anger that craves the other person's suffering or death. This reaction creates systems and laws which make people scared to seek freedom. Any individuals or organizations which punish people for leaving the relationship or membership share something in common with these Zoramites. A church that creates a punitive theology that scares people into staying shares something in common with these Zoramites. Do not push people to fear the repercussions of liberation.

Zoram, the leader of the Zoramites, sends a message to the Anti-Nephi-Lehies threatening them and directing them to expel the converted Zoramites. He does not seem to have any understanding of who the Anti-Nephi-Lehies are and what they have lived through. They lived through genocide and did not pick up their swords. They abandoned their homes and land and started new lives among their former enemies. They already demonstrated their lack of fear of death and certainly will not be intimidated by a man threatening violence for welcoming oppressed people.

Instead of reacting in fear, they choose radical love. Verse 9 cannot be emphasized enough, and we ought to preach and teach it over and over again. In the face of threats, the Anti-Nephi-Lehies "did receive *all* the poor of the Zoramites . . . and they did nourish them, and did clothe them, and did give unto them lands for their inheritance; and they did administer unto them *according to their wants*" (emphasis added). They did not merely feed them; they nourished them. They did not simply house them; they gave them land for their inheritance, meaning permanent ownership. They did not only meet their needs; they answered their wants. This community moves to serve the least of these. Abundant hospitality overcomes the threats of hatred.

The Anti-Nephi-Lehies' godly love further enrages the Zoramites. They cannot stand that the people they treated so poorly found welcome somewhere else. In response, they go to the Lamanites and ally themselves against the Nephites for war. Importantly, the allyship of the Zoramites with the Lamanites is precisely the political move Alma was trying to avoid by going on his mission to the Zoramites.[165] In the end, Alma's actions not only failed to avert this event, they indirectly caused it. But although the Nephites feared a schism and alignment with their enemies, that fear does not stop them or the Anti-Nephi-Lehies from doing the right thing. They take a stand for justice, even when it is not politically expedient and even increases their physical danger. Although one of the initial purposes of the mission was to avoid war, they do not let war interfere with their protection of vulnerable people.

Alma 35:13–14

Because of their covenant of nonviolence, the Anti-Nephi-Lehies move out of the land of Jershon as it becomes a war zone and the Nephites move in to provide defense. Although the text claims this is "a war betwixt the Lamanites and the Nephites" (v. 13), that statement reads far too reductive. It is a war of Nephites protecting former Lamanites against Lamanites and former Nephites. This is not binary nationalism. The groups have split off and realigned so many times that these labels serve only the purpose of identifying opposing sides.

The poor Zoramites experienced second-class citizenship in the land of their birth. They were driven from their homes for their choice to follow God. But then they received land—good land which

---

165. Alma 31:4

would belong to them and their descendants forever. Poor in their former land, they become wealthier as refugees. They lost what little they had, only to find something much better than before. God upsets expectations and changes narratives.

Alma 36:1

The following seven chapters record Alma's words to his three sons. They approach at a time when Alma feels particularly sad, faces war against his people, and nears his own death. These chapters exemplify prophetic testimony mixed with the love and concern of a parent. The way Alma speaks here differs from how he preached to crowds in previous sections. He weaves together his experiences with an ancestral narrative and a blessing on his children.

Chapter 36 begins and ends with a promise that "inasmuch as ye shall keep the commandments of God ye shall prosper in the land." In between, Alma unpacks what this phrase means, giving it far more complexity than readers may initially assume it contains.

Alma 36:2

The foundational principle of Alma's sermon references an ancestral legacy of miraculous liberation. In verse 2, and again in verses 28–29, Alma speaks of God delivering God's people out of literal and metaphorical bondage. Starting a family story at a point of captivity and afflictions offers a powerful beginning.

The beautiful repetition of names reminds the reader that the God of Abraham is also the God of Isaac and Jacob and Alma and Helaman. Readers can name God this way for themselves in their prayers and sermons. *The God of Abraham is also the God of Fatimah and the God of Margaret.* We can place our own ancestors in relationship with God as well, naming God as the God of our mothers, grandmothers, and great-grandmothers. Substituting those names reminds us that God knows us particularly and personally. Giving three generations symbolically reminds us that God is whole and complete, and we are made so through God. How might you make Alma's invocation of God your own?

Alma 36:3–4

These two verses give two clarifications about Alma's call to prosper in the land. First, he says the righteous "shall be supported in their trials, and their troubles, and their afflictions" (v. 3). Alma does not start off with a message of joy, nor does he promise that prospering in the land means an easy life. Those who trust God will still have trials, troubles, and afflictions, just as those who do not trust God. God does not remove the struggles. The difference is that the former have divine support through hard times. This is, indeed, Alma's own story—he faced prison, torture, trauma, and grief. His life does not look like one of prosperity, but he knows God dwells with him.

Second, Alma explains that his knowledge of God comes through spiritual means, not temporal. He clearly distinguishes between the two, focused on helping Helaman understand the difference. In a context of a discussion on obeying the commandments and prospering in the land, Alma seems to clarify that God's support will be spiritual, not physical. Prosperity is "not of the carnal mind but of God" (v. 4).

Alma 36:5–11

Although the text gave an account of Alma's initial conversion and also referenced him telling other people about it, here we read a description of it in his own words. It reveals some interesting points, particularly in comparison to the record in Mosiah 27. Both accounts share the detail of describing the angel speaking with a "voice of thunder"[166] (v. 7). As we wrote in the section on Mosiah 27, God speaks in many different ways, including shouting—reverence is not limited to silence or solemnity. Limiting God's voice to certain circumstances

---

166. Mosiah 27:11 in the original account.

or ways of speaking results in a kind of spiritual tone deafness in which we might miss much of what God says.

Alma describes the three days and nights he lay unmoving as a kind of semi-unconscious paralysis in which he attempted to speak and move but could not (v. 10). During this time, his community gathered around him, fasting and praying for his recovery.[167] While Alma could not speak, his people prayed for him. He could not physically pray, but that did not stop prayers from being uttered. Although he could not move, his community fasted in his stead. They stayed present for him even when he had not been acting right by the church. In this way, Alma's experience was communal, not just individual. However, Alma narrates the story here—in comparison to the version in Mosiah—*as if* it were an individual journey, not mentioning the people who stood around him. Perhaps, for him, the salient moments were those when he felt left alone in the dark and despair of the confrontation of his own failures. Often, even the most harrowing moments of our lives are not devoid of communal care, even if we do not notice it. Alma omits his folk from his story, but as readers, we know they were there for him.

Alma's personal account states that he missed most of the encounter with the angel. After the angel's first line—"If thou wilt be destroyed of thyself, seek no more to destroy the church of God" (v. 11)—Alma collapsed and heard no more. He specifically notes that his companions heard more from the angel due to his unconscious state. Yet in the original account, the angel said a great deal to the entire group—none of which matches the line repeated twice in Alma 36:9 and 11—and departed before Alma's collapse.[168] The somewhat conflicting reports of the same incident speak to how spiritual experiences can be interpreted differently by separate people, or even by the same person, years later. Alma and the sons of Mosiah were all present at this incredibly important moment in their lives

---

167. Mosiah 27:21
168. Mosiah 27:17–18

and yet no singular account exists of what happened. An inbreaking of God is personal and individualized, even during a shared experience. Our journeys with God do not and should not conform to a single narrative. A great joy of mortality includes talking about unique experiences and appreciating the rainbow of divine diversity.

Alma 36:12–16

One of life's most important ethical rules is to do no spiritual harm to another person. It is a kind of spiritual Hippocratic oath ("First, do no harm"), one that respects the contours of someone else's faith. Hurting someone else's faith proves a particular kind of destruction. Any commitment to the social good understands the importance of not tearing down another person. Alma's spiritual torment comes from feeling God's displeasure for the ways in which Alma hurt people's relationship with God. His vivid description of suffering paints one of the more painful pictures in the Book of Mormon, including Alma's account of torture and imprisonment. Alma carries a specific, heavy grief for his actions. Deliberately harming people's faith goes against justice and grace.

Alma 36:17–19

Into Alma's pain and sorrow comes the memory of his father's words about Jesus Christ. After recalling his sins and grieving, now he remembers the promise of the Atonement. Memory and remembrance have the power to bring the greatest torment and the balm of relief at the same time. Memory work, harrowing and healing, invokes both captivity and liberation. LDS Church President Spencer W. Kimball said that possibly the most important word in the world is *remember*.[169] Part of memory's power comes from the fact that even bitter memories can still bring blessed relief. To add com-

---

169. Spencer W. Kimball, *Circles of Exaltation*. Speech delivered at Brigham Young University, Provo, UT, June 28, 1968. https://www.churchofjesuschrist.org/study/

plication, Alma states that the memory of his father's words allowed him to "remember [his] pains no more" (v. 19). Memory worked to make him no longer remember. This bewildering contradiction permits an omniscient God to not remember the sins for which we have repented. God moves in a divine power of memory in ways beyond what our human imaginations can comprehend. God knew us before we were formed in our mothers' wombs[170] and completely forgets our sins.[171] Divine grace and power allows certain times to disappear from memory.

Alma 36:20–27

Once again, Alma wraps joy and pain/suffering tightly together. The coupling of joy and grief runs throughout his narrative, which he clearly articulates in verse 21 as he compares the "exquisite," bitter pain and sweet joy of his conversion. These two feelings bound together play significant roles in his testimony and sense of self. A few verses later, Alma explains that he built his ministry on that encounter of tasting joy and his desire for other people to have the same experience. Ministry and missionary work can be an effort to share joy. And yet, Alma's life could be considered tragic in so many ways. He witnessed unspeakable horrors. He experienced loss, physical suffering, and disappointments. His whole ministry struggled against communities enmeshed in pride, idolatry, and violence. He consistently acknowledges those hard times: "I have been supported under trials and troubles of every kind" (v. 27). However, he also describes the great joy of his work and celebrates that "many have been born of God, and have tasted as I have tasted" (v. 26).

---

manual/teaching-seminary-preservice-readings-religion-370–471-and-475/circles-of-exaltation

170. Jeremiah 1:5

171. Hebrews 8:12

Alma 36:28–30

Alma brackets this sermon on prospering in the land with a second reference to an ancestral legacy of captivity and divine liberation. By reminding Helaman that he "ought to retain in remembrance, as I have done, their captivity" (v. 29), he also reemphasizes memory work. An essential part of what it means to prosper in the land means recognizing the hand of God in liberative movements.

Finally, Alma repeats his promise that keeping God's commandments leads to prospering in the land. Yet he interprets the phrase in a way very different from how superficial readers might. He ties it to an ancestral history of bondage, invoking memory work, and describing how joy interweaves with pain. As a final definition, he gives an inverse statement of what prospering is not: "inasmuch as ye will not keep the commandments of God ye shall be cut off from his presence" (v. 30).[172] Prospering in the land by keeping the commandments means tasting the joy of being in God's presence and remembering the blessings God has given you and your ancestors.

Alma 37:1–12

These verses include one of the few times the narrator speaks about the record itself: the value of the plates, their purpose, how to care for them, and what Alma thinks about them. While some of the authors in Jarom and Omni wrote about receiving and passing on the record, Alma's instructions to his son have far more detail and personal feeling in the description. Two important themes emerge. First, Alma emphasizes the importance of keeping the record safe and "retain[ing] their brightness" (v. 5), which seems to mean keeping them dynamic and relevant. Alma describes keeping scriptures bright through memory work, changing behavior, and having a relationship with God. Second, Alma repeatedly describes "a wise purpose" (v. 2) which he seems to understand only in part. Through

172. Alma 9:13

admitting the limitations of his own knowledge, Alma leaves open the door for greater understanding of the purpose of scriptures. People who continue to expound scripture, moving in text to expand their meaning and purpose, can reveal additional wise purposes for the text. Alma leaves room for further revelation.

What would it look like for scriptures to lose their brightness? Alma's counsel to Helaman implies that human action would have an effect on the brightness of the record, meaning the need to protect the value of the content, not just the safety of the physical object. The worth of scripture does not exist in a vacuum; humans dim or brighten scripture through use. The value of scripture hinges on how it is kept and applied. In particular, Alma values holy text's ability to enlarge our memories and change our ways (v. 8). So much of scripture is ancestral inheritance and memory. Scripture not only revives our memories of our ancestors; it also gives us access to their collective memories through their stories. As our own stories intermingle with their stories, a dialogue emerges and our memories enlarge. As we read others' stories and see ourselves in the good *and* the bad, we understand our role in repeating the mistakes of the past. These first two goals of scripture (enlarging our memories and convincing us of the error of our ways) are requirements for the third: to bring them to "the knowledge of their God unto the salvation of their souls" (v. 8).

Alma has at least a general sense of the mission of the Book of Mormon. The account of the people is to eventually go forth to teach the entire world (v. 4), an astonishing claim for a man in a small nation on the edge of a wilderness. Because he has access to Nephi's record, Alma also knows the Nephites will eventually die out, making the claim even more audacious. Yet he maintains his faith in the future of the plates without, apparently, understanding the particulars of the scriptures' mission. After vaguely referring to "a wise purpose" (v. 2, 12) multiple times, Alma specifically says the future of the text is a mystery to him and he refuses to speculate (v. 11). He believes they exist for a critical reason, even if it is not the purpose he desires. Alma seems to wish, rather than expect, the record to be the means of converting the Nephites after the success of the Anti-Nephi-Lehies (v. 9–10). This man spent his ministry among his own people and had to face their failures and sins. He appears unsure whether the text can hold the same power for the Nephites as it did for the Lamanites.

Knowing the future of the Nephites gives every prophet in the Book of Mormon a certain amount of hopelessness because they know their people will ultimately fail. In this moment, Alma seems to have little hope in the future of his own people. But he surmounts despair by looking into the far distant future and believing in a wise purpose he does not know. The work he does in engaging with the plates tells readers that scripture sometimes tells us both what we do not want to hear but also that things will work out in ways we do not understand or necessarily desire.

Alma 37:13-17

Alma repeats his promise from 36:30 that those who keep God's commandments will "prosper in the land," introducing the idea with a repeated, "remember, remember" (v. 13), which emphasizes the importance of his words. In the following verses, he connects his concept of prospering with access to scripture, linking the two with a reminder to "remember" (v. 14) and a parallel promise. Just as Alma inverted the promise of prospering by also giving the description of *not* prospering, "If ye will keep my commandments ye shall prosper in the land—but if ye keep not his commandments ye shall be cut off from his presence" (v. 13)—so he describes the guarantee of holy text: if we keep the commandments, "no power of earth or hell can take them from you" (v. 16), and if we do not keep the commandments, then "these things which are sacred shall be taken away from you" (v. 15). Alma connects prospering in the land with having sacred text, which brings with it the presence of God.

Alma 37:18–25

Alma's multiple references to "a wise purpose," his warnings about the spiritual state of the Nephites, and even his description of the thousands of converted Nephites all point to a poor emotional state. He seems almost desperate as he repeats promises that his work will be preserved for something outside of what he has lived and known. His life and difficult ministry have been full of disappointed hopes, among them a wish that the Nephites might repent like the Lamanites did. At the end of verse 25, he references "every nation that shall hereafter possess the land," indicating his knowledge of the Nephites' future destruction. As he reviews the past of the Jaredites and looks at the present state of his people, he puts his hope in unknown people of the future. He has to believe that his record will someday be able to completely fulfill its mission. The dark words of this chapter reflect a grief and sorrow for his people.

Alma 37:34–37

God offers the possibility of finding rest while also doing good work. We cannot simply will ourselves "to never be weary of good works" (v. 34), since mortality requires rest and relief. To do good works without weariness requires divine intercession. God has not asked us to run ourselves down to the point of compassion fatigue and soul exhaustion. In fact, stepping in to go beyond what we can do alone is antithetical to God's promise of grace and community. We are not meant to give more than we have, but when we ask continually for support, counsel, and direction, God shows us ways to serve beyond what we expect or comprehend.

Alma 37:43–47

Alma holds competing ideas in tension so masterfully. Just as he often speaks of joy and sorrow together, in this chapter, he describes the land of the Nephites as "promised" (v. 44) and cursed (v. 28). In verses 38–42, he discusses the miracle of the Liahona and also the failure of Lehi's family to live obediently and the hardships which followed. Although he insists on "the easiness of the way" (v. 46), things are never simple or straightforward for Alma in his rhetoric or testimony. The complexity he sees gets reflected in his explanation "that these things are not without a shadow" (v. 43). A shadow is not the opposite of an object. It takes the same form as whatever creates it and inherently cannot exist without that thing. A person and their shadow coexist naturally. For a man who sees joy and sorrow as two parts of the same experience, a cursed land is simply the shadow of a promised land. The same land can carry a curse and a blessing simultaneously because a shadow always follows.

This offers a powerful template for our own study of history and social systems. We should *expect* to see the shadows—meaning weakness, failures, or sins—of people, institutions, and organizations. Our land can be a land of promise *and* a land which has lived into a curse of oppression and violence. Acknowledging the shadows of our countries, churches, or heroes is not a lack of loyalty; it accepts that "these things are not without shadow." It recognizes Alma's counsel that only "the words of Christ, if we follow their course, carry us beyond this vale of sorrow into a far better land of promise" (v. 45).

Alma 38:1

Alma repeats his alternative definition of prosperity from 36:30. Alma's nuanced definition of prospering in the land marks one of the most important works of his in the Book of Mormon. How could Alma's repetition of prosperity as a relationship with God shift our understanding of blessings, divine protection, joy, and success?

Alma 38:2–15

This lovely chapter mixes Alma's roles as prophet and parent. His love for and relationship with Shiblon is clear: Alma finds "great joy" (v. 2) in his son for all of Shiblon's virtues and good works. Alma repeatedly calls Shiblon "my son" with affectionate and personal language. Alma rehearses his personal story of conversion and reminds Shiblon that wisdom must be learned through a relationship with God (v. 9).

Alma's words also give additional insight into what happened to him and his companions in the land of the Zoramites. Shiblon was tied up and stoned for his work during that time. And because Alma always mixes joy and grief together, he expresses joy from watching Shiblon's faithfulness, diligence, patience, and long-suffering during those harrowing experiences, events which must have caused Alma terror and distress at the time.

These verses essentially offer a guidebook on testimony. Alma explains how to walk in power and not hurt others with it. His counsel to simultaneously gain wisdom but avoid pride is foundational for how to fulfill spiritual call and be a good human while doing it. Alma makes clear that merely preaching impressive sermons is not enough; meekness and humility are critical components of a healthy spiritual life.

Alma 39:1–14

As Alma shifts his attention from Shiblon to Corianton, the tone and message change significantly. Shiblon has been an obedient, faithful child while Corianton has struggled. Although the problems and sins Alma describes seem straightforwardly focused on sexuality, a closer reading reveals greater complexity.[173]

Several signs point to Corianton's problems being more complicated than solely a relationship with a prostitute named Isabel. Alma chides Corianton for his pride, vanity, and materialism. Alma repeatedly calls his son to humility and modesty, rebuking him for "boasting in thy strength and thy wisdom" (v. 2), reminding him to "suffer not yourself to be led away by any vain or foolish thing" (v.

---

173. For further reading, see B.W. Jorgenson, "Scriptural Chastity Lessons, Joseph and Potiphar's Wife; Corianton and the Harlot Isabel," *Dialogue: A Journal of Mormon Thought* Vol. 32, No. 1 (Spring 1999), 7–34.

11), and finally counseling him to "seek not after riches nor the vain things of this world" (v. 14). Alma also corrects his son for abandoning their ministry among the Zoramites, which harmed Alma's efforts to preach (v. 11). Putting this chapter in the context of Alma's words to Shiblon reveals another important issue: the mission to the Zoramites included terrible experiences of persecution. Alma praised Shiblon for the patience and long-suffering Shiblon displayed in the face of binding and stoning.[174] When Corianton forsook his ministry, he left behind his brother and companions to face the violence of the Zoramites alone. God called him to minister in Antionum, and Corianton betrayed that trust. He was not where God asked him to be and where his brother needed him. Corianton's pride and boastfulness carried him away from his ministry and his poor actions had a deleterious effect on the entire mission. Corianton's heart lost focus on God and community. Perhaps this failure proved a greater sin than Corianton's actions with Isabel. Possibly the "abominable" sin (v. 5) Alma describes is ignoring God and abandoning companions. Corianton's pride and selfishness harmed his brother and friends as well as the Zoramite society.

Of the three named women unique to the Book of Mormon—Sariah, Abish, and Isabel—only Isabel has no voice of her own. The only references we have of her span two verses, Alma 39:3–4, so she easily serves as a passing embodiment of sin. Although these verses offer almost no information, many readers of the Book of Mormon have condemned Isabel for acting as a stumbling block to Corianton's spiritual life. In the absence of any information about her, she gets reduced solely to the role of a sex worker. While claiming guilt or innocence for her would be purely speculative, consider how other sacred texts treat women like Isabel. Rahab, from the Book of Joshua, looks quite similar to Isabel: both are women, harlots, foreigners (Rahab is from Jericho; Isabel is from the land of Siron). Just as Rahab lived on the border with a house that was "upon the town

---

174. Alma 38:3–4

wall,"[175] Isabel lived on the border of the land of the Lamanites. Both women physically and socially inhabit the margins of their communities. Rahab's testimony and bravery saved the Israelites and she became one of the ancestors of Jesus Christ through her son, Boaz. While the Book of Mormon fails to give the complete history of Isabel, her story may have been just as complex, unexpected, and important. Reducing her to a single point in her life and a few lines of text marks an unfortunate loss.

Reducing Corianton's sin to fornication signals a sexist interpretation of the text, given that Alma only states that Corianton went "after the harlot Isabel" (v. 3) and "after the lusts of [his] eyes" (v. 9). Assuming that because Corianton lusted after Isabel—and assuming fornication occured because Isabel was harlot—gives no space for Isabel's will or self-determination. It assumes that because Corianton wanted her, he must have gotten what he wanted, because a harlot would never reject sexual advances—an offensive and incorrect inference. There are unlimited possibilities about what occurred between Isabel and Corianton in this story, including a non-sexual passing encounter or rape. Because the narrative gives only a few vague lines from someone who was not present and entirely silences one of the participants, we would be wise to exercise caution in drawing conclusions about the text.

Finally, readers may be tempted (as in a status quo reading) to assume Alma's ranking of sins as universal, placing sexual sin as the worst offense to God behind killing people and denying the Holy Ghost. As explained previously, Alma may have been referencing the pride and self-centeredness which pulled Corianton away from his community and call, rather than solely sexual sin. However, it is better to avoid attempting to create hierarchies of sin, especially as universal categories.[176] God moves differently with each individual,

---

175. Joshua 2:15

176. Jorgenson, "Scriptural Chastity Lessons," argues that what Alma calls the sin "most abominable above all sins save it be the shedding of innocent blood or

and creating a fixed order is too rigid. God gave the Israelites the Law of Moses and then upended the law with Jesus and a new set of commandments. God forbade stealing but then asked Nephi to steal the plates. We should not be so attached to the ordering of laws that we miss how a dynamic God moves and rewrites and changes for new circumstances and people. The scriptures show the commandments as far more complex than a simple checklist. And while Alma counsels that repentance may not be "easy" (v. 6), he does not describe it as impossible. In fact, Corianton appears to eventually grow out of this period of spiritual immaturity and accept his call to preach, as Alma 43:1 explains that "the sons of Alma did go forth among the people, to declare the word unto them."

Alma 40:1–26

In chapters 40–42, Alma addresses Corianton's confusion and doubts about the resurrection. He understands that his son has questions, and this section contains a lovely dialogue to address those concerns. Multiple times, Alma uses the phrase "I perceive that . . ." and describes a certain point of theological confusion his son experiences. It is unclear how Alma receives these insights: is it purely prophetic insight into his son's mind? Is he intuiting questions from Corianton's behavior? Or has Corianton openly expressed his doubts to his father? The dialogue lacks Corianton's questions, although the questions are implied through the answers. Having the entire exchange would lend a deeper understanding of how the discourse came about and what precisely Alma tried to address with his responses. If the questions were part of the text, such as in Doctrine and Covenants 77 or 113, readers would have a more complete understanding of the answers.

---

denying the Holy Ghost" (v. 5) is actually a kind of spiritual murder, that of leading people away from God—something Alma would understand well. If that is the case, then the three sins Alma names would be murder, denying the Holy Ghost, and the destruction of others' testimonies. We discuss the serious problems involved with damaging others' faith in the section on Alma 30:13–17.

When Alma answers questions, he shares his testimony and what he knows about God. But he is also quick to share what he does not know or what he is unsure about. Here, Alma uses most of the chapter to explain the resurrection, but he begins with the limitations of his knowledge: "I unfold unto you a mystery; nevertheless, there are many mysteries which are kept, that no one knoweth them save God himself. But I show unto you *one thing* which I have inquired diligently of God that I might know" (v. 3, emphasis added). Alma makes clear that although he is a prophet and speaks with angels, he does not know all things. In fact, he has had to work diligently to know this one thing. Alma models how to be comfortable with not knowing. Despite his incredible testimony and a close relationship with God, he repeats again and again that he lives in some uncertainty or ignorance. In verse 20, for example, he couches his theological explanation in the phrase, "I give it as my opinion," making clear the limitations of his knowledge; he does not wish to conflate his opinion with fact. In verse 21, he again goes to some effort to separate what he knows from what he does not know: "But whether it be at his resurrection or after, I do not say; but this much I say. . . ." Alma shows awareness of the parameters surrounding what he knows and can comfortably identify and what he does *not* know. This template engages truth while recognizing limitations and imperfections. Alma weaves together a beautiful testimony with an acknowledgement of not knowing. Vulnerability does not mar truth.

Alma 41:1–15

Alma continues to explore complex doctrinal and philosophical questions about the tension between justice and mercy, what divine forgiveness looks like, and whether unrighteous people can be happy. Clearly, although speaking to Corianton, Alma is processing some of his own personal history, particularly his past experiences as a wicked man who fought against God. His conclusion in verse 14, that we should be merciful, "deal justly, judge righteously, and do good continually," pulls together four of Alma's core life values and finds a nice balance in the pull between justice and mercy. Justice moves in concert with mercy to increase our compassion and to push us to "do good continually." As philosopher Mark Wrathall has written about this section of Alma, "The ultimate purpose of justice, the work that justice aims to produce, is to help us find mercy—not just to receive acts of kindness or pity but to be transformed so that we become merciful. . . . We find mercy when we become beings who no longer seek after our own interests and rights but seek instead to compassionately relieve others of their unhappiness without thought for their dessert."[177]

Alma 42:2–8

In using the account of Adam and Eve to do the theological work of explaining mortality and redemption, Alma does not use Eve's name. He references Adam and uses "first parents" to describe them both, but the plural reference is inconsistent. For example verse 5 seems to speak only about Adam, although it's about both Adam and Eve, while verse 6 seems to reference both Adam and Eve, although it repeatedly uses "man" to describe both people. In the original Genesis story, Eve is a visible and critical part of the narrative. Here she is essentially erased. And while this may not seem to matter, when engaging in the work of exegeting scripture, it is critical to use precise and inclusive language. Vague or exclusive language compromises the doctrine. Rhetorical choices and doctrinal understanding are not separate. Alma's choice to not name Eve in this story makes his reading of the story incomplete.

Alma 42:13–25

Alma does some interesting work here on the relationship between justice and mercy. As Wrathall has noted, "the defining event in the

---

177. Mark A. Wrathall. *Alma 30–63: A Brief Theological Introduction*. Provo, UT: Neal A. Maxwell Institute, 2020. 105.

life of Alma the Younger—the event that transformed his understanding of himself and of his relationship to God and to the world—was
an event of unexpected, overwhelming mercy."[178] Yet Alma's ministry has been filled with events of terrible injustice: women and
children being burned alive, genocide against nonviolent believers,
and the exclusion of the poor from Zoramite synagogues, to name a
few of the most dramatic. In those cases, the law did not ultimately
enact justice, leaving observers to wonder when justice would occur.
Alma's own personal experiences with mercy give him a testimony of
its critical importance. He has lived into God's mercy. But his ministry has taught him the need for divine justice. This chapter reveals
his efforts to hold those two things in tension and understand which
ultimately prevails in the nature of God. As Wrathall writes, "Alma's
doctrine places the conflict between justice and mercy at the heart of
human redemption."[179] As a whole, Alma's exploration of justice and
mercy reveals what Alma wants to see from God, which may be why
he repeats so frequently in these verses that "God would cease to be
God" without the work of justice.

Alma states clearly that undiscriminating mercy is intolerable.
Although forgiveness is part of the work of Christ, it cannot be an
end in itself. Justice must be part of the equation or else God would
no longer be divine. While many of us, including Alma, come to God
for mercy, the oppressed and disenfranchised come to God for justice. Alma's work as a witness to some of the atrocities of human
behavior understands that this makes justice one of the ultimate and
immovable characteristics of God. Ultimately, Alma cannot believe
in a God without believing God will someday make right the terrible
things Alma has seen and set in order the injustice humans create.

The final note on these verses is Alma's interesting choice to
gender justice and mercy in verse 24. Female pronouns appear so
infrequently in the Book of Mormon that their use seems inten-

---

178. Wrathall, *Alma 30–63*. 88.
179. Wrathall, *Alma 30–63*. 91.

tional and worth examining. Alma names justice as a masculine trait—"justice exerciseth all his demands"—and mercy as a feminine one—"mercy claimeth all which is her own." Although Alma may be associating justice with strength and fortitude, many ancient and contemporary cultures connect justice with female figures. Ancient Egypt had Maat, the personification of order, justice, and truth. Rome's mythological Justitia and ancient Greece's Themis provided the imagery of the blindfolded goddess of justice which appears in many American courtrooms today. If justice and mercy are going to be gendered—and they needn't be—perhaps justice ought to appear as a representation of the most marginalized member of society, the person who is most in need of relief from injustice.

Alma 42:29-31

This is a fascinating conclusion to Alma's exploration of justice and mercy. Alma does not want his son to rest peacefully in the concept of mercy. As scholar Mark Wrathall writes, "In Alma's experience, mercy can be correctly understood only if it is accompanied by a full recognition of one's just condemnation under the law." Mercy should not be a calming agent that allows us to not worry about our salvation. Instead, it should motivate us toward repentance. Wrathall continues, "Alma's doctrine places the conflict between justice and mercy at the heart of human redemption."[180] Alma states clearly that there are good kinds of trouble; we ought to be troubled by the things that trouble God. Justice pushes people toward a "remorse of conscience"[181] while mercy can "bring you down to the dust in humility" (v. 30). Justice and mercy therefore have the same goal and act in partnership to move us toward God. Ultimately, Corianton is still called "to preach the word of God unto this people" (v. 31), despite his failures and doubts. Alma worships a God of justice who has a plan of mercy.

---

180. Wrathall, *Alma 30-63*. 91.
181. Alma 42:18

Alma 43:1

At certain times in the Book of Mormon, Alma and other prophets deliberately rest from their work, such as when Alma nurtures
Amulek after their trials in Ammonihah,[182] or when Alma and his
companions withdraw to the land of Jershon after preaching to the
Zoramites.[183] Alma also taught the concept of a divine rest for those
who have faith.[184] Yet here, Alma cannot rest. Perhaps this is because
the situation is so grave as the nation moves toward war or maybe it
is because Alma realizes he is close to the end of his life. Regardless,
Alma is a beautiful example of someone who appreciates the critical
value of rest while fully dedicating himself to his mission.

The sermons Alma gave his sons also offer readers insight into
the individual personalities of Helaman, Shiblon, and Corianton.
Knowing a little bit about their unique struggles and triumphs makes
this verse more powerful as they all "go forth" to preach the gospel.
Despite their different journeys with God, they are all called to the
work. This section of the Book of Mormon has many messages about
community, including this example of a group of preachers. Alma,
Amulek, the sons of Mosiah, and the sons of Alma form a kind of
abundant community of discipleship.

Alma 43:4–13

Although the text claims that "the Zoramites became Lamanites" (v.
4), and repeatedly describes the "extreme hatred of the Lamanites"
(v. 11) toward the Nephites, this is an oversimplification of the social
dynamics. The text makes this clear in verse 13 when it goes into a
more complex definition of who falls under the broad category of
Lamanites, but in the remaining verses, the more reductive label is
employed. The Zoramites and Amalekites ally themselves with the

---

182. Alma 15:18
183. Alma 35:1
184. Alma 12:36–37

Lamanites, but both groups were originally Nephites—the Amale-kites are descendants of the priests of Noah and the Zoramites only recently separated themselves from the Nephites. However, these two groups don't fully integrate into the Lamanites, as they remain distinct enough to be named as "chief captains over the Lamanites" (v. 6). The reason given for the Lamanite leader Zerahemnah's appointing Amalekites and Zoramites as chief captains was to "pre-serve [the Lamanites'] hatred towards the Nephites" (v. 7) and "stir up the Lamanites to anger against the Nephites" (v. 8). The Amale-kites and Zoramites have such an egregious lack of humanity that they become the leaders of a military designed to be as violent and full of hate and anger as possible. This force is organized with the design of fomenting animus and the ultimate goal to bring people into slav-ery. It is the deliberate creation of oppression through stoking hatred and anger via war. Dissenting Nephites and descendants of Nephites play a critical role in this attempt. The language of Lamanites hat-ing Nephites does not adequately describe the hatred of Nephites for other Nephites. The narrator does not fully address how some of their own people are now their enemies, making the Nephite/Lama-nite distinction increasingly irrelevant. This battle started because the Zoramites left the Nephites and allied themselves with the Lama-nites in order to attack Jershon, which is occupied by Lamanites who left their people and became allies of the Nephites.

Remember that this conflict did not involve the Lamanites until the Zoramites joined them. The battle started because of the schism of the Zoramite society. When the wealthy Zoramites expelled those who followed Alma and his companions, the dissenting Zoramites found asylum in Jershon, where the Anti-Nephi-Lehies gave them land and cared for them.[185] The converted Zoramites thrived in a space with-out their former ruling class oppressing them, which enraged the elite Zoramites so much that they joined the Lamanites. This kind of anger, fueled by liberated people prospering without the shackles of the aris-

---

185. Alma 35

tocracy, is not foreign to modern history. It appeared in the 1921 Black Wall Street massacre in Tulsa, Oklahoma, in which white attackers destroyed 35 blocks of one of the few financially successful Black communities in the country. Power that relies on people remaining as an underclass will quickly resort to overt violence in order to survive.

Alma 43:18–21

Though the Nephites and Lamanites have comparable weapons of war, the Lamanites lack protective gear, which the narrator cites as one of the major factors in their loss.[186] However, the Zoramites and Amalekites, who are the chief captains of the Lamanites, have more protective clothing than the Lamanites. So the Zoramites and Amalekites started this conflict, have historically acted to stir up the Lamanites to conflict, are in leadership roles in order to foment hatred and anger, and now have better protective gear than the rank and file soldiers. They clearly knew of the clothing the Nephites wore, as they are Nephites and wear that clothing themselves, yet they did not prepare the Lamanites with that kind of security. The chief captains have protections for themselves that they do not offer those below them. This scripture tells us that the Zoramites and Amalekites are using Lamanite bodies for their own ends. Their alliance with the Lamanites is not one of cultural affiliation or shared values, but of exploitive power. This does not take away the agency of the Lamanites; they have responsibility for their own decisions. But the fault of this war does not fall equally on all participants.

Alma 43:22–26

At other times in the Book of Mormon, God specifically directs the prophet about military strategy in order to flee from enemies or regain captives. This is the first time the prophet goes to God and receives explicit instructions about where to go to attack and kill other peo-

---

186. Alma 43:37; 44:18

ple. However, it is not unique to scripture; the Old Testament has multiple examples of military leaders consulting with prophets about strategy and how to effectively win in battle.[187] This link between God and bloodshed and placing God as a crucial part of winning a military victory deserves careful evaluation. It is possible that God gave Alma specific instructions in this moment—after all, the text explains that the Lamanites were about to "commence an attack upon the weaker part of [the Nephites]," (v. 24) making it possible to argue that Moroni's attack ultimately prevented a greater assault against innocent civilians. We also want to be careful to not casually strip God from other people's stories, particularly during dark periods of their lives. But any religious text that ties God to the work of death and violence requires strict scrutiny. People throughout history have claimed divine sanction of their military campaigns, often with horrific consequences. Also, while placing God into the victories of war is easy, it runs the risk of the same people feeling abandoned by God during periods of struggle, as the Nephites experience a decade later.[188] Part of our work as readers is to find the ways in which humans narrate God into human endeavors and justify our own actions by shielding ourselves behind our claim of God's approval.

Ultimately, it is not possible for readers to definitively decide whether God truly instructed Alma on where and how to kill Lamanites. Possibly this was a revelation, or maybe it was Alma inserting God incorrectly into his own experience. As seekers, what is important is to carefully interrogate the scriptures rather than simply believing what the narrator claims, particularly in sections that tie God to violence. While we need to be careful to not cherry-pick scriptures to satisfy our own ends, attentively evaluating messages about God sanctioning warfare is an important work of reading scripture for the least of these.

---

187. For example, Barak and Deborah in Judges 5:2–31; Saul and Samuel in 1 Samuel 13:8–23
188. Alma 58:7–9

Alma 43:30–54

The text repeatedly reminds readers who is good and who is bad in this story. The delineation is clear: "it was the only desire of the Nephites to preserve their lands, and their liberty, and their church" (v. 30) and "the Nephites were inspired by a better cause, for they were not fighting for monarchy nor power but they were fighting for their homes and their liberties, their wives and their children" (v. 45). It is possible, even likely, given the events of the narrative, that these claims are accurate. But remember that it comes from a single perspective, one person with a bias in an extremely emotional, fraught period. Be wary of texts in which all morality exists on one side, particularly during a violent conflict. Rhetoric in the midst of war is often far too reductive, leading people to justify their violent actions. Mark where this language occurs and notice when it is right before or after a description of death and destruction.

These verses are disturbing even if the reader accepts the premise that the Lamanites bear all the responsibility for the conflict. The author does not shy away from the gruesomeness of war, calling it "the work of death" (v. 37) and describing how the Lamanites' lack of protection allows the Nephites to destroy Lamanite bodies. The Lamanites' terror as they repeatedly try to retreat, only to meet more of the Nephite military, is palpable. The river Sidon, the same site where only thirteen years earlier the Nephites killed innumerable Lamanites and dumped their bodies,[189] is again the location of a horrifyingly bloody war. It is probable that some people who fought in that original battle on the banks of Sidon fought in this one as well. It prompts a feeling of hopelessness and stagnation, as if the people have made no significant progress toward peace. They are simply stuck on an endless loop of repetitive violence. The grief this prompts may make readers want to turn away and focus instead on more hopeful, uplifting scripture. But the Book of Mormon does not shield

---

189. Alma 2:34–3:3

its readers from the great failures of humanity. It does not excuse us from awareness of the grief and injustice of the world. It is a text which knows humans' capacity for horrific actions and asks readers to look at it clearly. War, enslavement, genocide, rape, and torture all appear in its pages, reminding us that these things occur throughout history and also every day in our modern world. God cares about the worst of humanity. Our scriptures tell us to not look away.

Alma 44:1–2

Moroni clearly states that the Nephites do not want to be "men of blood" (v. 1) or exert their power over the Lamanites. He wants them to surrender so that he can let the Lamanites go free. The repugnance he feels for death and slavery guides his military decisions. Yet despite the statement of his wishes, the Nephites do end up as men of blood when the Lamanites refuse to surrender. The description in verse 18 of the Nephites' swords wiping out the Lamanites stands in stark contrast to Moroni's words in these verses. This is one of the great tragedies of violence: people frequently have to make choices they do not want to make in order to defend themselves. Violence prompts sequences of events in which people must go against their principles and desires in order to get through a terrible situation. This compelled behavior often leaves lasting scars in the additional victimization of a survivor.

According to the narrative, this battle began when some of the Zoramites converted, left their land, and found refuge in Jershon. So while Moroni's claim that the Lamanites are "angry with us because of our religion" (v. 2) is true in that religion played a role in the conflict, it does not capture the full complexity. The Zoramites are angry because they lost the underclass of their society, thereby losing authority. The Lamanites seek to enslave the Nephites. This battle is about social hierarchy, resources, and power. The Zoramites/Lamanites aren't interested in the Nephites converting; in fact, they refused entry to their synagogues, which is the opposite of evangelizing. They want to subjugate the Nephites in order to increase their power and wealth. Religion is the reason the converted Zoramites left, but it is their liberation through religion that is the true threat to warring Zoramites. This is typical of violent conflict, in which religion is frequently used to strengthen group identities, amplify grievances, and dehumanize others in order to justify violence. Human needs and the struggle for power and resources are the true causes of conflict; religion is merely a tool used by those who benefit from contention.

Alma 44:3–5

Any claim of God's protection or deliverance from harm raises difficult theological questions. On the one hand, Moroni's ability to see God in dark places is beautiful, and can offer divine hope to those struggling under oppression. On the other hand, it prompts questions of why and how God participates in violence. Narrating God's presence into victory implies that God is always on the side of the winner. Was God on the side of the citizens of Missouri who chased 19th-century Mormons out of their homes? Was God absent for the 200 years America enslaved people? The world is full of atrocities in which God did not physically rescue innocent people. So while we can respect Moroni's particular claim, we ought not to expand it into a universal teaching. In addition, tying God to specific actions has historically been used as an excuse to do terrible things under the banner of spirituality. From the crusades to schools for Indigenous children, the language of God has been weaponized to enact terrible harm.

Moroni's words raise two extremely difficult theological questions: What do we do about cases in which God does not deliver people? And does God help people to kill other people? Humans have wrestled with these questions for millenia without definitive answers. Rather than offering conclusions, the Book of Mormon presents opportunities to wrestle with these difficult ideas. The Nephites' experiences can push us to reflect on how violence permeates our own societies. Moroni's claims can prompt our own examination of the ways we narrate God into our own lives, particularly in periods of conflict. Rather than simply pinning God to certain outcomes of victory or denying Moroni's testimony of God's presence in difficult times, readers can use the Book of Mormon's war chapters to engage in complicated and worthwhile conversations.

Alma 44:6–8

The only requirement Moroni gives is for the Lamanites to surrender their weapons and promise to not attack the Nephites again. Zerahemnah agrees to the first but not to the second. While he's willing to give up his tools for immediate war, he will not sacrifice his ability to attack and attempt to enslave in the future. What is most precious to him, even more than his life, is to subjugate others. Although it seems extreme, Zerahemnah is articulating a mindset which has appeared in other places in human history, in which those in power are so attached to power that they say, like Zerahemnah, that they will "perish or conquer" (v. 8). The American confederacy, French colonizers in Algeria, and the Afrikaaners in South Africa are all examples in which people were so committed to subjugating a population that they accepted death and destruction for the right to pursue their cause. They were willing to die for their right to have ownership over other people.

In some ways, Zerahemnah is remarkably self-aware. He realizes that his desire to enslave the Nephites is so powerful that he will break any oath he might make about preserving peace. He also knows that his people are raising their children with the same entitlement and love of power that has prompted this battle. This is a multigenerational cultural commitment to oppression.

Alma 44:12–16

Before the Nephite soldier scalps Zerahemnah, Zerahemnah seems to speak for his entire army, insisting that none of them will make a covenant of peace with the Nephites. After the scalping, the soldiers are able to choose for themselves and they make individual decisions about whether to continue fighting. At least a large number of them want to simply go home and not die, while those that remain need Zerahemnah to "stir [them] up to anger" (v. 16) in order to fight with passion. Given that the Zoramites and Amalekites originally became chief captains of the Lamanites in order to "preserve their hatred of the Nephites,"[190] this war does not seem to be a motivating cause for the Lamanite foot soldiers. Lacking protective gear and having watched their companions die, their willingness to risk death dwindles. Yet Zerahemnah understands that the rhetoric of violence is an art form. His ability to preserve hatred and anger is remarkably powerful. Although the text does not share the language he used to convince the remainder of the Lamanite soldiers to continue fighting, it's worth imagining what it was like. It likely sounded similar to the rhetoric used to preserve hatred and anger today. Recognizing how political leaders, certain members of the media, some corporate executives, and conspiracy theorists utilize the language of hate and anger as a rallying cry could help us respond, and eventually bring peace to our world. What kind of language prompts people to risk their lives in order to score points against their political or social opponents? What moves us collectively toward rage and resentment? Those are the words that Zerahemnah likely used.

Alma 44:17–22

As noted earlier, Moroni did not want to slaughter the Lamanites, yet that is exactly what happened. Yet, barring a willingness to die or be enslaved, he didn't have a real choice because of Zerahemnah's actions. People fighting for liberation have historically engaged in violence. The Book of Mormon indicates that the question of whether that violence is morally justified should be placed in the context of their situation. In the end, the surviving Lamanites make a covenant of peace to the Nephites. Yet the victory is not unambiguously trium-

---

190. Alma 43:7

phant. The number of dead is so great that they do not count them, and yet again they dump the bodies in the river Sidon. The feeling of futility is palpable. Although the Nephites merely desired to defend their lives and freedom, the violence has left lasting wounds.

Alma 45:1

This verse is interesting in comparison to Alma 28:5–6, which also describes the Nephite community following victory in a terrible battle in which innumerable people died. In both accounts, the people fast and pray, but in prior verses the tone is solemn and full of grief while the latter speaks of joy and worship. It seems likely that in the wake of war, people would feel joy, grief, relief, and solemnity all at the same time. Even believing God has led them through this terrible time would not prevent them from feeling the burden of the human cost involved. Tying these verses together gives a more complete picture of the likely emotions of the Nephites at this time.

Alma 45:2–8

Helaman's simple yet beautiful answers to Alma's questions immediately give the reader insight into who he is and his relationship with God. These verses offer a condensed version of chapter 36, the speech Alma gave Helaman about memory work and prospering in the land. In that chapter, Alma's definition of prospering in the land—having access to God's presence—reflects his promise that because Helaman has faith and obedience, he will prosper. Once again, the blessing is spiritual, not material.

Alma 45:9–14

Again, we must keep in mind as we read the Book of Mormon that the prophets and authors know their people are doomed to unbelief, war, and extinction. Every one of them fulfills their missions in serving, converting, and leading the Nephites with an awareness that their work is ultimately futile. Alma has the record of Nephi's vision,[191] but here he speaks with much more specificity about the destruction of the Nephites. It seems likely that Alma took Nephi's record, pondered it, and sought additional revelation about what would happen to his people. If so, this exemplifies the scriptural record acting as a catalyst for questions that reveal more light and knowledge. Whether examining Joseph Smith studying the Book of James or Nephi reflecting on the words of Lehi, the prophetic mind inquires and always searches for more and better understanding. These efforts of struggle are necessary to the ongoing cause of the restoration and serve as an example for anyone who wants to know God better.

Alma 45:15-17

Alma "blessed the earth for the righteous' sake" (v. 15) and then, immediately after, announces that the land is cursed: "yea, this land, unto every nation, kindred, tongue, and people, unto destruction, which do wickedly, when they are fully ripe" (v. 16). Alma simultaneously leaves a blessing and a curse on the land, and specifically states that the curse will hold for any people who inhabit the land in the future. This seems to reflect his understanding that the Nephites will eventually die out, but it is useful to think of his words continuing down through the centuries. A land can be choice and cursed at the same time. What people do on the land, how they act as stewards, and how they treat God's children will determine whether the blessing or curse prevails. Once again, the land itself is a character in the Book of Mormon, seeming able to react according to the actions of its inhabitants.

At this dramatic end to his ministry, Alma navigates two extremes and, once again, pulls oppositional concepts into tension. He blesses his sons and the church while prophesying the demise of the Nephites. He blesses the earth while knowing it will move against the wicked.

---

191. 1 Nephi 12

And he does this while looking into the far distant future, linking his own moment in time to generations ahead. Alma does not frame his final sermon for his present time. He clearly and deliberately connects his own people to the unknown people of the future, separated by time but sharing a common land. Just as he previously interwove joy and grief or justice and mercy, he pulls together the present and the future and a blessing and a curse in a beautiful end to his work.

Alma 45:20–46:2

As the efforts of Helaman and his brethren show, the work of the church requires constant maintenance. Alma spent his ministry preaching to the Nephites and reorganizing church leadership in order to address the constant erosion of faithfulness and commitment. The text explicitly states that conflict—"wars with the Lamanites and the many little dissensions and disturbances which had been among the people" (v. 21)—accelerated this erosion. The last two verses of chapter 45 provide critical context for understanding the schism described in chapter 46.[192] The Nephite society is susceptible to the cunning and flattery of Amaleckiah because they have grown proud from their "exceedingly great riches" (v. 24). The violent conflict erupts, rooted in a belief of superiority stemming from wealth. The breach splits the community to such a degree that the people are willing to fight and kill their own brethren (v. 1–2).

The Nephites' desire to kill the prophets is not uncommon in scripture. Truth-telling frequently provokes violence and makes people like Nadia Murad, Mahatma Gandhi, Malala Yousafzai, Leymah Gbowee, and Wangari Maathai the targets of hatred and brutality. Speaking God's word proves a dangerous work. Helaman's life is in danger at the very moment when he has lost his father because he inherited Alma's call to preach to the Nephites. He does not have time to process that loss before a threat to his own life emerges.

---

192. There were no chapter breaks in the original text, so this is one fluid story.

There is no reprieve for Alma's sons as they struggle with this enormous shift in their lives; their sacred work in the wake of loss gets met with terrible violence.

Alma 46:3–7

The Book of Mormon describes the physical stature of only a few people, most of whom are righteous men such as Nephi, Gideon, and Moroni. Why does the author include a reference to Amalickiah's physique? One possible reason is that, combined with his ability to flatter people, his physical characteristics give Amalickiah unearned and dangerous influence over others. As a tall, strong, charismatic man with a gift for words, Amalickiah conforms to the social expectations of who ought to have authority. He looks and sounds like a leader in the same way Moroni does, only he uses his talents in self-serving ways. The scriptures often defy assumptions about authority—Joseph was a younger brother, Moses was slow of speech, and Jesus was the son of a small town carpenter. Yet even today, humans struggle with the tendency to choose leaders who are tall, wealthy, good-looking, and charismatic. Amalickiah shows the danger in that.

Amalickiah's most compelling flattery promises power to the "lower judges of the land" (v. 4). Interestingly, these people already enjoy a certain degree of power and prestige through being judges. While they do not belong to the group with the most authority, presumably they have more than the general population. Yet, Amalickiah successfully lures them away with the promise that "he would make them rulers over the people" (v. 5). His most susceptible audience consists of people who want more privilege rather than recognizing what they already have. This depicts a key divergence between justice work and the rhetoric of Amalickiah. Like Amalickiah, the rhetoric of justice sometimes tells people they deserve more than what they have. But the objectives could not be more different. Justice speaks to people who have been denied equal opportunities and decent treatment, telling them that they have human rights and deserve dignity. Amalickiah taught people who had power that they should have even greater power in ruling over others. While the language may superficially look similar, crucial differences lie in the social location of the listener and the use of power. We must distinguish flattery, which tells a privileged class that they deserve more in order to exercise power over others, from social justice, which tells the marginalized they deserve more so that they can experience equality.

Although Amalickiah's efforts to influence the lower judges seem at first to be a political move, the issue quickly evolves into a religious one. Verse 7 explains that "there were many in the church who believed in the flattering words of Amalickiah, therefore they dissented even from the church." His desire for political power almost immediately impacts the spiritual health of the community. This exemplifies the womanist claim that the personal is political. Insisting that the church operates in a separate sphere from politics ignores the ways they have deeply affected each other for millenia. It also allows people to ignore or deny injustice by pretending that God does not care about political, social, or economic issues. Our religious lives do not operate in a vacuum separate from the rest of our lives.

Alma 46:8–10

The Nephites did away with a monarchy for the precise reason described in verse 9: one person with too much power can do extraordinary damage to a society. Yet the system of judges Mosiah created has not managed to avoid the contention and violence he feared. The Nephites still struggle with the human desire to simply follow and trust one person. Regardless of the political structure, one person can still create a divisive and dangerous movement. This verse names Amalickiah as a "very wicked man," one of only three *very wicked men* in the Book of Mormon,[193] all of whom happen to be Nephites.

The text, as we see with other individuals who seek to lead people away from God and beloved community, lays that fault at the feet of Amalickiah. While tempting to point to a single person as the cause of great social failures to protect and care for one another, even the most cunning person has limited power in a society rooted in righteousness. One person must have followers to help them exploit and expand existing weaknesses and fissures. There will always be people who aspire to lead by tapping into the basest parts of humanity, the parts rooted in oppression, pride, and a hunger for power. If individuals and organizations have not utilized a gospel which pushes them to examine, interrogate, and confront those parts of their humanity, they make easy targets for people like Amalickiah. An evil person cannot gain power without appealing to the brokenness of the community. If a society is healthy and follows God, one man like this cannot get power because the people recognize efforts to stir up oppression and hatred and they do not accept them. We see a powerful example of this when Korihor attempted to appeal to the Anti-Nephi-Lehies and they immediately rejected him.[194] They could recognize a threat to Zion in their midst because they had invested in love and care for one another.

Alma 46:11–18

Moroni is passionate, impetuous, and very human. His feelings, like the anger he shows in verse 9, seem to always be near the surface. Like Peter of the New Testament, he makes mistakes in his impulsivity, but he is also eagerly searching for God. He embodies one of the

---

193. The other two are the chief ruler of the Zoramites (Alma 35:8) and pre-conversion Alma (Mosiah 27:8). Turley, *Alma 1–30*. 30.
194. Alma 30:19–20

characters of the Book of Mormon who emphasizes the complexity of human disciples.[195]

Although Mormons frequently think of and depict these "title of liberty" verses as a bold, loud, masculine moment, the crucial moment in this story happens in verse 13, when Moroni "bowed himself to the earth, and he prayed mightily unto his God." The text returns to this prayer again a few verses later, describing Moroni as having "poured out his soul to God" (v. 17). This language of a deep longing for God to answer the wickedness of the dissenting Nephites speaks to the emotion Moroni so often displays. Before the public rally, Moroni pleads to God with a kind of anguish for what the people have already been through and what they are about to face. Even in all his armor, with the title of liberty in hand, this illuminates a vulnerable moment before God. Moroni's words clearly show he knows Alma's words and final prophecy, and he understands the peril of his own people.

Moroni's prayer stems from Alma's teachings in three ways: first, he begins with memory work. Alma frequently invoked ancestors, such as Abraham, Isaac, Jacob,[196] or Lehi.[197] Moroni, like Alma, understands the importance of remembering God as part of his ancestral legacy, and the title of liberty reflects that emphasis on memory. Second, Alma's last prophecy left a blessing on the land as well as a recognition of a curse on the land. Moroni explicitly ties the land into his prayer, naming all the land as "a chosen land, and the land of liberty" (v. 17). Moroni understands the land acts as a character in the Book of Mormon and the potential it carries to bless or curse its inhabitants. Finally, Moroni appears to know that the Nephite nation is eventually doomed to disbelief and extinction. When he pleads with God to not allow them to be destroyed "until we bring it

---

195. For further reading on Moroni's character, see Hardy, *Understanding the Book of Mormon*.

196. Such as in Alma 36:2

197. Such as in Alma 36:22

upon us by our own transgressions," he references a future in which the Nephites will fail. Like Nephi, Alma, and other Book of Mormon prophets, he works to delay the inevitable.

Alma 46:19–22

The Nephites who follow Moroni form a new covenant, with their torn clothing as the token, to"not forsake the Lord their God" (v. 21). They also build into the covenant their own consequence if they fail to follow the covenant, saying that God "may cast us at the feet of our enemies, even as we have cast our garments at thy feet to be trodden under foot, if we shall fall into transgression" (v. 22). It appears the people not only write their own particular covenant with God, they also enact a penalty on their own transgression. They set up parameters to govern their behavior, as if they know their own weaknesses. This is similar to the Anti-Nephi-Lehies' decision to bury their swords in the ground to avoid the temptation of going to war again.[198] The Anti-Nephi-Lehies knew their own proclivity for violence, so they built structures in order to bolster individual will. The Nephites know their own tendency to wander from God, so they imagined their own covenant and included accountability for their actions. The church does not tell people the terms of the covenant; the people write their own because of their desire to be closer to God. This covenant shows the spirit inspiring people to confront what they need to change as a community, and God appears to honor that choice.

Alma 46:23–27

Once again, Moroni roots his rhetoric in memory work, this time reminding listeners of the story of Joseph of the Old Testament. This particularly appropriate ancestral story serves this moment because Joseph was a victim of his own brothers. Likewise, the Nephites face

---

198. Alma 24:15–16

aggression from other Nephites, kin who have chosen power over family and community. It is a civil conflict, with the Nephites facing a threat from their neighbors, family, and fellow church members. Invoking the story of Joseph feels particularly pertinent.

Alma 46:29-30

The people following Amalickiah "were doubtful concerning the justice of the cause in which they had undertaken" (v. 29). This indicates that part of the flattery Amalickiah used to convince them to rebel mimicked language of justice. Sometimes evil uses the same language as righteousness in order to deceive people. We can separate rhetoric meant for justice and rhetoric designed for oppression by carefully examining the goal of the speaker. Importantly, the Amalickiahites begin to doubt the rightness of their cause when they see that they are in the minority. People standing up and vocally opposing Amalickiah and the lower judges, publicly stating the injustice of their campaign, plant the seed of doubt in the minds of Amalickiah's followers. Amalickiah understands the power of people speaking out against corrupt and wicked movements, which is why he removes his followers from the land of Nephi and separates them from their friends and family who could convince them of the wrongness of their actions. The outspoken folk model the importance of taking a visible stand against injustice and oppression, particularly at their inception. A vocal majority—or even a handful of truth-tellers—can sway people to make better choices.

When the Amalickiahites leave, Moroni fears a repetition of the events of the Zoramites and other dissenters who allied themselves with the Lamanites. This kind of schism has become a pattern in the Nephite society. The text recognizes this, describing the Amalickiahites as acting to "stir up the Lamanites to anger against them"

(v. 30), language identical to that used about the Zoramites' actions among the Lamanites.[199]

Alma 46:36–38

The title of liberty, more than a symbol of war or even victory, represents a token of the covenant the Nephites made to not forsake God. The Nephites' rending of their own clothes "in token, or as a covenant,"[200] was in similitude of Moroni's cloth. Therefore, placing the title of liberty on "every tower which was in all the land" (v. 36), rather than intending to send a triumphant or aggressive message, reminds the Nephites of their own need for self-reflection and repentance. It leads the Nephites to humility, which causes the peace the society briefly experiences. The continual symbolic reminder of their covenant helps them make choices which lead to "peace and rejoicing" (v. 38).

Alma 47:1–3

This is the third time within a short period of Nephite history that a group has broken off from the Nephites and then deliberately incited anger and hatred within the Lamanites in order to provoke war. The first time occurred when the Amulonites and Amalekites convinced the Lamanites to rebel against the Lamanite king and attack the newly formed Anti-Nephi-Lehies and, subsequently, the Nephites.[201] The second happened when the Zoramites and Amalekites became chief captains of the Lamanites in order to "preserve [Lamanite] hatred towards the Nephites," with the goal of enslaving the Nephites.[202] Although this third conflict shifted into a political conflict, with Amalickiah's conspiracy to become king, it began with an argument

---

199. Alma 43:8
200. Alma 46:21
201. Alma 24:1–2 and 25:1–3
202. Alma 43:4–8

over church leadership. The first faction broke off after Helaman and his brethren appointed priests and teachers for the churches and a certain group felt dissatisfied.[203] The dissenting Nephites established a pattern of tapping into preexisting animus and conflict to exacerbate and encourage it for their own ends. They exploit contention with the goal of gaining power. These stories—recorded in detail and placed next to one another in the record with similar rhetorical phrases, such as "stirring up to anger and hatred"—are meant to be understood together. These signify not individual incidents, but a recurring and fundamental societal problem. The "war chapters" between the Nephites and Lamanites actually offer a complex, faceted struggle of multiple, interwoven identity groups so heavily burdened by pride, greed, and lust for power that they destroy beloved community.

A group of Lamanites hesitate to follow the order of their king to attack the Nephites. Although the text cites only the Lamanites' fear of death as the reason for their reluctance (v. 2), it is also possible that they wish to adhere to the covenant of peace they made a mere two years earlier after Zerahemnah's campaign failed.[204] It seems likely that some of the soldiers of that battle have returned to their families and wish to live in peace for multiple reasons, including the covenant they made. However, the Lamanite king, determined to enter war, places Amalickiah at the head of the military. Once again, a Nephite heads the Lamanite army in order to increase the likelihood of violence. Dissenting Nephites have shown a remarkable capacity to spread hatred and anger in their search for power.

Alma 47:4–8

Amalickiah's strategy usurps the power of a people he tries to exploit in order to subjugate a nation. He comes to the Lamanite king with the appearance of friendship, but with a secret plan to not only start

---

203. Alma 45:23–24
204. Alma 44:19–20

war, but also to overthrow the Lamanite government. The Nephites repeatedly show themselves to be untrustworthy and dangerous allies for the Lamanites. While the Book of Mormon tells many stories of Lamanites entering Nephite land and disrupting peace and stability, it is important to notice the times in which Nephites enter Lamanite lands and cause problems. Ammon and his brethren's remarkable promise of servitude to the Lamanite kings[205] runs counter to so many other encounters of the Nephites in Lamanite land.

In this case, Amalickiah's actions cause a full schism of Lamanite society, prompting the military to turn against its own people as they flee conscription. The moment when dissenting Lamanites seek refuge in Onidah and their own army chases after them echoes the Anti-Nephi-Lehies' flight into Jershon because they desired nonviolence. The Lamanite cultural understanding of violence and war points to dissension and conflict in this society.

Alma 47:9–19

Lehonti's desire for power ultimately paves the way for his downfall. Amalickiah was clearly hesitant to attack the dissenting Nephites in their stronghold on top of the mountain. Lehonti's willingness to trust Amalickiah stems from his interest in becoming the captain over the entire Lamanite army. Amalickiah manages to deceive Lehonti and the Lamanite king through exploiting their ambition and widening the social fractures he helped create. It is a kind of "divide and conquer" strategy of coming into a community, sowing divisions, then playing the groups off one another as the leaders vie for dominance. Powerful people seeking even greater power have replicated the actions of Amalickiah, the Lamanite king, and Lehonti throughout human history. And while one or the other man seems, at certain moments, to have emerged victorious, the ultimate losers are the Lamanites, many of whom do not want to go to war but who

---

205. Alma 17:25 and 22:3

suffer as pawns in the hands of their leaders. As the three men work duplicitous schemes against one another, the people suffer the most.

Alma 47:21-30

The "token of peace" (v. 23) that the servants of Amalickiah exploit to kill the king came originally from the Nephites. The text does not explain how the Lamanites adopted this significant ritual; possibly it came from the covenant of peace the Lamanites made to Moroni,[206] or maybe it came by cultural transmission from the Zoramites or other dissenting Nephites. The relevant feature is that Amalickiah adopted an action signifying peace and used it to commit violence. This betrays not only of the king, but the entire Lamanite community, because it defiles something sacred and symbolically powerful.

Following the murder, Amalickiah and his servants use lies and deceit to create confusion and infighting among the Lamanites. They deliberately spread a false narrative in order to fracture the community, turn people against one another, and reap power. This perfectly models Jesus' teaching that "he that hath the spirit of contention is not of me, but is of the devil, who is the father of contention, and he stirreth up the hearts of men to contend with anger, one with another."[207] Amalickiah uses conflict to wedge communities apart and create rifts in which one group fights the other to defend lies. This is not unique to the Book of Mormon or Amalickiah. Around the world today, we see politicians using a playbook of lies and contention to manipulate and control. When confronting the most destructive conflicts in our communities, it is worth asking what lies are being shared and who benefits from them. Who gains or maintains power through social divisions? What kind of deceit might they use in order to exacerbate hatred and anger? These questions can help de-escalate violence and restore justice.

---

206. Alma 44:19
207. 3 Nephi 11:29

One final point to note in this section is the reference to Jershon, which once again plays the role of sanctuary. It operates as the moral compass of the entire land, a place that both Nephites and Lamanites can retreat to for safety. Since Lamanites and Nephites have found refuge there, we know that it is a diverse community of people who might otherwise be at war with one another. It appears to be the only place where, as a land settled by former Lamanites and protected by Nephites, integration of the two nations works. Jershon exemplifies a society that actually lives up to ideals of welcoming the stranger, ideals reminiscent of the words of the poet Emma Lazarus, "Give me your tired, your poor / Your huddled masses yearning to breathe free."[208] Jershon is a place rooted in nonviolence, and all downtrodden and hunted people know they can go there for safety.

Alma 47:32–35

The queen seems to understand her precarious situation as well as Amalickiah's duplicity. Her first response to his message reveals her appreciation of the threat, her bravery, and her commitment to her people. Before anything else, she asks Amalickiah to "spare the people of the city" (v. 33). Her second priority is to find out what happened, and she asks for witnesses beyond Amalickiah himself. The text does not make clear how she ultimately decides to marry Amalickiah or whether she is convinced by the lies of the servants. However, her options appear severely limited and it is possible she seeks to protect more than just herself. Her marriage to Amalickiah helps save her people from slaughter and also may have shielded any children she had from her marriage to the Lamanite king. Interestingly, this is the Book of Mormon's third Lamanite queen wielding power, directing people, and asking difficult questions of a Nephite.[209] While the

---

208. Emma Lazarus, "The New Colossus" *Emma Lazarus: Selected Poems and Other Writings*, Ed. Gregory Eiselen. Peterborough, ON: Broadview Press, 2002.

209. The first was the wife of Lamoni, who questioned Ammon about whether her husband was dead and testified of Jesus (Alma 18). The second was the queen who

characters and fates of the three Lamanite queens drastically differ, they share a sense of self-assurance and bravery.[210] No other female characters use their authority so boldly in the Book of Mormon.

Alma 47:35–36

Although the text frequently reduces the complexity of this conflict to the reductive labels of "Lamanites" and "Nephites," it also repeatedly interjects a reminder that the people are much more complex. Here, the book introduces group names which have previously gone almost completely ignored: Lemuelites and Ishmaelites, as well as "all the dissenters of the Nephites, from the reign of Nephi down to the present time" (v. 35), implying numerous other unnamed schisms. The author uses harsh language to describe the dissenting Nephites, calling them "more hardened and impenitent, and more wild, wicked, and ferocious than the Lamanites" (v. 36). This comparison demands pause. Readers have already seen how dissenters have capitalized on conflict and exploited people for their own personal gain. Their animosity toward their own people provides the fuel for much of the warfare between the Lamanites and Nephites. Yet in all of the condemnation of the vile Nephite dissenters, the author does not mention their clothing, skin color, personal appearance, or cultural practices. This crucial omission belies the text's earlier claims tying Lamanite wickedness to these things.[211] The Nephite dissenters are allowed to practice evil as individuals while the Lamanites are

---

believed that Aaron and his brethren had attacked her husband and ordered the servants to slay them (Alma 22:19–25).

210. Joseph Spencer notes the parallels of two Lamanite queens (Lamoni's wife and the Lamanite queen from Alma 47): Lamoni's wife meets Ammon, a royal Nephite, while the latter queen meets Amalickiah, a would-be royal Nephite. Ammon respects the queen's authority while Amalickiah seizes and manipulates it. In the former case, it *appears* as if the Nephite has killed her husband but he is innocent; in the other, it *appears* as if the Nephite has not killed her husband but he is guilty. "The Structure of the Book of Alma," *Journal of Book of Mormon Studies* 26 (2017): 278–79.

211. Such as 2 Nephi 5:21–24, Enos 1:20, and Alma 3:5–6

judged as a monolithic group whose culture must be condemned in its entirety.

Alma 48:1–5

Amalickiah, tragically, accomplishes his designs. His ultimate goal—to rule over the Nephites—is made clear by his immediate move to attack "as soon as" (v. 1) he comes into Lamanite power. While Amalickiah's thirst for power makes him happy to assume the Lamanite throne, ultimately his efforts there are merely a means to an end. The Lamanites become a casualty of his hatred for his own people. And as Amalickiah "inspire[s] their hearts against the Nephites" (v. 2) and "blind[s] their minds, and stir[s] them up to anger" (v. 3), the Lamanites become pulled into a war that many of them sought desperately to avoid. Notice the word "inspire" in verse 2. These verses offer a detailed description of what happens to the human soul when inspired by evil. James Cone describes this deliberate effort of people wishing to see others as less deserving of certain rights and opportunities by dehumanizing them.[212] The resulting blindness ignites anger that can move people to violence. Rage, not mere anger, moves a person to risk oneself for others; rage hardens the heart and decreases empathy, allowing people to do terrible acts of brutality. This blindness and rage go together and both turn a person inward, centering a person entirely on themselves. Rather than thinking about the suffering of others, Amalickiah convinces the Lamanites to become blind to others around them and less aware of the humanity of the Nephites.

He does so with the goal of enslaving the Nephites. He uses the propagandist tools at his disposal—in this case, the Lamanite "towers" (v. 1)—to preach hatred, anger, and disdain for others. This deliberate campaign moves people to violence in order to subjugate others. When Amalickiah forms his military, he appoints Zoramites—

---

212. Cone, *The Cross and the Lynching Tree.*

Nephite defectors who have attacked the Nephites in the past—as chief captains. This war was instigated by a Nephite, and is led by Nephites. It is, essentially, a civil war with Lamanites pulled into the conflict.

Alma 48:7–10

Although comparisons rarely serve the people of the Book of Mormon well, this one makes a useful point: while Amalickiah launches an active campaign of hatred, Moroni points the people toward God and works on strengthening their defenses. He puts the focus of their resources toward the weakest places in their land, eroding the power of the Zoramites' knowledge of the Nephites' cities. This beautiful metaphor illuminates how a community can decide to allocate resources equitably. By focusing on the most vulnerable, poorest, most fragile neighborhoods, schools, and individuals in our society, we can bring them up until they become our strongest places. That kind of work protects the entire population. When a society focuses its resources on the most crime-ridden, least-educated, most poverty-stricken areas and turns them into strongholds, then their enemies will be confused and denied. The Nephites' willingness to spend resources analyzing their own weaknesses, acknowledging them, and fortifying them was the key to the entire nation's preservation.

Alma 48:11–19

The author's commentary of Captain Moroni veers occasionally so hyperbolic that it serves as a reminder of the human filter of the writing of the Book of Mormon. No mortal, excepting Jesus Christ, has "perfect understanding" (v. 11). And while Moroni may have been an extraordinary human, he most certainly sinned and made mistakes, which undermines the claim that if everyone was identical to him, "the devil would never have power over the hearts of the children of men" (v. 17). The tribute to Moroni proves useful as a list of virtues to emulate. He not only did his work, but his "heart did

glory in it; not in the shedding of blood but in doing good, in preserving his people, yea, in keeping the commandments of God, yea, and
resisting iniquity" (v. 16). We can find life purpose in these beautiful things. He also teaches the Nephites to defend themselves but to
never use violence in any other situation (v. 14). Yet, while the author
also notes that Helaman (the prophet of this time) and his brethren
who risk their lives by preaching to the people, are "no less service-
able" to God, none of the other men mentioned (including Alma,
who the text says was taken up by the Spirit[213]) get the extravagant
praise Moroni receives. That does not mean it is a problem, it simply
serves as a useful reminder of the human element of the text. The
author—likely Mormon, a military leader himself who named his
son Moroni—clearly admired Moroni. His personal love for Moroni
shines through on the page. Just as that human filter influences the
exaggerated rhetoric about Moroni, so the entire text gets shaped
and formed by the authors' and editors' personal experiences and
feelings. The Book of Mormon offers a powerful record of their own
understanding of their journey with God, described in their own
terms, and it includes their own mistakes.

The definition of "prosper in the land" contained in verses 14–16
deserves another mention. The text lays out a commitment to nonviolence except in specific cases of self-defense. It then ties this
philosophy to God, saying, "this was their *faith*, that by doing so God
would prosper them in the land" (v. 15, emphasis added). This adds
another new aspect of prospering in the land in the Book of Momon.
It claims that part of qualifying for God's prosperity blessings means
decisively choosing peace. Verse 15 also gives an additional definition
of prospering in the land: "God . . . would prosper them in the land; yea,
warn them to flee, or to prepare for war, according to their danger." So
while the Nephites tie God's grace to military success, they equally tie
the phrase to fleeing from a dangerous situation. Prospering does not
necessarily mean fighting and winning. It may mean God telling them

---

213. Alma 45:19

to become refugees in the wilderness. Having God with you does not guarantee traditional victory, even when linked to warfare. This offers an important enlargement of the concept of prospering in the land.

Alma 48:20–25

They work constantly during this period to bolster the church, convincing people to repent and return the communal focus to God. The efforts of Helaman and his brethren manage to convince the Nephites to "humble themselves" enough to avoid intracommunal violence for four years (v. 20). The gospel uproots enough pride in their society that they can focus on love and unity rather than on power and control. However, readers should not forget that while the text describes the conflict beginning in verse 21 as being with the Lamanites, that vastly oversimplifies the struggle. As previously described, the involvement of Amalickiah and the Zoramites makes this war as much Nephites against Nephites as Nephites against Lamanites. That important nuance offers understanding of the tragedy and violence which follow.

Alma 48:22–25

Despite "much reluctance" (v. 22) from the Nephites and their efforts to fortify their cities, and thereby deter the Lamanites from battle, the Nephites still find themselves at war. They have worked so hard spiritually and physically to keep peace, but their partners in conflict have insisted on violence. Great grief comes with building community, living a righteous life, reaching out in goodwill, and still finding oneself at war. They desire peace for themselves but they also desire peace for their enemies, as the text says they grieved at the thought of the deaths of the Lamanites (v. 23).

Finally, the text clarifies again that while it continues to use the term "Lamanites," this word inadequately describes the people involved in this conflict. They are "those who were once their brethren, yea, and had dissented from the church, and had left them and had gone to destroy them by joining the Lamanites" (v. 24). "Joining" also seems deficient in characterizing the role Amalickiah and the Zoramites play in this war, particularly, as the text describes, with their propensity to "rejoice over the blood of the Nephites" (v. 25). Ultimately, Amalickiah and the Zoramites bear the greatest responsibility for the bloodshed which ensues.

Alma 49:3

The Book of Mormon previously gave conflicting explanations for the destruction of Ammonihah. First the text attributed it to the will of God through Alma's visionary promise that God would destroy Ammonihah unless the people repented.[214] Then it claimed Ammonihah's ruin was due to the anger of the Lamanites because of the conversion of the Anti-Nephi-Lehies.[215] This verse seems to support the first claim, saying the Lamanites destroyed Ammonihah "because of the iniquity of the people." This seems a fascinating contrast in competing claims of divine intervention in military events. The text puts God into the first attack on Ammonihah, even hinting that God used the Lamanites to annihilate the city. Did God create the rage within the Lamanites that led to their desire to destroy Ammonihah? Yet in this second attack, the text claims God's protection against the Lamanites because the Nephites have become a more (although not altogether) righteous people. The military history of the city itself bears testimony of the complexity of narrating God into violence.

Alma 49:4–9

Bondage as a theme runs throughout the books of Mosiah and Alma and becomes particularly relevant to this story because of Amalickiah's obsession with enslaving the Nephites. The central conflict in this war is not over natural resources, possession of a city, or who is

---

214. Alma 8:16
215. Alma 25:1–2

next in line for the monarchy. It is whether the Nephites will become the slaves of the Lamanites and Zoramites. This signals a very particular reason to go to war.

Much of the language in this chapter's almost farcical descriptions of the Lamanites sets up an intellectual battle between the Lamanites and Moroni. As a group, they vacillate between "uttermost astonishment" (v. 8) and great "disappointment" (v. 4) so frequently that the text edges into caricature, flattening the Lamanites into a sub-human group. What was the goal of the author in using this hyperbolic language? How does it reflect his social location? Although it may be due to the author's love for Moroni and a hatred for the Lamanites, it is worthwhile to not take the description of collective shock and astonishment too literally.

The last point to note in these verses is how the text struggles with what to call the people attacking the Nephites. Is it fair to call them Lamanites when their leaders who have caused hostilities are Nephite defectors? On the other hand, does the leader change an entire people's identity, especially when some of them did not want to go to war in the first place? The complexity of this nation's identity, again, cannot be reduced to a single label, although the Book of Mormon and this book employ it for the purpose of simplicity and readability. Yet names and identities are fundamentally crucial to know and remember.

Alma 49:10–25

Moroni's leadership focuses on making the previously weak places strong. Fortifying these fragile places ultimately protects the entire society. His approach has two components which work together: the first is to alter the geographical landscape of the place through walls and ditches. The text describes this in detail, with references to the "ridge of earth" (v. 4), "forts of security" (v. 13), and a high "bank which had been thrown up" (v. 18) as protection. These structural changes alter the very earth on which they stand. The second component is to give the individual people the resources they need to prepare themselves: they have "stones and arrows" (v. 19) as well as "swords and . . . slings" (v. 20). These two strategies must work together in order to be effective. Stones would not have helped much without a wall, but neither would a ditch have done anything without people armed with arrows. In a similar way, those building beloved community must simultaneously address the structural problems that leave vulnerable populations exposed while also giving individuals resources to meet their specific challenges. Preparation for threats looks like protecting people on multiple fronts.

These verses also provide contrasting insight into the Lamanite leadership, which looks very different. Amalickiah, consistently willing to sacrifice Lamanite bodies in his quest to rule over the Nephites, is never even present on the battlefield. The text emphasizes this, noting that "he did care not for the blood of his people" (v. 10). The Zoramite chief captains also do not appear to care for the lives of the Lamanites as they decide to honor the oath they made to destroy the city of Noah (v. 13), even when it becomes clear that proceeding with their assault is foolish (v. 17). The tragedy of the Lamanite soldiers in this story should not go unnoticed. Amalickiah and the Zoramites spend Lamanite lives freely and without restraint. Perhaps it should not come as a surprise that when the Zoramite chief captains die, the Lamanites surrender (v. 23). The text accentuates the divergence in identity and values between leadership and soldiers in verse 25, saying, "when the Lamanites saw that their chief captains were all slain they fled into the wilderness. And it came to pass that they returned to the land of Nephi, to inform their king, Amalickiah, *who was a Nephite by birth*, concerning their great loss" (v. 25, emphasis added). As if readers could not recall, the book reminds us that Amalickiah and the chief captains were born Nephites, and their defection is the primary source of this tragedy.

Alma 49:28

The Nephites thank God for "delivering them from the hands of their enemies." God has extraordinary power to deliver people who invest in protecting the most vulnerable. In this verse, the Nephites worship the God of the least of these, a God whose miraculous power pours down on people who recognize those among them with the least chance of surviving and thriving, and who then invest in ways to prepare and protect those people. The question is not whether God delivered them in this moment, but whether they shifted their ways of thinking so that they could recognize the ways in which God has always protected and cared for the marginalized. When the people reoriented their own focus and priorities, seeing the weak not as the weak but as part of a whole that needed fortification, they could let God prevail in their lives.

Alma 49:30

Notice that Corianton acts as part of the group of righteous people playing a crucial role in the ministry to the Nephites. Although he struggled in the past, he is still called and chosen. Note here that although the text invokes "great prosperity in the church," which might imply material wealth, the phrase gets followed up by naming the children of Alma and their mission to preach the gospel. Alma's unrelenting message was that prospering means having the blessing of God's presence. Readers can assume that Alma's children would teach the same understanding of that phrase. This would also fit with the verse's explanation of peace and prosperity as a consequence of the people's "heed and diligence which they gave unto the word of God."

Alma 50:1–6

With more time to prepare, Moroni organizes defenses for "*all* the cities, through *all* the land which was possessed by the Nephites"

(v. 1, emphasis added). Although the most vulnerable places came first, once he has enough resources, Moroni includes everyone in his defensive strategy. Notably, the text does not mention preferential treatment for the wealthiest or most powerful cities. The weakest came first, then everyone else. This depicts an equitable endeavor of preparation and security.

Tragedy lurks inside this extraordinary effort of manpower and resources in engineering and defensive strategy. The incredible industry and innovation described in these verses raises the question of what these people could have accomplished if they did not have to put all of their efforts into preparing for war and trying to stay alive. One of the great casualties of living on the edge of survival is the loss of creative accomplishments that accompany human thriving.

Alma 50:7–15

According to the text, some pockets of land near Nephite areas acted as neutral Lamanite territories—and possibly provided fruitful trade and intermingling areas—in the "east wilderness" (v. 7). Without clear cause, Moroni orders his army to force all the Lamanites from their homes in that wilderness area and into the clearly defined Lamanite territory. The Nephites then colonize the east wilderness and the borderlands and build settlements along the frontier (v. 9–10). They not only build defensive structures, but cities that apparently include women and children (v. 13–14), a typical sign of settlers' intentions to permanently occupy land.

Claiming land and this kind of hardening of borders typically signals a community moving toward violence, and it is not without unintended consequences. As scholars Patrick Q. Mason and J. David Pulsipher have written, while Moroni's decision has "compelling logic" in short-term thinking, violence "provides the seeds for its own perpetuation" in the long term. From the Lamanites' perspective, the Nephites' action was highly aggressive. Evicting Lamanites from their homes and then building cities on land which borders theirs could easily appear threatening. Mason and Pulsipher conclude, "The Lamanites direct their first attacks toward the new Nephite settlements, presumably in what they consider a justified act of reconquest to drive out the invaders and occupiers of their native land. Violence can—and often does—rebound on itself."[216]

Alma 50:17–23

The wealth of the Nephites described in these verses acts as a hinge between the settlement of cities on the border—which will be the sites of much bloodshed and sorrow in the coming chapters—and yet another schism and outburst of violence. Although the riches are not necessarily a problem (the Book of Mormon describes periods of time in which the people use their wealth to build Zion[217]), the placement of the verses in the middle of these problematic actions indicates something amiss in the Nephite society.

Verses 18 explicitly defines prosperity as exceeding riches, which puts it in tension with verses 19 and 20—even while the text seems to intend for them to cohabitate. Verse 20 quotes Alma's definition of prosperity as having "the presence of the Lord."[218] By putting verse 18 with verses 19 and 20, the text acts as if exceeding riches and having the presence of the Lord are the same thing. The author does a very dangerous thing by conflating the two concepts and muddying Alma's definition of prosperity. Wealth is not inherently bad, but in no way is wealth synonymous with God's presence.

The author again reveals bias and confusion in verses 21–23, which include some important truths mingled with statements undermined by the text itself. Verse 21's note about the Nephites' own contentions and sins which have "brought upon them their wars and their destructions" offers an important counterbalance to the narrative of Nephite protagonists and Lamanite villains. Particularly during the

---

216. Mason and Pulispher, *Proclaim Peace.* 81.
217. Such as in Alma 1:26–31
218. Alma 9:13; 36:30; 37:13; 38:1

war chapters of the book of Alma, dissenting Nephites have been the greatest cause of violence. Yet this moment of introspection gets undermined by the claim that "those who were faithful in keeping the commandments of the Lord were delivered at *all* times, while thousands of their wicked brethren have been consigned to bondage, or to perish by the sword" (v. 22, emphasis added). Clearly not all faithful people in history, or even in the Book of Mormon, experience deliverance. Abinadi, the women and children of Ammonihah, and the Anti-Nephi-Lehi martyrs offer examples of people who died for the faith. Although one could argue that the text intends deliverance to mean spiritual salvation, not deliverance from oppression or struggle, the text's own examples in the same sentence—bondage and perishing by the sword—indicate that the author meant otherwise. A claim about spiritual salvation is not supported by the text.

While the Nephites may have felt particularly happy during this time (v. 23), the surrounding context betrays serious underlying problems in their society that they did not confront and repair during this time. In the subsequent verses, they erupt into a conflict over land which quickly turns deadly. That is not a sign of a healthy, peaceful society, despite the text's pronouncement of happiness.

Alma 50:25–27

Following on the heels of the explanation in verse 21 that the sufferings of the Nephites stem from their own contentions and bad behavior, they once again face a schism. This time, the fighting takes place in the colonizing cities on the border and centers on ownership of territory. The number of times in the Book of Mormon that the Nephite society violently separates and turns on itself illustrates that the nation as a whole, particularly during this period in the book of Alma, is not well.

Alma 50:28-36

The Nephites have good reason to believe that Morianton's flight north would bring calamity (v. 30), having experienced similar tragedies several times in recent years. Defecting Nephites do not seem able to leave peacefully; they return with a thirst for blood and desire to enslave their former kindred.

The hero of this story is an unnamed maid servant who suffers domestic violence and then risks her life to warn the Nephites of Morianton's plans. The battery she experienced, described as serious, was likely not an isolated incident. Abusers tend to escalate greater acts of violence over time. Her status as a servant, a woman, and a survivor of abuse all put her on one of the lowest levels of the social caste system, making her decision to become a spy one of the bravest actions in all of the Book of Mormon. Perhaps Morianton's name, and not hers, ought to be lost to history.

Verse 35 describes Morianton as being inspiring and having flattering words. Other wicked men, such as Sherem, Alma the Younger prior to his conversion, and Amalickiah also had the gift of flattery.[219] Wickedness often masquerades as charisma, and flattering words frequently lead to people's downfall in the Book of Mormon. Morianton, an abusive, brutal man without regard for human life in his public or private life, can inspire and flatter people.

When the people who followed Morianton promise to change, the Nephites accept them back into community in an extraordinary moment of grace. Not only are they not prosecuted, but they "were also restored to their lands" (v. 36). The Nephites allow the followers of Morianton—people who earlier "were determined by the sword to slay them" (v. 26)—to return to their homes and land and form "a union . . . between them" (v. 36). What does this scene add to our understanding of the balance between justice and mercy when navigating a rupture to community?

---

219. Jacob 7:4, Mosiah 27:8, Alma 46:5

Alma 51:1–8

This chapter begins with yet another fissure in the Nephite nation, this time over what system of government they should use. The reign of the judges, only twenty-five years old at this point, has been an extremely turbulent quarter century for the Nephites. Perhaps some of them long for the peaceful period under the rule of king Benjamin. But the driving force of the movement comes from "those of high birth" who "sought to be kings" (v. 8). This raises questions of what kind of social strata exist in the Nephite society. We already know from the story of Morianton that their culture has an underclass of servants. Here, it appears that not only do they also have an upper class of rulers, but that those people qualify for their position through their birth. These elites wish to consolidate their influence by narrowing the number of people who hold power and creating a monarchy. The text makes their wishes clear: the king-men not only desire power, they want "authority *over* the people" (v. 8, emphasis added). They do not wish for power in order to empower others or to use their power to lift up others or build community, as king Benjamin did. They do not seek to strengthen the vulnerable around them and help others have the ability to live fuller lives. The king-men want power for the purpose of oppressing and marginalizing others. That dangerous, corrupting force threatens the Nephite nation.

Alma 51:9–21

The timing of this political crisis proves disastrous for the Nephites because they simultaneously face an internal and an external threat. The self-serving king-men "were glad in their hearts" when the Lamanites attacked, and "refused to take up arms" to help protect their kinsfolk (v. 13). These people decide that because they did not get the political policy they wanted, they will watch their neighbors die and even rejoice in it. Their people face a particularly difficult external threat and they choose to compound the vulnerability because of their unwillingness to make any sacrifice for their community.

On the other side of the conflict, thousands of Lamanites have died in recent battles with the Nephites (v. 11). Yet this appears to be no great loss to their leader, Amalickiah, because he does not care about the deaths of the Lamanites.[220] His focused thirst for power and personal hatred of the Nephites endangers an entire nation. The parallels between him and the king-men are clear: their selfishness and pride become the all-consuming forces in their lives. When they do not get what they want, they indifferently make other people the casualties in their quest for power. Amalickiah's oath to drink the blood of Moroni[221] offers an inversion of covenant-making. Covenants are often intended to be about sacrifices the person making the covenant is willing to make. In contrast, Amalickiah's oath causes the sacrifice of other people's lives. Both he and the king-men act only for themselves at the expense of community.

Within this context of the king-men and Amalickiah deliberately and indifferently sacrificing the lives of people around them for their own selfish pursuits, Moroni becomes angry (v. 14). The intensity of Moroni's anger is unique in the Book of Mormon, and it is worth questioning why the text gives space for Moroni's fury in a way that is different from other positively-viewed Nephite leaders. Of all the Nephite protagonists, only Moroni exhibits extreme anger. Outrage is not despair, grief, fear, or disgust, although it is related to all of those things. It seems unlikely that in the centuries of Nephite history only Moroni has felt the kind of wrath that the Book of Mormon articulates in these verses and elsewhere in his narrative. But anger is universal to the human experience, and given the scenes other Nephite leaders have witnessed (genocide, human sacrifice, abuse of family members, and war crimes, to name a few) they likely felt the kind of wrath that Moroni feels in this moment. What is more probable is that the text allows Moroni to feel and act upon anger because he serves as a general, not a prophet. He gets described as a man of God, but funda-

---

220. Alma 49:10
221. Alma 49:27

mentally he acts militarily, not as a spiritual leader. The book seems to give him space to experience these intense negative emotions not otherwise narrated into the stories of Nephite leaders.

This depiction holds importance because anger is an inevitable part of working in the cause of justice, particularly when a person labors with their own people on issues of great importance. Moses grew so angry with the Israelites that he smote a rock and cried to the Lord in frustration.[222] When your own community acts against its own best interests and makes everyone vulnerable, passionate feelings naturally follow. So many prophets throughout the Book of Mormon found themselves in the situation of trying in vain to stop their people from slipping into patterns of oppression, injustice, and deep harm. They must have felt anger, as well as other inescapable negative emotions, during that process. It comes with the work.

None of that excuses Moroni's actions, even if it gives readers empathy for his rage. Moroni watches people in his own community—people who already enjoy comfort and many privileges in their lives—rejoice in the impending deaths of their neighbors, and he realizes they prove a greater threat even than the Lamanites. His choice to compel people to fight or face death (v. 15) is indefensible, yet offering a better option proves hard in the crisis of war. Regardless, violence is always a choice, even when the alternatives seem problematic or insufficient. The horror of this level of killing, let alone within one's own people, is hard to imagine: four thousand people killed and even more put into prison without trial (v. 19). This episode makes Moroni one of the truly complicated figures of the Book of Mormon.

Alma 51:22–28

Although Moroni's violent efforts may have helped the Nephite nation survive the Lamanite onslaught, he cannot force them to

---

222. Exodus 17

build beloved community. His individual struggle in "subjecting them to peace and civilization" (v. 22) cannot substitute for a collective effort. Regardless of how righteous and powerful he is, he cannot force them into peace. Without their collective belief in the value of protecting the vulnerable and caring for one another, Moroni proves utterly unable to cultivate Zion. All his petitions and the full force of his military cannot replace soft hearts and a love for others.

The speed with which the Lamanites claim the new Nephites cities indicates how the internal strife weakened the nation. Unsurprisingly, compelling people to fight against their will did not create an effective military force. Damaged by the infighting, contentions, and subsequent lack of trust and goodwill, the Nephites sustain enormous casualties and lose their "strongly fortified" cities (v. 27). Moroni faced real-world consequences when he had to decide what to do with the dissenters. He knew people would die. The decisions of the king-men affected not only their own lives but those of the innocent people around them. We can draw a direct line from the choices of those of "high birth" who "sought to be kings" (v. 8) to all the men, women, and children who die in Nephi, Lehi, Morianton, Omner, Gid, Mulek, and the other cities. This makes this story a tragedy. By deciding to center their lives on themselves and their interest in power over others, the king-men's choices had ramifications for the entire Nephite society, particularly on much more vulnerable people.

Alma 51:31

Here we see another example of the author's military rhetoric becoming so hyperbolic that it betrays the human bias through which he writes. It is not reasonable to claim that "*every* man of Teancum did exceed the Lamanites in their strength and in their skill of war." If the weakest Nephite warrior was stronger and more skilled than the strongest Lamanite warrior, then these war chapters would be much shorter. The flourish the author uses, particularly when referencing his military heroes, reveals that scripture is not without human foibles. The Book of Mormon, in particular, contains doctrine mixed with human narrative, creating a complex and subtle book of scripture.

Alma 52:8

Quite a bit happens in the following chapters about prisoners and soldiers who surrendered. It is worth paying attention to how these groups of people get treated. The rhetoric around the vulnerable people—their living conditions, and their (lack of) treatment as human beings—all changes depending on the current context and the person in charge.

Alma 52:11

Too much hardship following tragedy takes a toll on relationships, as described in this verse. Moroni's desire to help his friend is clear, but he faces too many burdens of his own. In a community overburdened with poverty, lack of rights, war, a pandemic, or other long term struggles, there may be periods of time in which everyone feels so exhausted by their own trials that they cannot come to the aid of their neighbors. They feel the needs of those around them and desire to reach out in love but have no extra capacity to help. That causes an emotional strain on individuals and on relationships over time. To have to say, "I would come unto you, but behold . . . I cannot come unto you" as Moroni writes here underscores a particular kind of loneliness.

Alma 52:33–35

Once again, the Lamanites are led by a defected Nephite, Jacob, who is unwilling to compromise or surrender, regardless of how many Lamanites die in the process. The text has yet to name a single Lamanite in a position of leadership in the current military or Lamanite government. Verse 35 seems to encapsulate the war chapters of Alma, with Moroni wounded and Jacob killed. No one escapes from these conflicts unharmed, even the victorious armies. Death and destruction surround everything, with Nephites in leadership positions on every side. The tragedy lies in how avoidable the suffering was.

Alma 53:2

Joseph Smith taught that "Friendship is the grand fundamental principle of Mormonism."[223] The Bible offers many examples of close, essential friendships: David and Jonathan; Naomi and Ruth; Elijah and Elisha; Mary, Martha, and Lazarus; and Paul, Priscilla and Aquila, to name a few who were loyal and true to one another. Although the Book of Mormon only faintly hints at female companionship, it offers several beautiful examples of male friendships that exhibit nurturing love and kindness. Alma and Amulek protect and feed one another in their homes.[224] The sons of Mosiah travel and preach together. Here, the text offers a small insight into the love Moroni has for his friend Lehi and how he has maintained that friendship over distance and the struggle of war. These lovely examples depict the importance of male relationships.

Alma 53:8–9

With Moroni gone, the Nephites once again slip into infighting. Although "intrigue" (v. 8) makes the conflict sound like a soap opera, the situation is clearly more serious, as verse 9 cites the "iniquity" among them and verse 8 points to the loss of land (and presumably loss of life) that follows. Although the text never clarifies the cause of the conflict or who participates, this offers another example of a community unwilling to work and sacrifice as a unified whole. One of the important lessons from the war chapters of Alma is that a sin-

223. "Discourse, 23 July 1843, as Reported by Willard Richards," p. [13], The Joseph Smith Papers, https://josephsmithpapers.org/paper-summary/discourse-23-july-1843-as-reported-by-willard-richards/3
224. Alma 8:27, 15:18

gle individual cannot substitute for community. Regardless of how righteous and capable Moroni appears, he cannot force the Nephites to invest in their community. Zion cannot rest on the backs of a few people, and at this time the Nephites, as a whole, too narrowly focus on their individual interests to work cooperatively. So while Moroni travels from place to place trying to shore up the nation, the effort proves unsuccessful because too many of the people refuse to care for their neighbors. It shows a striking contrast to the Anti-Nephi-Lehies in the following verses. Moroni does not need to go to Jershon because the culture there is radically different. They established a beloved community of care and do not appear to depend on one individual's leadership.

Alma 53:10–15

As we described in the section on Alma 27:4, "moved with compassion" (v. 13) marks an important phrase in scripture. Jesus was moved with compassion when he performed some of his most important miracles.[225] Joseph Smith cried out for God to be moved with compassion when he sat miserable in Liberty Jail.[226] Perhaps most importantly for this story, the only other time this phrase appears in the Book of Mormon is when the sons of Mosiah act to protect the Anti-Nephi-Lehies from the Lamanites by migrating them into the Nephite land. Decades later, the Anti-Nephi-Lehies are so moved with compassion that they offer to break their own covenant with God to protect the Nephites. Miracles happen in scripture when people are moved with compassion.

Although Helaman shares the same faith as the Anti-Nephi-Lehies, they did not make the same covenants. Yet he honors the covenants the Anti-Nephi-Lehies made, *even though it comes at his own people's expense*. The Nephites are in dire danger, yet Helaman

---

225. Matthew 9:36, 14:14; Mark 1:41, 6:34
226. Doctrine and Covenants 121:3

acts so vigorously to protect their covenant that he actually "over-powers" (v. 14) the Anti-Nephi-Lehies efforts to break it. He is willing to die for their journey with God.

How do we do that for one another? How do we help someone else keep their commitment to God, even when it does not look like our own?

Alma 53:16–22

This society raised children who have not made the same covenants as the previous generation who then act out of love and compassion for the people who have protected them. The sons of the Anti-Nephi-Lehies understand and appreciate what the Nephites have done for them over the decades and take action not only on behalf of their own families, but for those who have guarded their parents. This society likely has many single mothers. The Anti-Nephi-Lehies suffered an enormous amount of death earlier in their history, which may be part of the reason that these young men particularly cite learning from their mothers.[227] After many of them endured widowhood, war, and immigration to a new land, the mothers of these young men built a beloved community with sons deeply committed to protecting them.

The Anti-Nephi-Lehies chose their name deliberately,[228] and this book has argued for the importance of respecting their choice. Here, although their sons clearly revere their parents, the children of the Anti-Nephi-Lehies decide to give up that name and "call themselves Nephites" (v. 16). They have the choice to name themselves and to choose their own covenants, regardless of how important those same decisions were for their parents. Helaman and the Anti-Ne-phi-Lehies each exhibit extraordinary respect for the different faith journeys their kinsfolk take.

---

227. Alma 56:47–48
228. Alma 23:16–17

The young men's decision to change their name to Nephite also further undermines any kind of biological meaning to the Nephite/Lamanite labels. With a Nephite on the Lamanite throne and Zoramites serving as the chief captains of the Lamanites military, Noahite/Nephite priests intermarrying with Lamanite women, and now former Lamanites taking on the Nephite name, any idea that these two people are ethnically different is simply a social construct. The sons of the Anti-Nephi-Lehies can *choose* to be Nephites. Rather than functioning entirely as a circumstance of their birth or lineage, it is what they call themselves. And in this moment, when many of the Nephites struggle to understand the responsibilities of community, these young men actually act to redefine the name of Nephite, bringing new honor, hope, and covenant to the label.

The last note from these verses is that the Anti-Nephi-Lehies "never had hitherto been a disadvantage to the Nephites" (v. 19). Regardless of the resources it took to protect the Anti-Nephi-Lehies, the Nephites never saw them as a burden, even before their sons came to help. Caring for this vulnerable population was not seen as a weight or a hardship; they were simply a part of their community.

Alma 54:3

In the coming chapters of Alma, pay particular attention to what happens to the women and children. In the last few years of this bloodthirsty war, women and children get pulled more deeply into the conflict—such as later in this chapter, when Moroni threatens to arm them for battle (v. 12)—and get named more frequently as victims and captives.[229] Here, the Lamanites have taken women and children prisoner while the Nephites have captured only soldiers. This may be a deliberate choice on the part of the Nephite military, or it may be a function of the war occuring on their land and the Lamanites occupying Nephite cities. Regardless, this conflict does

---

229. Alma 56:30–31, 60:13

not take place in designated battlefield sites, out of the range of non-combatants. The capture of cities and the movement of violence into living spaces creates a new kind of casualty. The destruction is no longer limited to a death count. While the text frequently cites the number of soldiers killed, readers must imagine for themselves the other kinds of carnage occurring.

Alma 54:5–14

Moroni's epistle to Ammoron demonstrates how his tendency toward anger, rashness, and being emotionally charged does not always serve him well. Much of the language he uses, such as calling Ammoron "a child of hell" (v. 11) is unlikely to get him the exchange of prisoners he professes to want. He invokes a lot of language of the justice of God, calling on Ammoron to repent (v. 6) and threatening him with hell if he does not (v. 7) while claiming the Nephites as "the people of the Lord" (v. 8). These stark lines do not build the connections a negotiator usually creates. This is a pattern for Moroni, who also told Zerahemnah to surrender because the Nephites would dominate through righteousness.[230] His argument proved unsuccessful in both cases. Moroni excels at motivating people who already agree with him, but when he is in an adversarial relationship, he merely escalates the conflict. He repeatedly resorts to force, either physically or rhetorically, and he uses God as an adversarial weapon. The way he calls people to change repeatedly fails, giving a warning for those in conflict today. Using this kind of angry rhetoric in calling others to justice merely makes people angry in return and widens divisions. Is this about proclaiming a God who invites people to repent?

In addition, Moroni's threats of arming women and children, usurping Lamanite land, and obliterating the Lamanites (v. 12) undermine his own claims of moral authority. Although the text seems to underscore the point that the Lamanites, unlike the Nephites, have

---

230. Alma 44:1–5

taken women and children as prisoners of war (v. 3), using children as combatants seems a far less ethical practice. Even threatening such an idea is inexcusable. By warning the Lamanites of his willingness to take their land and commit genocide, Moroni increases fear and distrust. His letter indicates a decisive move from a defensive to an offensive posture. He no longer acts in justice when he acts in rage. His years-long witness to the ravages of war influence his rhetoric. His own language and behavior here, although it fits with his tendency to act rashly and harshly, does not square with what he values and what he has said about himself. This epistle reads similar to his assertion in Alma 55:3 that he "will seek death among [the Lamanites] until they shall sue for peace," but contrasts sharply with his words a decade earlier, when he told Zerahemnah that the Nephites "do not desire to be men of blood."[231] Ten years of seeing and engaging in terrible violence has taken a toll on Moroni. The death, rape, and starvation he has witnessed had consequences. Living that kind of life affects even a man committed to righteousness.

Alma 54:15–24

Ammoron's letter contains striking claims about identity, family legacy, and right to reparations. These issues are complex for Ammoron. Although he could be called a disaffected Nephite, he has completely rejected this label and calls himself a Lamanite, adopting their grievances as his own. Although his own brother killed the Lamanite king,[232] Ammoron tells a narrative in which he is not complicit in the ongoing violence.

Notice the pronouns Ammoron uses to distinguish who belongs to whom in these verses: the Lamanite army belongs to him (v. 16), although his brother usurped the crown. The Nephite ancestors, however, have nothing to do with him (v. 17), despite the high likelihood

---

231. Alma 44:1
232. Alma 47:24

that he is at least distantly related to Moroni. When he writes of how the Nephites "did rob [the Lamanites] of their right to the government when it rightly belonged to them" (v. 17) he seems to make no connection to Amalickiah's murder of the Lamanite king and marriage to the queen. And when he closes his letter, he claims to be "a bold Lamanite" (v. 24), despite having just claimed descendancy from Zoram (v. 23). He shifts quickly between identities, seemingly having no good sense of who he is or where he belongs. He has only hatred toward the Nephites and a desire to exercise power over other people, roots too shallow to sustain a secure existence. Despite claiming identity with the Lamanites, he simultaneously understands he is not truly a part of them: when he explains why this war started, he writes that it is "to avenge *their* wrongs" (v. 24, emphasis added). His language makes clear that because of his choices, he is a king without a people.

Verse 23 deserves a significant pause in our reading. In his account, Nephi described Zoram going willingly into the wilderness with Lehi's family.[233] Hundreds of years later, that narrative comes back to haunt the Nephites. It is impossible to know where the truth lies: how freely Zoram went with Nephi, whether the Zoramites carried this narrative of harm through the centuries or whether Ammoron only recently recreated the story to set himself apart in the narrative. More important than what factually occurred, however, is how stories of violence, ethnic identity, and trauma ripple out in unexpected and uncontrollable ways. While the biological difference is certainly nonexistent, the social divisions among these groups consistently and repeatedly exacerbate these issues, with tragic results.

Language around violence and power in Ammoron's epistle deserves notice. According to the text, this war began because of Amalickiah's desire to bring the Nephites into bondage,[234] a claim confirmed by Ammoron's call for the Nephites to "subject your-

---

233. 1 Nephi 4:35
234. Alma 48:4

selves to be governed by those to whom the government doth rightly belong" (v. 18). This indirectly describes slavery, although his claim of a "right" to their personhood is consistent with historical justifications for oppression. His threat of "eternal" war (v. 20) is also consistent with abusive behavior. Eternal war reads like a corrupted version of immortality, with war and slavery that goes beyond death. Wishing for such reveals a deep depravity.

Alma 55:4-9

Again, the text reveals how the terms "Nephite" and "Lamanite" have become increasingly irrelevant through time as various factions separate and merge: a Lamanite is part of the Nephite army (v. 5), while a disaffected Nephite leads the Lamanite army. A few verses later, the soldier Laman leads Nephite soldiers into a Lamanite camp carrying strong wine in order to intoxicate the warriors and set free their prisoners (v. 7-8). The Lamanites' inability to recognize Nephites in their midst—or perhaps the normalcy of estranged Nephites allying themselves with the Lamanites—further points to the lack of significant difference between these groups. The barriers between them are a social construction, inherited hatred and prejudice passed down through generations willing to continue enacting violence.

Alma 55:19-25

Despite Moroni's earlier rage and his promise of "seek[ing] death among [the Lamanites] until they shall sue for peace,"[235] his actual plan of action does everything possible to avoid killing people. His principles seem to win out over his anger in this case. He chooses the path of nonviolence, even when his enemies are drunk and unconscious before him and he has the opportunity to easily slaughter them. In the end, he gets what he wanted, with the chief captains

---

235. Alma 55:3

"pleading for mercy"(v. 23)—or, in other words, suing for peace— but without death and destruction.

This scene offers an interesting comparison to Nephi's murder of Laban. Nephi and Moroni both faced life-and-death decisions about what to do with a dangerous adversary who was drunk and helpless. While the morality of Nephi's decision proves difficult to weigh, it is interesting to note that his choice to kill Laban put Nephi in additional danger by triggering fear from Laman, Lemuel, Sam, and Zoram,[236] Moroni's determination to keep the Lamanite prisoners alive allows him to make use of them to keep the Nephites safer. The nonviolent route appears to have fewer unintended disadvantages and better outcomes.

Alma 56:1

Up to this point, the war chapters of Alma have focused on Moroni's narrative, but in this chapter the account shifts to Helaman. Although readers sometimes think of Moroni as a prophet, the text names him as a military man who seeks God. Helaman is a prophet who, because of his circumstances, has to take on the role of a general. While the two men share some leadership roles, they do their jobs in fundamentally different ways. Pay attention to these differences, noting how Helaman's role as the keeper of the records and pastoral guide for the people orients him in a slightly divergent direction.

Alma 56:2–3

Helaman frequently offers open expressions of love and concern to those around him, and the opening words of his epistle to Moroni depict an excellent example. Calling Moroni "beloved" (v. 2) and offering up comfort in the midst of the suffering of war, Helaman opens with compassion and humanity. He quickly expands that in verse 3 by tying the Anti-Nephi-Lehies, the Lamanites, and the Neph-

---

236. 1 Nephi 4:28–30

ites to Lehi, their common ancestor. By using the Anti-Nephi-Lehies as a bridge between the Lamanites and Nephites, Helaman employs legacy as a tool of peace instead of as a weapon of war. While Ammoron and other militants use the origin story to inflame conflict, Helaman emphasizes the groups' shared heritage.

Alma 56:5

The Anti-Nephi-Lehi young men *chose* Helaman as their leader. Given the need for fighters, they could have chosen to follow any of the great Nephite military minds, such as Moroni, Teancum, or Lehi. These men, descendants of Lamanites, make the significant choice of selecting a Nephite man with spiritual, not military experience. This meaningfully compares to the current situation of the Lamanite army, which is commanded by a Nephite who has forced himself into leadership. There is an additional layer of comparison in the Anti-Nephi-Lehies' decision to willingly take on the name of Nephite to help their community[237] while Ammoron has violently claimed the title of Lamanite,[238] to the detriment of the Lamanite people. Individual, ancestral, and social names matter. The ways we utilize those names and the narrative we build around where we belong and which names belong to us plays an important part in social justice.

Alma 56:11

This section of the Book of Mormon repeatedly ties God and country together, as if the causes were one and the same. Womanist theology pushes back on this linkage, insisting that the forces that demand loyalty to the state are often the same that confine women and oppress marginalized populations.[239] Some Christian denomi-

---

237. Alma 53:16
238. Alma 54:24
239. Elizabeth Shüssler Fiorenza, "Feminist Studies in Religion and the The*logy In-Between Nationalism and Globalization," *Journal of Feminist Studies in Religion*, Vol. 21, 1 (Spring 2005). 111–119.

nations also claim that while patriotism may be fine, it ought to be kept entirely separate from faith. For them, putting the two on the same platform signals a type of idolatry because it implies that the two things are equal in importance.[240] A country's laws and the laws of God may sometimes run in opposition to one another. A social justice reading of these chapters asks readers to ponder the linking of those loyalties and the way those links have been and continue to be weaponized against vulnerable populations. How do we separate them in our own lives?

Alma 56:16–17

Despite fighting "valiantly by day and toil[ing] by night," the Nephite army is "depressed in body as well as in spirit," having suffered "every kind" of affliction (v. 16). This marks a dark time, even though they have worked hard for a just cause. Though committed to their cause, they know that God does not guarantee them victory and they may die in their efforts (v. 17). To be depressed in both body and spirit characterizes a particular kind of struggle, one that many readers may relate to during particular times in their lives. Fighting against oppressive forces is a wearying work.

Alma 56:27–32

Although they cannot fight, the Anti-Nephi-Lehies bring food, not only to the Nephite soldiers (v. 27) but also to their families (v. 28). The deliberate inclusivity of this act, although it puts additional

---

240. Anabaptists have long believed in a clear separation between church and state, along with their commitment to nonresistance. "In contrast to the church, governing authorities of the world have been instituted by God for maintaining order in societies. Such governments and other human institutions as servants of God are called to act justly and provide order. But like all such institutions, nations tend to demand total allegiance. They then become idolatrous and rebellious against the will of God." *Confessions of Faith from a Mennonite Perspective*, Article 23. Scottsdale, PA: Herald Press, 1995. 85.

strain on the land of Jershon, reflects the Anti-Nephi-Lehies' commitment to holistic community. They care about all the people, not just the ones who can wield a weapon.

The Lamanites, however, see the food as a threat (v. 29), and this triggers a Nephite strategy to lure the Lamanite army away from the city of Antiparah and stealthily surround them. Notice the multiple paradoxical pieces to this subterfuge: to lead away "the most powerful army of the Lamanites,"[241] the Nephites use food, a simple item that addresses a basic human need, yet which is perceived as a threat. The food was supplied by the nonviolent resisters of a land known to welcome refugees, and it is carried into the wilderness by youth with almost no military experience. This entire story centers around an authority losing its position of strength through the power of food, young people, and noncombatants.

Alma 56:37–41

Helaman's army does not have the strength to confront the Lamanites, so they simply run into the wilderness. Without a plan aside from the Nephite commander, Antipus, overtaking the Lamanites, the young men must simply march directly ahead as fast as they can. This is God in flight, on the run. Unwilling to sacrifice his sons, Helaman's only strategy is to stay on the move. Here we see yet another example in the Book of Mormon of people finding safety by running into the wilderness.

Alma 56:43–45

Somewhat surprisingly, Helaman asks his inexperienced troops if they will go to battle. Unsure whether he faces a trap, he wants to know their desires because he does not know the best answer. This exemplifies how Helaman's leadership differs from other military generals. Just as the Anti-Nephi-Lehies have invited him to be their

---

241. Alma 56:36

leader, he invites them to help decide what to do. Helaman's focus seems to be on the relationships he has with these young men and his investment in them as people.

His description of their courageous response seems worthy of notice. When Jesus healed the servant of a centurion, he marveled at the man's faith, claiming that he had "not found so great faith, no, not in Israel."[242] The centurion was an outsider to the community, but Jesus recognized a particular kind of faith in him. Similarly, Ammon sees faith in the queen of the Lamanites unlike anything he has ever experienced "among all the people of the Nephites."[243] Something incredibly powerful happens in engaging with people who are unlike you and witnessing their journey with God. As Helaman sees courage different from anything among his own people, it brings him joy and strength.

Alma 56:46-48

Once again, Helaman emphasizes his close relationship with these young men of Jershon. They have chosen the name of Nephite and asked him to be their leader; now they apply the name of father to him, and he repeatedly calls them his sons. There is a kind of closeness to this family. Given the history of war and genocide against the Anti-Nephi-Lehies, many of these soldiers' fathers are likely dead. They choose to love Helaman, and he loves them in return. Yet their relationships do not stop there. The young men describe the Lamanites as "our brethren" (v. 46) and voice their desire for peace with them. Even in the midst of fleeing from them, they do not rhetorically treat them as enemies; in fact, they recognize them as family. While they recognize their responsibility to help the army of Antipus, their words and actions are bound up in language of compassion and the preservation of life.

---

242. Matthew 8:5-10
243. Alma 19:10

After naming Helaman as their father and the Lamanites as their brothers, they then turn to their mothers. The Book of Mormon only twice gives a glimpse of the work women do: the first is when it describes the women in Lehi and Sariah's family bearing children and eating raw meat in the wilderness.[244] The second is here, a moment that implies decades of teaching and nurturing. As a child of a single mother, these verses gave one author of this book (Fatimah) a chance to see her own family in scripture. She recognized the strength of her own mother, who accomplished extraordinary things in the face of oppression, and connected it to the Anti-Nephi-Lehi women. And while we may wish for a thousand times more information about the women of the Book of Mormon, it seems that when they do appear, they do so in moments of pivotal need where they show strength beyond imagining. These women's lives deserved to be recorded.

In their invocation of the faith of their mothers, the sons seem to imply their own imperfect faith. They "do not doubt [their] mothers knew it" (v. 48) rather than announcing their own convictions. While they may not be sure of God, they do not doubt their mothers, and they are willing to hang their faith there. Sometimes testimony is choosing your mother. Sometimes it is not doubting what your grandmother said. Sometimes the faith of young men rests on the fact that they believe their mothers. At no other point in the text does a man point to a woman as an anchor or example for himself. But the people of Jershon have a particular kind of community, different from anywhere else in the Book of Mormon.

Alma 56:55–56

Helaman goes looking for every single one of the two thousand soldiers because that is what families who have chosen one another do. He feels bound to them not only out of duty but out of love. Signifi-

---

244. 1 Nephi 17:2

cantly, having God's power with them resulted in less violence and death, as the Lamanites were so frightened they did "deliver themselves up as prisoners of war" (v. 56).

Alma 57:6–12

Provisions drive much of the narrative of the war chapters, who has them, where they are going, and who can control them. Provisions, a shorthand term for the necessities of life, are always crucial for survival. But during times of increased stress, such as war or severe poverty, provisions become a more focused priority. Scarcity underscores their value. It is therefore worthwhile to track the provisions in these chapters and consider how they get used as a stand-in for power. In these verses, the Nephites go to great lengths to (successfully) intercept the Lamanites' provisions and redirect them to Zarahemla (v. 11). Despite their difficult situation, the Lamanites "were still determined to maintain" their strategic position (v. 11), yet only a few days without provisions causes them to give up hope and surrender the city (v. 12). Controlling access to the things that maintain life shows a kind of power not only over people's bodies, but over their ability to sustain hope.

With that understanding of the power of provisions, consider how resources get controlled, allocated, and intercepted in geographic spaces today. Do our poorest neighborhoods have access to clean water and healthy food? Do they have what they need for life to thrive or are provisions being intercepted and redirected? Communities that are denied provisions will weaken and lose hope over time.

Alma 57:13–15

The Nephites consistently face the problem of what to do with prisoners of war during this era, and they come up with various approaches of relief, including using them for labor,[245] swearing them to a cove-

---

245. Alma 53:5

nant of peace,[246] and/or sending them to Jershon to start new lives.[247] Only one account exists of them being massacred, although the casualness of the reference and the regularity of the problem means it likely occurred more than once. These are difficult verses to wrestle with. In other verses, it seems the Nephite leaders have gone out of their way to minimize the death count of Lamanites, creating a clear implication that they (and the God they worship) value all life. Here, they deliberately choose to kill people who are powerless to defend themselves. Complicating factors of insurrections (v. 14) and a lack of sufficient food (v. 15) add layers to the ethical dilemma. But for anyone committed to minimizing and containing violence, the actions Helaman and the Nephites take in these verses are disturbing.

Alma 57:21

In this incredibly important moment in the Book of Mormon, Helaman watches the Anti-Nephi-Lehi young men and remembers the witness they gave about their testimony and what they learned from their mothers. As he watches their example, he recalls their testimony about what was valuable and significant in their lives. In chapter 56, we noted that this example of young Anti-Nephi-Lehies referencing their mothers is the only time in the Book of Mormon that men point to women as spiritual anchors. Significant evidence suggests that the Nephite culture was patriarchal and hostile toward women.[248] Not only is the Nephite prophet now also indirectly learning from these women, he is learning from women who are ethnically Lamanite. Their conversion, as well as mutual love, has possibly allowed Helaman to suspend his own prejudices and allow women to be spiritual leaders in his life.

---

246. Alma 44:19
247. Alma 62:17
248. "The Book of Mormon undeniably presents a depressing picture of the situation for Nephite women." Joseph Spencer, 1 *Nephi*, 104.

Alma 57:25–26

Joy and grief, as well as the value and frailty of life, are bound up together in these verses. Helaman rejoices that all the Anti-Nephi-Lehies survived the battle, yet all of them "received many wounds" (v. 25). So while they apparently had God's protection, they also suffered the reality of a brutal war. They emerge wounded but praising God for their preservation. God could have sheltered them from any harm at all, but that is not what happened. Still, they see the miracle in their experience.

Alma 57:36

When considering the souls of those who have died in battle, Helaman does not seem to distinguish between the Nephites and the Lamanites, but rather trusts "that the souls of them who have been slain have entered into the rest of their God." The prophet offers a prayer for everyone who died that day, not only his own people. And the hope he gives for them is a rest; those who have truly had to struggle in mortality look forward to an eternity of peace, where they can set down their labors at the feet of God. Those who face oppression in this life often hope for the rest of God in the next.

Alma 58:1–12

The first seven verses of this chapter describe a period of stalemate, and the word "wait" appears several times. As time goes on, circumstances become dire and it seems the Nephites might die of starvation (v. 7). We see an honest, brutal description of what happens in war between battles. Not knowing why he does not receive help, Helaman begins to fear for the survival of his people, and to wonder whether God is punishing the Nephites (v. 9). In a few chapters, the record will reveal the reasons for the lack of support: an insurrection in the capitol forced the chief judge, Pahoran, from power. The cause of the Nephites' hunger is not God's anger, but rather the consequences of a difficult political struggle. But the Book of Mormon is partially a record of the human effort to make sense of suffering when there seem to be no reasons for the deprivation, violence, hunger, and fear in the world. For Helaman, a man of faith living in the midst of war, the questions of *"Where is God?"* and *"What does God want from me?"* are very real. One of the most powerful gifts of scripture is locating how people narrate their own journeys with God.

As Helaman's people pray, they receive peace, faith, and hope (v. 10). Yet what they asked for was strength, support, and deliverance (v. 9). Possibly, they hoped for manna at their doors or a lightning strike against their enemies. Instead, God gave them spiritual gifts. But this seems to have reinvigorated them and given them the imagination to think differently about their situation. While previously they believed they did not have enough resources to confront the Lamanites, in the following verses they use clever strategy to improve their situation. The gift of hope proved pivotal for them.

Alma 58:28–31

The women and children in the cities captured by the Lamanites are "taken prisoners and carried off" (v. 31). What happened to them? The text never clarifies, nor does it explicitly state what being "carried off" means. Yet there is good reason to believe that "carrying off" implies rape. Rape is a common tactic of war and the Book of Mormon has a precedent for using the term in this way. These verses echo of when the men of Limhi offered up their daughters to the Lamanites, who "took them captives and carried them back to the land of Nephi,"[249] as well as the priests of Noah who "carried [the Lamanite daughters] into the wilderness."[250] As in this case, the text equivocates about the sexual violence that seems apparent to anyone concerned about the women and children in this society. But later

---

249. Mosiah 19:15
250. Mosiah 19:5

in the text, Moroni describes the Lamanites "carrying . . . away captive" the Nephite women and children and "causing them to suffer all manner of afflictions,"[251] a phrase which more explicitly suggests a multitude of different forms of violence, including rape.

The narrator claims these battles occurred "without the shedding of blood" (v. 28), a remarkable achievement that points to the Nephites' efforts to avoid fighting. But this does not mean it was without severe and lasting violence and trauma.

Alma 58:34–37

Helaman's response to the suffering caused by a lack of support differs significantly from Moroni's fiery epistle to Pahoran in Alma 60. While Moroni's anger is not necessarily wrong (although it is ultimately misplaced), Helaman's reaction seems much more tempered. He remains curious, asks questions, and he appears worried. But ultimately, he decides that whatever happened does not matter because his faith is in God for deliverance, regardless of what form that takes.

Alma 58:39–41

As is typical for Helaman, he frames his epistle with affection, expressing love for the sons of the Anti-Nephi-Lehies and Moroni. But the most important sentence of his closing comes in a short phrase between two commas: "may the Lord our God, who has redeemed us and *made us free*, keep you continually in his presence" (v. 41, emphasis added). God makes us free, no matter what happens on the battlefield or in the government. Helaman knows he is and always will be free. This is the prayer of Black church, for people who have not always known freedom. The faith of oppressed people must rest in the knowledge that God has inherently made their souls free no matter what their mortal conditions, and they pray for God to be with them as they fight for earthly liberation.

---

251. Alma 60:17

Alma 59:3

What does it mean to miraculously prosper in wartime? The authors of the Book of Mormon use various definitions of prosperity throughout the text, with prosperity sometimes being equated with population growth, or wealth, or having God's presence. In wartime, prosperity seems more likely to be tied to retaining lands through battle, as described by Jarom or Amaron.[252] These multiple definitions of prosperity ought not to be used interchangeably. Alma clearly meant something very different when he used "prosper in the land" in his doctrinal teaching[253] than when the author uses it in a military setting here.

Alma 59:11–12

Because the Nephites are in another losing position in the war, the leaders again begin to wonder whether God is angry with them or whether God will punish them. This shows the double-edged sword of narrating God into the terrible tragedies of mortality: it raises questions of whether God allows suffering because people deserve it. This continues to be a human tendency today, with witnesses blaming the victims of calamities as somehow bringing God's wrath upon themselves. If we reject that thinking, then what do people of faith do in the midst of genocide, ethnic cleansing, natural disasters, or pandemics? Where does God belong in these stories? In this text, readers can clearly see Helaman, Moroni, and the chief captains struggling with these exact questions that may weigh on us today.

There are no easy or correct answers to these questions, which is why humanity continues to ask them. To say God is absent in these terrible events denies survivors divine hope. To claim that those who emerge victorious had God's favor means allying oneself with those who have committed acts of horror. Those who seek for God and

---

252. Jarom 1:9; Omni 1:6–7
253. Alma 36

work for justice must therefore name the complexity of having faith while witnessing horrible situations. We need not rush to answers, but rather let the questions sit with us as we journey with God. This is why the war chapters prove valuable in the Book of Mormon and why readers must not simply skip over them. Violence is, sadly, a fundamental part of the human experience. The text asks us to not look away from the questions it raises.

Alma 60:1

Moroni's letter to Pahoran is well-known for being based on incorrect assumptions about the state of the government and Pahoran's loyalties. Moroni judges too quickly and with inadequate information. However, while he may have misunderstood the situation, his demands of social institutions, including the government, still seem useful for a social justice reading of the text. For any *capable* government that is indifferent to the suffering of its citizens, Moroni's epistle offers a useful example of speaking truth to power. While Moroni's anger led him to act in an undiplomatic way, it is worth putting his words in the context of the starvation and death he witnesses and experiences daily.

Alma 60:2–9

Moroni's condemnation begins with the implied questions, "*What have you done with your authority? How have you helped the people you are obligated to serve?*" He points out that Pahoran has been appointed to gather and distribute resources to those in need. What is he doing with his power? And while Moroni knows the "hunger, thirst, and fatigue" of himself and his men (v. 3), his real complaint centers the thousands of unnecessary deaths due to lack of support (v. 5). They would have been willing to suffer if they felt they had a government who saw them and cared. Enduring terrible conditions and facing institutions that have the capacity to help but simply do not care feels unbearable. Moroni condemns the "great neglect" (v. 6), a charge which makes clear that doing nothing in the face of suffering commits a sin in itself.

Moroni uses blunt language in verse 7: "Can you think to sit upon your thrones in a state of thoughtless stupor, while your enemies are spreading the work of death around you?" This question could apply to so many modern-day movements in which governments have failed to intercede and prevent enormous loss of life: the Syrian refugee disaster of 2015, the AIDS epidemic in the 1980s, the Jim Crow South, the climate crisis, or the Rwandan genocide to name only a few. When thousands or millions of people die who "have looked up to you for protection, yea, have placed you in a situation that ye might have succored them" (v. 8) and you do nothing to help, that signals a grave failure.

Alma 60:10–14

The cry "ye ought to be beloved" (v. 10) reveals such a heartbreaking statement. It is a plea for people to be a part of community. Moroni tells them: you should be connected enough to your own humanity that you choose to care for others around you. When he writes, "ye ought to have stirred yourselves more diligently for the welfare and the freedom of this people," he communicates that their own internal moral compass should move them to action. During the civil rights era in the American South, critics described the white activists who helped protest and register voters as "outside agitators" who were "stirring the pot," or looking for trouble. Moroni's message, through a modern-day lens, shows that social institutions should be so eager to bring about justice that they stir the pot themselves.

Moroni also speaks against the sometimes common idea within religion that we can wait for God to fix the injustices of the world. First, he makes clear that God cares about each individual wound: "for known unto God were *all* their cries, and *all* their sufferings" (v. 10, emphasis added). Then, he puts the responsibility of changing the circumstances of that anguish on people. God's "exceeding goodness" (v. 11) will not deliver those who have the capacity to relieve misery and choose not to. Allowing death and suffering to become the cultural norm is unacceptable. Have we or our social institutions shown "exceeding slothfulness" (v. 14)? Toward whom?

Verse 13 wanders into issues of theodicy, or the problem of evil, doctrinal points Moroni processes during his experiences of war. This language sounds similar to that of Alma as he watched the women and children burn before him in the city of Ammonihah: "for behold the Lord receiveth them up unto himself, in glory; and he doth suffer that they may do this thing, or that the people may do this thing unto them . . . that the judgments which he shall exercise upon them in his wrath may be just."[254] Alma's and Moroni's experiences seem similar; both men witness gruesome deaths around them and are helpless to stop it. How do we explain the existence of God to those caught in the worst kinds of violence in our world? Moroni's answer, while imperfect, may feel more right to him than any other answer he can find.

Alma 60:15–18

While Pahoran is not, as Moroni believes, actually a deserter, the king-men truly were traitorous. Their thirst for power and authority, and their disinterest in who they harmed, caused ripples of harm far beyond their original intentions. They created fractures in the society and patterns of violence that triggered the current neglect. Though to Moroni's knowledge they are not directly responsible for the present situation, their violent actions continue to affect the community. This striking example shows how a small number of people opting out of the social contract can have devastating and lasting consequences to social cohesion. They exploited the weakest points of their nation, allowing an external threat to take hold.

---

254. Alma 14:11

Alma 60:19-23

The series of seven rhetorical questions which Moroni answers decisively in the negative in verse 23 depicts a forceful calling out of a lack of action in the face of injustice. Moroni comes from the center of power and likely came from privilege,[255] but he has chosen a life on the margins of society—both literally, fighting on the borders of the land, and figuratively, burdened with the hardships of war. He is acquainted with the hierarchies of power and has access to its highest levels. So his questions begin with a comparison of his own social location: *does your indifference come from not having to see what I witness every day? Are you so privileged that you have the ability to simply not think about it?* With his final question in this series, "Do ye suppose that God will look upon you as guiltless while ye sit still and behold these things?" (v. 23) Moroni decries the tendency to create narratives that allow us to see something and look away.

In verse 20, Moroni also invokes the work of remembrance that previous prophets emphasized: "Have ye forgotten the captivity of our fathers?" Again, this is why memory is so crucial to social justice. We have to remember where we came from, the struggles of our own ancestors and the help they received, or it becomes too easy for us to take for granted the advantages we may have inherited while "thousands round about in the borders of the land" (v. 22) decline.

Alma 60:27-36

Moroni's fiery final words against Pahoran threaten to overthrow a government that does not act to protect the least of these. He makes his threat and demand explicit: "I will stir up insurrections among you" (v. 27) "except ye do bestir yourselves in the defense of your country and your little ones" (v. 29). Once again, food and provisions play a key role in the narrative, as Moroni's desperation seems significantly driven by hunger: "God will not suffer that we should perish

---

255. Hardy, *Understanding the Book of Mormon*. 174.

with hunger; therefore he will give unto us of your food, even if it must be by the sword" (v. 35). This man lives among people on the edge of starvation and scrutinizes a government that does not seem to care. His rebellion stems from the torment of vulnerable people. Rather than seeking power and honor (v. 36), his work focuses on dismantling institutions that allow neglect.

In verse 33, Moroni writes that God has spoken to him and told him to rebel against the government unless the leaders repent. Yet readers will find out in chapter 61 that Moroni is mistaken and that Pahoran remained loyal and committed to their shared cause. If Moroni had divine direction, why did he miss key information about what was actually happening in Zarahemla? Even though he received a message from God, Moroni still lacks complete understanding, leading him to make violent threats against a friend. This serves as a reminder that even spiritual promptings do not lend us divine and whole perception; we are always limited by our mortality.

Alma 61:2–9

This extraordinary letter from Pahoran offers such an example of a humble, charitable individual laboring to make a system work for people. Pahoran sees people struggling and "it grieves [his] soul" (v. 2). Although Pahoran is in the right and would be justified in answering with hostility, his lovely, nonviolent response to Moroni exemplifies compassion. He understands the extreme burden Moroni carries all the time, and it grieves him. He names this twice, an important detail because there is a group of Nephites who take joy in seeing the destruction of their own people (v. 3). People who take satisfaction in the afflictions of others' lives are at the heart of the Amalikiahite wars. Their desire for power tears this community apart. Pahoran's gentle-hearted response stands in stark contrast to their callousness toward others.

Instead of escalating the conflict, Pahoran reassures Moroni that rather than anger, he feels gratitude for the "greatness of [Moroni's] heart" (v. 9). This highlights a stunning example of someone holding space for another's anger. Pahoran is the target of the justifiable but misdirected anger of someone who has suffered for many years and whose resentment just exploded. He sees the anger, gives Moroni space, comprehends the cause, and accepts its existence. Although Pahoran has his own struggles, he understands the greater burden Moroni has carried for a longer time. Can we offer a nonviolent response to those worn out by their burdens, even when we are tired ourselves?

Pahoran also states that, like Moroni, he is uninterested in power except to defend his people (v. 9). Both men redefine the concept of power, using their positions of power to liberate people rather than control them. Pahoran's final line from this verse is so important: "My soul standeth fast in that liberty in which God hath made us free." This echoes the words of Helaman a few chapters earlier, when he wrote, "the Lord our God, who has redeemed us and made us free."[256] Pahoran literally stands in exile, constrained by a horrible situation. But his testimony stands on the truth that God makes people free. When your body stands in places that are anything but liberated, your soul can rest on the assurance that God has already set us free.

Alma 61:14–21

In the remainder of the letter, Pahoran repeatedly offers love and comfort to Moroni and the other Nephite leaders, calling Moroni his "beloved brother" in verse 14 and telling him to remain strong in verse 21. He also puts forward a kind of integrated community of struggle against oppression. First, knowing they are on the edge of starvation, he sends food (v. 16). But he also asks them to send forces to help him (v. 17). Although Moroni wrote thinking he needed Pahoran, Pahoran sees they need one another.

---

256. Alma 58:41

Second, Pahoran rejoices in Moroni's letter, despite its false accusations (v. 19). Moroni's outrage gave Pahoran clarity to decide what to do with the insurrectionists. So while Moroni thought the divine direction he received meant one thing, it actually meant something entirely different. Pahoran's additional information provided the missing pieces Moroni lacked to complete the picture, while Moroni's determination gave Pahoran the determination he needed. We are the puzzle pieces to one another's work, even when we make mistakes. God can work miracles with imperfect people laboring together. In this case, God paired Moroni's anger with Pahoran's compassion and both men found the answer to their prayers. And while we might not expect Moroni's threats to be what Pahoran needed, the irony of God is that even in our mess, when we work alongside one another, God makes us well.

Alma 62:1–2

While Moroni rejoices over Pahoran's faithfulness, he mourns the insurrection in Zarahemla. Once again, the feelings of joy and grief go together in the Book of Alma.[257] These emotions exist interdependently.

Alma 62:4–6

So much of this war revolves around the Nephites' determination to avoid enslavement, which is why the title of liberty and the language of freedom unite and galvanize the people. They now simultaneously fight an external war with the Lamanites (led by dissenting Nephites and Zoramites) and an internal war with the king-men, both with the purpose of keeping people free. They are willing to die for one another to keep the population as a whole out of the power of an oppressive regime. People will often risk everything to avoid enslavement, indicating that for many bondage is the worst possible outcome.

---

257. Other instances include Alma 28:8 and 36:21.

The system of judges, in existence for less than thirty years at this point, is still relatively new to Nephite society. Before that, they lived relatively peacefully and successfully with a king. In addition, the system of judges is clearly not democratic or egalitarian in any way that modern readers would recognize. In drawing comparisons to our world today, direct comparisons to our political systems seem less useful. Instead, we can ask questions such as, *"Who is hungry for power and why? What are people willing to do to increase their political power? Who benefits from a certain kind of system? Who receives a benefit from returning to a previous way of life?"*

Alma 62:9–11

This kind of mass execution of king-men has occurred before, when Moroni ordered the army to kill or imprison all dissenters.[258] This case might seem marginally better since people are executed "according to the law" (v. 9) rather than without a trial, as before. They are also men who have already committed treason and installed a new king in the seat of government. However, the claim of peace being restored to the land of Zarahemla feels dubious at best, as that "peace" only comes through "having inflicted death upon all those who were not true to the cause of freedom" (v. 11). That exposes a bloody definition of peace, one enforced only through killing people. While it is difficult to positively claim there was a better path for Moroni and Pahoran to take, the tragedy of the situation is laid bare: all this violence, hunger, and death was unnecessary. The Nephites could have been different. They could have chosen each other. They could have decided they cared more about community than power.

Alma 62:16–17; 27–29

A pivotal development arises in the ongoing problem of what to do with prisoners of war. Rather than keeping them as prisoners or mas-

---

258. Alma 51:19

sacring them, the Nephites "caused [the Lamanites] to enter into a covenant that they would no more take up their weapons of war" (v. 16), something they have done in the past.[259] However, this time, rather than sending the Lamanites back to the land of Nephi, they go to the land of Jershon. Why would they do this? Perhaps because Ammoron, like his tyrannical brother Amalickiah,[260] would force the Lamanites to return to war, effectively breaking their covenant of peace. The Anti-Nephi-Lehies understand what it means to leave the battlefield and take on a covenant renouncing war.

Yet, even if they have empathy for these soldiers' position, welcoming 4,000 soldiers is still an extraordinary task for the people of Jershon. Just a few verses later, an additional unspecified number join their ranks (v. 27). Given that their own population of young men of fighting age amounted to only 2,000, we can assume this was not a large society. They struggled under the additional pressures of offering provisions for the Nephites during a time of war. Yet these people with deep convictions have consistently welcomed the marginalized, the oppressed, and those needing rest. Once again, they are the quiet heroes of the Book of Mormon, showing up and doing what is seemingly impossible. As they do so, their community seems to benefit: "the Lamanites did join the people of Ammon, and did begin to labor exceedingly, tilling the ground, raising all manner of grain, and flocks and herds of every kind" (v. 29). Their compassion helps create a more abundant society.

Over time, the land of Jershon has developed into a complex and diverse nation that has accepted Nephites and Lamanites in need of a new home. The people have repeatedly opened their borders to strangers, even to former enemies during wartime. This place serves as a home where people are not only tolerated, but are nurtured and given the resources they need to thrive. These new settlers

---

259. Alma 44:20

260. Amalickiah's efforts to compel unwilling Lamanites to go to war against the Nephites can be found in Alma 47–48.

of Jershon never get described as a burden; rather, their presence gets represented as a gift or reprieve to the Nephites, as in verse 29. Although frequently overlooked, Jershon shows one of the best scriptural examples of establishing Zion on earth.

The Lamanite soldiers, when given the opportunity, walk away from the war en masse. The text repeats that *"all* of the prisoners of the Lamanites did join" the Anti-Nephi-Lehies (v. 29, emphasis added). They do not wait for prisoner exchange in the hopes of continuing to fight. They abandon their nation, land, people, and government and choose a life of peace when they have the option to do so. This points to their original lack of conviction in fighting the Nephites, or perhaps simply a weariness of war after so many years. Importantly, the text only describes the movement of the soldiers to the land of Jershon, leaving out what happened to their wives, children, and parents in their native land. While it seems likely that the men would integrate into Jershon more peacefully with their families, the text remains characteristically silent about the narratives of women and children.

Alma 62:35–38

Teancum's anger in these verses gets explicitly attributed not to the Lamanites, but to Ammoron and Amalickiah. In Teancum's view, this war was caused by the two disaffected Nephite brothers. His choice to risk his life twice to assassinate them[261] underscores his belief that they bear responsibility for the instigation and continuation of violence. Perhaps part of this belief stems from having watched the Lamanite prisoners of war walk away from battle and join the Anti-Nephi-Lehies shortly before this moment, cementing Teancum's conviction that the Lamanite aggression was fueled by the leadership. And while Teancum dies in his mission, his efforts do appear to help stop the war: after more than a decade of fighting, the war ends

---

261. Teancum's assassination of Amalickiah can be found in Alma 51:34.

somewhat suddenly in verse 38. More than on the ending of the war, the text focuses on the "exceedingly sore afflictions" (v. 37) of the era. The toll that violence and hunger took on this people for many years will not be immediately healed by the cessation of bloodshed. While most of these chapters tell a sweeping story of a civilization, the individual story of Teancum and the anger he felt in these verses gives readers insight into the tragic harm those experiences did to a single person.

Alma 62:39–41

After describing the sins and terrible struggles of the Nephites, the text claims that "for the righteous' sake, yea, because of the prayers of the righteous, they were spared" (v. 40). Is this what being spared looks like? Living through famine, war, affliction, "murders, and contentions, and dissensions" (v. 40) for so many years may not be what we hope for when we pray to be spared. The people of the Book of Mormon do not emerge without scars, even when they recognize how they have been spared. Any kind of claim that God blesses the righteous materially must wrestle with these verses, which make clear that even with God's grace, good people will live through horrific events.

Verse 41 offers a fascinating description of how the society bifurcates in reaction to their ordeals. Many "had become hardened" while "many were softened." Trauma will act on people in very different ways, and not entirely by their own volition. Violence of this magnitude ripples out into a community, causing disruption within families and other personal relationships. What form did this hardening look like? Who were the victims? When we look at our society today, how does trauma cause some people to harden and others to soften?

Alma 62:42–47

The peace that follows the end of the war appears to be somewhat closer to positive peace and not just merely a ceasefire, as it has been at other times. The peace lasts for a few years and, as described in the following verses, the Nephites make efforts to create an equitable and just society. However, this is still a precarious time—made clear by the eruption of violence in the following chapter—and the peace was established through "a great slaughter"[262] of an uncounted number of people. This peace came at an incredible cost and remains shaky.

The three men who led the Nephites during the war take three different routes afterward. Moroni returns to his work in shoring up the most vulnerable parts of the Nephite nation[263] before retiring to his own home in peace, Pahoran returns to his role as chief judge, and Helaman goes to work reestablishing the church. After a period of upheaval and trauma, Helaman understands that the church needs to respond to what happened within the society. It cannot merely continue on as if nothing has happened because it is a social institution interwoven with people's lived experiences and relationships. The trauma of the people necessarily affects how the church can operate; therefore, it must adapt and change in a new era. What happens to the foundations of a church when a community is ravaged by years of violence? What is the church's new role and how should it move differently? How can a church address how a community has changed after war, racial strife, or widespread disease? In the wake of communal trauma and loss, how does the church re-establish itself and act in ways that will meet the new needs of its people?

Alma 62:48–51

While prosperity frequently signals a dangerous precursor to fragmentation and sin, here the Nephites remain humble and "remember how great things the Lord had done for them" (v. 50). The difference may lie in Helaman's commitment to responding to what happened in the community and reestablishing the church in response. The church's realignment led to a foundation strong enough to withstand

---

262. Alma 62:38
263. More can be read about these efforts in the section about Alma 48:7–10.

even the temptation of wealth. Helaman's willingness to confront and adapt to a new era led to a stronger, healthier community, one in which prosperity intertwined with the word of God.

Alma 62:52

We pause at the death of Helaman because he was such an extraordinary man who lived through some of the darkest years of the Nephite nation. He spent his ministry trying to hold his people together, only to watch them fragment into competing factions and dissolve into war, then finally begin to rebuild a community. He chose beloved relationships with the Anti-Nephi-Lehies, people who were different from his own, and they chose him in return. His work to shore up the church was consistently the backdrop of this period of violence. The death of Moroni a few verses later will signal the end of a generation of men who led the way during an extraordinarily difficult time. So while this depicts a period of peace, it is also a time of grief.

Alma 63:1–17

In many ways, a seemingly more satisfying end for the Book of Alma might be the death of Helaman in chapter 62, during a period of peace and with some hope for the Nephites to stay committed to community.

Instead, chapter 63 leads readers into another series of dissensions and wars. There seems to be a deliberate choice to end this book on a more despairing note as the people cycle back toward violence. The pattern appears identical to what has occurred repeatedly through the book of Alma: Nephite dissenters deliberately fomenting Lamanite anger against the Nephites and prompting war (v. 14–15). Recognizing the same actions recurring yet again underlines the epic tragedy of this people: they could have chosen beloved community, but they did not.

CONCLUSION

The repetition in the second half of the book of Alma is almost maddening. Again and again, certain Nephites dissent from their kin, stir up the hearts of the Lamanites to anger, provoke war, and pursue violence. The ending of the book heavily underlines this narrative, creating a feeling of despair as readers recognize the markers of a return to fragmentation and bloodshed yet again. By the conclusion, this nation—which felt so hopeful as it welcomed Limhi and Alma's people and gave sanctuary to the Anti-Nephi-Lehies—now feels to be on an inevitable path toward tragedy. As the scholar James Falcouner has written, "Though it happens over the course of more than a thousand years, the Book of Mormon is a story of a community that fails."[1] Readers may question if the Nephites and Lamanites have learned absolutely nothing in all their struggles and suffering.

This is, unsurprisingly, how our modern world frequently appears today as well. The same problems of racism, poverty, sexism, prejudice, and war persist generation after generation, even after moments when it seems we have finally reached a breakthrough or overcome the issue. The people of the Book of Mormon could comprehend the despair and grief we may experience as we look around us. Do we give into that despair or continue working on a labor which

---

1. James Falcouner. *Mosiah: A Brief Theological Introduction.* Provo, UT: Neal A. Maxwell Institute, 2020, 25.

may never end? The characters of the books of Alma and Mosiah offer a few different responses to the difficult burdens they face.

Alma the Younger shows us an example of lament. "O that I were an angel, and could have the wish of mine heart, that I might go forth and speak with the trump of God, with a voice to shake the earth, and cry repentance unto every people! Yea, I would declare unto every soul, as with the voice of thunder, repentance and the plan of redemption, that they should repent and come unto our God, that there might not be more sorrow upon all the face of the earth," he writes.[2] Shortly after, he again cries to God, "O, how long, O Lord . . .?"[3] His palpable sadness seems to move with him after all the terrible things he has witnessed in his ministry.

In contrast, Moroni and Teancum respond to the suffering around them with anger bordering on rage. They are swift to take action, hold people accountable, and accept risks for the cause of justice. While Teancum dies in his effort to kill Ammoron and Moroni survives to retirement, they both give their lives to the cause of liberty for their people. For good and ill, anger frequently directs their choices.

Finally, the Anti-Nephi-Lehies build community and offer sanctuary for anyone in need of it. Whether they welcome the expelled Zoramites or disaffected Lamanite soldiers, the Anti-Nephi-Lehies consistently build a place of diverse inclusion and safety for all who need it when faced with injustice.

None of these reactions is wrong; they are simply human. One of the gifts of the Book of Mormon is its description of the diversity of experiences and responses. We will not and do not need to all react the same way to the wrongs of the world. Through this group of people, readers can witness a diversity of faithful responses. They are all ways in which individuals and communities have journeyed with God in the midst of death and violence. While they each look a little different, each are absolutely worthy of our careful attention.

---

2. Alma 29:1–2

3. Alma 31:26

Many of the heroes in the books of Alma and Mosiah pass away without seeing the conclusion of the causes for which they labored. This does not mean they failed. We honor the witness of their lives and realize their work was not for nothing. Those who strive for causes of justice in the world might begin to wonder to what purpose they sacrifice and toil if the problems will only persist. But we praise those who remain valiant in doing right during a lifetime of struggle, even if they did not get to see the ends of their efforts. Desmond Tutu's life was not wasted because racism continues. Dorothy Day's work is not lessened by the endurance of violence and poverty. Pauli Murray's brilliance is not diminished by the recycling of the prejudices she faced during her lifetime. It may be that, as the health care activist Dr. Paul Farmer said, we fight "the long defeat."[4] But that does not take away from the beauty and importance of living in righteous ways in the face of injustice. The book of Alma teaches us that while the same circumstances may come around again and again, those who fight for justice have a charge to remain constant.

In the most hopeful periods of the books of Mosiah and Alma, individuals and nations choose each other. The Nephites welcome the Anti-Nephi-Lehies into their land, despite the political and military risks that decision carries. The sons of the Anti-Nephi-Lehies, in turn, choose Helaman as their adopted father and leader, and he embraces them as his sons. Although Limhi initially reacts to Ammon with distrust and fear, he eventually learns to trust him and treat him as kin. Alma and Amulek meet as strangers but learn to care for one another as brothers. King Mosiah rejoices as the people of Alma the Elder and Limhi wander out of the wilderness and into Zarahemla. He offers them a safe home and eagerly listens as they tell their stories.

Although the end of Alma seems hopeless, as if the people travel an irresistible track toward catastrophe, in reality they do not. They always have the opportunity to choose differently. As LDS scholar

---

4. Tracy Kidder. *Mountains Upon Mountains*. New York City: Random House, 2004.

Kylie Turley has written, "It is always the right time to begin living a life in God's time."[5] It is never too late for us, either. We can still choose God. We can still choose one another. We can still find justice.

---

5. Kylie Turley Nielson. *Alma 1–29: A Brief Theological Introduction*. Provo, UT: Neal A. Maxwell Institute, 2020, 18.

ACKNOWLEDGEMENTS

Our sincere thanks to the team at BCC Press. There are not many presses in the world that would be interested in publishing a social justice reading of the Book of Mormon written by two women. They have offered us the flexibility and space to make this project precisely what we envisioned, and that is an extraordinary gift. We are particularly grateful to our editors, Lori Forsyth and Rachel Rueckert, whose effort and skill have been invaluable.

Mikenzi Jones at Kenzi Studio Co. generously shared her work for the cover art. We were thrilled to find a Black LDS woman making art that spoke to our feelings about this section of the Book of Mormon. Our reading of the books of Mosiah and Alma focuses on the creation and destruction of community and how people are fundamentally interconnected. Jones' piece portrays that message perfectly. More of her beautiful work can be found on Instagram @kenzistudioco.

The text benefited enormously from people who read drafts along the way. We are grateful to Val Hemming, Alice Hemming, Abby Parcell, Emma Olsen, Natalie Prado, Steven Olsen, John Olsen, Jill Austin, and Jared Hickman for their feedback. We are particularly indebted to Joseph Spencer, whose feedback greatly improved the book.

Our siblings, parents, and friends offered encouragement, support, and faith in us in some of the most difficult periods of producing this work. Our children—who struggled through a pandemic literally alongside us—are interwoven into every paragraph and idea. This book did not happen in spite of them, but rather through them.

Finally, our partners, Eric and Patrick, who read drafts, made us laugh, shared brilliant ideas, listened, and encouraged us to go on an unexpected journey with a wild God. Thank you for being there alongside us.

REV. DR. FATIMAH S. SALLEH was born in Brooklyn, NY to a Puerto-Rican and Malaysian mother and an African-American father. Dr. Salleh received her PhD in Mass Communication from the University of North Carolina at Chapel Hill. She also earned a master's degree from Syracuse University in Public Communication and a Master in Divinity from Duke University. She launched A Certain Work in 2018 in an effort to provide racial equity consultation and training for organizations and churches. In 2021, she launched Salleh Ministries Inc., a religious non-profit, to focus on wellness and well-being for clergy and activists. She is married to Eric Sorensen and they are the parents of four children.

MARGARET OLSEN HEMMING is an independent scholar, author, and editor. The former editor in chief of *Exponent II*, she is the art editor of *Dialogue: A Journal of Mormon Thought* and sits on the advisory board for the Center for Latter-day Saint Arts. She earned a master's degree in International Peace and Conflict Resolution from American University. She and her husband Patrick Hemming are parents and foster parents in North Carolina.

Made in the USA
Monee, IL
20 April 2022